ELVIS COSTELLO AND THATCHERISM

For Louis Edwards and Bertie Pilgrim

"If they give you ruled paper, write the other way"
Juan Ramón Jiménez

Elvis Costello and Thatcherism
A Psycho-Social Exploration

DAVID PILGRIM
RICHARD ORMROD

ASHGATE

Published by
Ashgate Publishing Limited
Wey Court East
Union Road
Farnham
Surrey, GU9 7PT
England

Ashgate Publishing Company
110 Cherry Street
Suite 3-1
Burlington, VT 05401-3818
USA

www.ashgate.com

British Library Cataloguing in Publication Data
A catalogue record for this book is available from the British Library

The Library of Congress has cataloged the printed edition as follows:
Pilgrim, David, 1950-
  Elvis Costello and Thatcherism : a psycho-social exploration / by David Pilgrim and Richard Ormrod.
    pages cm.—(Ashgate popular and folk music series)
  Includes bibliographical references and index.
  ISBN 978-1-4094-4962-1 (hardcover)—ISBN 978-1-4094-4963-8 (ebook)—ISBN 978-1-4094-7208-7 (epub) 1. Costello, Elvis—Criticism and interpretation. 2. Popular music—Great Britain—History and criticism. 3. Popular music—Political aspects—Great Britain—History—20th century. 4. Thatcher, Margaret. 5. Great Britain—Politics and government—1979-1997. I. Ormrod, Richard, 1973- II. Title.
  ML420.C685P56 2013
  782.42166092—dc23

                                                                2013002719

ISBN 9781409449621 (hbk)
ISBN 9781409449638 (ebk – PDF)
ISBN 9781409472087 (ebk – ePUB)

Printed in the United Kingdom by Henry Ling Limited, at the Dorset Press, Dorchester, DT1 1HD

Contents

List of Tables and Music Examples

Tables

Music Examples

General Editor's Preface

The upheaval that occurred in musicology during the last two decades of the twentieth century has created a new urgency for the study of popular music alongside the development of new critical and theoretical models. A relativistic outlook has replaced the universal perspective of modernism (the international ambitions of the 12-note style); the grand narrative of the evolution and dissolution of tonality has been challenged, and emphasis has shifted to cultural context, reception and subject position. Together, these have conspired to eat away at the status of canonical composers and categories of high and low in music. A need has arisen, also, to recognize and address the emergence of crossovers, mixed and new genres, to engage in debates concerning the vexed problem of what constitutes authenticity in music and to offer a critique of musical practice as the product of free, individual expression.

Popular musicology is now a vital and exciting area of scholarship, and the *Ashgate Popular and Folk Music Series* presents some of the best research in the field. Authors are concerned with locating musical practices, values and meanings in cultural context, and may draw upon methodologies and theories developed in cultural studies, semiotics, poststructuralism, psychology and sociology. The series focuses on popular musics of the twentieth and twenty-first centuries. It is designed to embrace the world's popular musics from Acid Jazz to Zydeco, whether high tech or low tech, commercial or non-commercial, contemporary or traditional.

Derek B. Scott,
Professor of Critical Musicology,
University of Leeds, UK

Acknowledgements

In part, we put this book together because of our chance meeting in The Jam Factory in Darwen, Lancashire, so thanks to all our fellow players in the band! Gratitude is also due to Mark Cresswell from the Department of Sociology, University of Durham, for his views on the potential applicability of Bourdieu's notions of 'field' and 'habitus' to Elvis Costello, as well as prompting our reflections on the auteur role in recent culture. John Wainwright from the School of Social Work, University of Central Lancashire provided some helpful advice about the draft chapter on race and nation.

At the start of the project, colleagues in the Department of Music at the University of Liverpool generously gave their time and advice, especially Anahid Kassabian, Marion Leonard and Giles Hooper. Particular thanks go to Freya Jarman-Ivens for allowing the less musically competent one of us to sit at the back in her undergraduate lectures on listening to music. Thanks to Rus Pearson for reading through the analyses and providing valuable feedback, and to Diane Hart for providing a non-musician's perspective. Finally, candid feedback on several draft chapters was given by Steve Pilgrim, whose inside view of the music industry and healthy caution about academic approaches to performance were helpful at all times.

Any faults or inaccuracies in the book are nothing to do with any of the above and are ours alone.

David Pilgrim and Richard Ormrod

Introduction

This book is about Elvis Costello the young artist and his work, rather than Declan Patrick MacManus, even though his childhood is considered, at times, for its relevance. Put simply, what were the conditions of possibility for the style, content and success of the first dozen years of Costello's career? What did his work reflect about a time and place we have now come to label as 'Thatcherism' or, for some, just 'the 80s'?

As we noted in the preface, answering this sort of question is less an exercise in typical musical biography and more about the exploration of an artist, his work and their particular social context.[1] In the latter were: controversial strikes; a recrudescent civil war in Ireland; in-fighting on the British left; the rise of the New Right with a fresh devotion to finance capitalism and a rejection of 'One Nation Toryism'; and the refusal of fascism to rest in Hitler's bunker, with the continuing electoral ambitions of the National Front and the British Movement. In this early period of Costello's success, Margaret Thatcher was elected and post-war consensus politics, built around Keynesian economics and social democratic reforms underpinning the modern British welfare state, were fragmenting. The crude cash nexus and consumerism were defining relationships in civil society and public policy in Britain, which was sliding into a new cultural norm of selfish individualism. It has never fully recovered from this revolution of the right.[2]

The period being considered was also a time when the gains and losses of modernism in science and the arts were giving way to cultural fragmentation. Now, in the shared legacy of the latter, at the time of writing, social science has lost confidence in grand narratives (about anything). This can lead to the disadvantages of partiality and even nihilism; what can we ever now say with certainty about anything, and does any knowledge claim about people in society now ever matter? There is an upside to this recent academic context though, which is more liberating. We now might offer a few illuminative insights tentatively, drawing on different perspectives and disciplines, which encourage readers to appreciate

---

[1]   This approach to the relationship between the lives of people and their situating contexts was articulated at its best by Sartre in *Search For A Method* (1958). Many approaches in social science now respect this movement to and fro between person and context, some tend more to the sociological and others the psychological in their emphasis.

[2]   Ironically, at the time of writing, we now have a Conservative Prime Minister, David Cameron, whose response to that selfish cultural legacy, in a context of the most recent capitalist crisis, is to make a moral exhortation for us all to join 'the Big Society' and to assert that 'We are all in this together'.

popular music products and their producers in their social context. In this book some social science is mixed with some musical analysis to this end.

Interpreting Costello's early work

Having emphasised that the book is about the relationship between Costello's early work and what in Britain we now think of as the regime of Thatcherism, some clarifications about our way of understanding that relationship will be presented immediately to establish our intent and reader expectations. At the outset, we consider that *both* Costello's work as a text *and* the context it emerged from, and he worked in, are important (Moore, 1993; Middleton, 1990; cf. Frith, 1988; Hebdige, 1979). By 'text' we mean his recorded and performed music, whether penned by himself or others. This requires some attention to his music, lyrics and voice, also his performance persona, reinforced by public accounts of his work. By 'context', we mean the embeddedness of these textual considerations in the life of the young artist. This includes some aspects of his personal history as well as the contemporary setting in which he produced his work. The latter included Costello's working relationships with fellow musicians, who were the *de facto* co-producers of his work in the studio and on stage, record producers, co-writers and the character of the music industry of the period.

This declaration of our orientation of understanding is provided now, given the tensions in the study of popular music between positions that can be taken up about the autonomy of the musical text on the one hand and those about social determinism or social intelligibility on the other. From our perspective, musical texts are semi-autonomous (so their inner workings can be understood to an extent in their own right). However, the possibility of their production and appreciative consumption must be contextualised to avoid partiality and to make fuller sense of any work being considered.

Our starting point then is not one of an 'either/or' about text and context but one of a 'both/and' relationship. To draw an analogy to illustrate our starting premise, popular music can be explored in the same way as food. We all can taste it and know what we like; hence there is a plurality of tastes or preferences. However, our particular cultural context has *shaped* our enjoyment of some dishes and not others. It has also *limited* what we can taste, because of the time and place we have inhabited to date only including the presence of some dishes and ways of cooking and not others. (Context is about absence as much as presence.) Also, in any context some of us, but not others, *expertly prepare and produce* food and a range of experts can examine how dishes work or fail, whether they are tried and tested or innovatory, and so on. The ingredients can be *analysed* and the wisdom or otherwise of their combination can be *documented and debated*.[3]

In other words, food, like music, has immanent qualities that can be analysed and reflected upon, but ultimately whether a dish recurs on the menu of a culture over protracted periods of time is a result of a set of socially embedded judgments. In relation to Costello's music, Griffiths (2007) explains that there is a transition from 'taste' (immediate and subjective) to 'value' (considered evaluation by those with the authority to do it) which determines whether or not artistic products survive in a 'canon'. In the case of Costello, for a range of reasons, the jury remains out about this progression.

However, for our purposes this question of Costello's aesthetic worth is a consideration not in and of itself but only in relation to understanding it in time and place and the artist's claims about his own products. It becomes relevant, for example, when looking at his position about his own long-term value and in relation to the mirroring or relevance of his songs in their particular context. For example, whether 'Peace in Our Time', which we examine in Chapter 5, is or is not to one's taste and whether it will be remembered or develop an honoured reputation is an open question. But a question we *can* address with much certainty is its meaning in relation to Anglo-American militarism in the 20th century. This is also the case with other Costello songs such as 'Pills and Soap' and 'Shipbuilding'.

There is a sociological argument that this question about of taste, value and reputation is hopelessly focused on the character of the music, when all that really matters is how it is apprehended in a range of contingent listening contexts (Martin, 2006). This would leave us with no interpretative prospect about a common time and place about the production of music and limits us only to its consumption. We disagree with this *limited* focus on the listener(s) and argue in this book that the content and production of music also deserve proper consideration.

It is possible to accept the polysemic character of multiple listeners (Grossberg, 1983) and still search for common features and influences in their shared context. A purely psychological argument about unending varieties of subjective listening experience is logically and intuitively defensible but it risks nihilism about any form of sociological account about music, rather than its audiences. On the other hand, it is clearly logically and psychologically untenable to assume that we can interpret the production and consumption of popular music by *only* seeing them as epiphenomena of deeper social processes. Musicological reductionism is risked by ignoring the social context of musical production and consumption but sociological reductionism is also a risk; hence our declared aspiration to take both text and context seriously.

---

and the production and listening context remains challenging for all students of popular music. This can lead to the multiple risk of musicological, psychological or sociological, reductionism. Even when some balance is attempted, someone will claim it is wrong, depending on their own point of critical emphasis (usually determined by their own disciplinary background). For a range of views about disciplinary privileging (and its risks of reductionism), see amongst others: Langer, 1942; Meyer, 1958; Nattiez, 1975; Hebdige, 1979; Adorno, 1990; Moore, 1993; Leppert and McClary, 1987; Feld, 1974; and Shepherd, 1991.

This contestation about text and context is also highlighted when Moore (1993) suggests that some sociologists might assume homogeneity of the listening experience in order to make manageable knowledge claims. He notes that Frith (1983) privileged the general social meaning of popular music over an appreciation of its technical qualities and features. Moore makes the completely fair point that some sociologists avoid the primary text because they simply lack the musical competence to deal with it. Thus our orientation towards music undoubtedly is shaped, at least in part, by our disciplinary preferences and aspirations for epistemological authority.

We assume, in debates about epistemological privileging, that readers favouring aesthetic arguments will tend more to psychological and musicological understandings. By contrast, those favouring social or cultural determinism will want the balance of interpretation to be tipped away from individuals (be they producers or consumers) and from much, if any, consideration of the immanent qualities of the music. Our hope is to offer something to both of these constituencies, in line with our 'both/and' rather than 'either/or' ambitions. We accept, though, that we may end up fully satisfying neither camp of readers.

The limits of our analysis

As we indicated in the preface, but this bears repetition, the book is not a pop music biography, in the traditional sense about good and bad performances and the salacious micro-politics of life on the road. It is also not a detailed accountancy-style review about Costello's abundance of recordings and concert set lists.[4] The chapters will provide some examples of Costello's songs and how they work musically to illustrate or stimulate our contextual discussion. However, we will not and cannot attempt a comprehensive analysis of all of the music he produced during the period of interest (this would fill several volumes, given his productivity, even in the first period of his career being considered).

Much has been written already about Costello by journalists, including versions of biography and views about his work. Moreover, this has been touched on in passing by cultural theorists considering pub rock, punk and 'New Wave' music. Serious offers from academic musicology and cultural studies have also been provided, which address themes in his music, more than simply telling the story of his life (Griffiths, 2007; Smith, 2004; Bookmens, 2004). A more journalistic account (as it contains no index, referenced citations or academic rationale) focuses quite elaborately on Costello's early lyrics rather than his biography (Gouldstone, 1989). The main messages from these types of academic and journalistic contributions will be utilised at different points in the book.[5]

---

[4]   He has been extraordinarily prolific, by any standard. Costello's industriousness is beyond question.

[5]   The distinction between some types of journalism and academic analysis is not always clear cut. For example, good investigative or 'guerrilla' journalism shades into

The content of the book

By Chapter 8, we place Costello's work at the cusp between modernism and postmodernism, when he was an early proponent of different musical styles and genres. His ambivalence about the type of artist he aimed to be, and experimented in being (including which stage name to adopt), speaks to a wider question (beyond him as an individual) about modernist and postmodernist themes. This question is about the distinctions but also continuities associated with those two worlds of cultural production, particularly about the feasibility now of a true musical 'auteur'. Also it is an opportunity to discuss the extent to which the pastiche and layering of music from past sources (for example, in the work of Costello) *really is* a uniquely 'postmodern' phenomenon.

Between the first and final chapters some key topics are chosen for exploration about the period we now associate with Thatcherism. It was in the context of the late 1970s that Costello appeared, and was highly appreciated, by a good few of his generation. From the outset, he made a pointed point about 'being his own man' and developed a public reputation for being angry and for his pleas for greater appreciation by critics. As we noted in the preface, this is why we use the term 'auteur' in our text not to unquestioningly validate Costello's assertive personality but to test out its plausibility, when his products, conduct and strongly expressed opinions are examined by us in their social context.

The chaos of his early career and the content of his songs emerged in a commercial environment, shared by all of his contemporaries. This made their class position or 'socio-economic status' ambiguous. If already rich or middle class, the temptations of music put them at risk of being rendered déclassé. If already poor or working class, a *nouveau riche* world beckoned. If these ambitious musicians were unsuccessful, humdrum work or the dole was their fate. However, if successful, lowly struggling musicians were beamed up to an opulent world only dreamt of by those left behind, where there were high earnings and, if desired, unending supplies of alcohol, drugs and sex. The huge pitfall of ego inflation also awaited them. Fawning fans and all of those depending on personal success in the music industry from the daily gofers to the more distant mandarins could stuff the hungry egos of artists to bursting point. We look at Costello's class position in Chapter 7 and we touch upon his ego inflation at different points.

Behind that largely irresistible temptation of narcissistic indulgence, earlier inner life remained. The early hungry ambitions and the particular family roots of artistic identity never left, remaining sources of both distress and creativity. Costello, like other male songwriters in the British post-war period, such as

academic ethnography. However, journalists tend to offer single author opinions and they are prone to entertain and sensationalise more than academic writers, who are governed by the cool conventions of scholarly probity (Kelly and McDonnell, 1999). Academics understandably complain that they tend to acknowledge the legitimate work of journalists but the recognition is not then mutual.

John Lennon, Paul McCartney, Paul Weller and the Gallagher brothers, were to experience this inner turbulence, as both victims and beneficiaries. The confluence of past insecure obscurity and untested ambition from childhood, with the shock of newly found adoration, helped to shape their music in both style and content. At times, the hedonistic excesses it encouraged put their mental and physical health at risk.

But this was not just about class, it was also about period. This was a time before the internet and the decline of the direct power of the record companies. It was a time when leading and responding to the young audiences buying records created successful careers for a few. For most there was commercial failure; the mood was misjudged or the product was not found original and exciting enough by the fickleness of youth. Then, as now, there were plenty of very talented musicians who went back to their day job or the dole, having sung or played their hearts out, as one-off wonders or never-made-its.

Costello did make it commercially, albeit without the full reputation he believed was warranted. But although he was a very talented musician, that alone cannot explain his considerable success. He did something in the *particular* style, content and performance of his songs (and tellingly sometimes those of others), which impressed and intrigued in a *particular* cultural context. By 1980, having achieved success, his capriciousness meant – maybe more by accident than design for a while – he was walking a precarious high wire in his career. Caught up in a row about racism and perplexing his New Wave generation, when he took refuge in Country and Western music, this was a challenging period for him and his fans. We explore these points in Chapters 3 and 6.

In that scenario of 1980, and the years either side of it, Costello seemingly was confused and confusing, fast and fascinating, at a time when his country of birth had, within the living memory of older people, successfully fought fascism. But the young generation who had benefitted from this victory had not been born to witness it. The extra twist at this point was that Costello was part of a post-colonial context, in which Britain also had a far less honourable history in global politics; culturally he was part of the Irish diaspora, with its accompanying musical sensibility about victimhood, attachment, loss and dislocation. His Anglo-Irish identity was thus a potential conduit for the ambivalent and often problematic relationship between Great Britain and Ireland, both culturally and politically. This tension is examined in Chapter 4 and touched upon as well in Chapter 5.

Fascism was a point of reference for him, his fans and beyond, but in an unclear way for his generation.[6] Costello's Irishness was to become a constant inspiration and fascination in his music. The Irish Republic had remained notionally, and for 'the Brits' suspiciously, neutral in the Second World War, with republicanism split between pro-fascist and anti-fascist elements (English, 2005). By the time Costello was growing up, the British ultra-right were happy to extend English

---

[6]   The initial but discarded title for Costello's album *Armed Forces* was 'Emotional Fascism'. See also Marcus (1993).

racism to the Irish, despite their white skin and proximity across the short stretch of water. Race was washing around in what we describe as Costello's *habitus*.[7] It was a theme in the upbringing of an intelligent, irritable and thin-skinned young man. Habitus is explored by Bourdieu (1993) and it includes what he calls a 'feel for the game'. As will be seen recurrently in this book, Costello certainly had an adept 'feel for the game' in the music industry. And the latter is an example of another concept from Bourdieu, that of 'field'. He defines this as:

> a separate social universe having its own laws of functioning independent of those of politics and the economy. The existence of the writer, as fact and as value, is inseparable from the existence of the literary field as an autonomous universe endowed with specific principles of evaluation of practices and works. (Bourdieu, 1993: 162–3)

Bourdieu is not arguing that the economic and political context is irrelevant (not at all) but merely that we need to understand what others, like Luhmann or Parsons might call social 'sub-systems' in society. This requires a *particular appreciation* of organising principles and practices in *one arena of activity* that are not present or applicable in another. For us, this means the music industry of the 1980s. In Chapter 7 we dwell on this particular point but it comes up sporadically in other parts of the book.

With post-colonial Britain in decline in the 1980s, Costello could look to those vanquished in the Second World War of 1939–45 and see reversals of alliances and fortunes in countries, which were now confident, prosperous and chic. Grey British life was, for most people, none of these. As Costello was to note in 'Peace In Our Time', 'now the disco machine lives in Munich and we are all friends and I slip on my Italian dancing shoes as the evening descends'.

The austerity of the 1950s, the decade of Costello's birth, had established a democratic consensus of sorts, offering the NHS as the jewel in the crown of the welfare state. Recent memories of the camaraderie of the war and the levelling impact of slow-to-disappear rationing were one side of this cultural experience. However, others, such as Margaret Thatcher, dismissed the period, when she recalled that 'No one ... could mistake the petty jealousies, minor tyrannies, ill-neighbourliness and sheer sourness of those years for idealism and equality' (cited in Marr, 2007: 385).

Moreover, radical conservatives like Thatcher, keen to snuff out any aspirations of the left about 'idealism and equality', had other ammunition. Through the 1960s there was plenty of evidence about the corruption and fiefdoms linked to

---

[7] 'Habitus' is used by sociologists like Elias and Bourdieu to describe the habits, values and aspirations associated with our *particular* childhoods – it is not solely a psychological concept (like 'personality') because it is situated in social relations of the period. It has both inner and outer aspects and it remains open to change, even after childhood, because of new social contexts for our lives.

'town hall socialism' on the one hand and the popular desire for US-influenced conspicuous consumption on the other. The ideology championed by Thatcher was even retained by New Labour's version of neo-liberal politics and the celebrity culture and atomised individualism still evident today. Indeed, although it is now the conventional wisdom, that Thatcher oversaw the end of post-War consensus politics, it is equally tenable to claim that she ushered in a *new* consensus; partly the economic governance of monetarism and partly the celebration of the cultural values of self-centred individualism emphasised in consumerism.

In the past thirty years, this has all required, or involved, a disavowal of social determinism and a conservative turning away from collective solidarity; hence Thatcher's famous rejection of society in the 1980s.[8] If a hungry creative artist could not make something of this real and immediate context, then arguably they did not deserve to succeed. But Costello did make something of it, and many cultural commentators, as well as his fans, appreciated his efforts.

Thus, there was indeed a special political and economic 'market niche' for Costello's work but to emphasise this monetary context alone risks understating the emotional and cultural value of his work. For those who he appealed to, he had anticipated a sympathetic 'community of affect' (Hebdige, 1979). That connection was not reducible simply to commercial opportunism, though the latter is an undeniable part of the reality as well. And opportunities can be understood in a different way for us here because, by 1980, there was a sense in which they had been, or were being, lost for Costello's generation.

Disenchantment was setting in all around about everything. Socialism was being abandoned, as a political aspiration, and peace and love, which were the touchstones for the young of the period of the mid-1960s to mid-1970s, were becoming passé. Angry rebellion was displacing this trend. Moreover, arguably the incipient aggressive individualism of the 1980s might have been found in part, albeit in a benign form, in the passing 'flower power', with its self-centred and inner-world preoccupations of cannabis use ('doing my own thing in my own time'). 'Hippy' youth culture[9] was giving way, instead, to a sneering angry form of anarchism.

---

[8]   In an interview in *Woman's Own* on 23 September 1987, Thatcher said: '… we have gone through a period when too many children and people have been given to understand "I have a problem, it is the Government's job to cope with it!" or "I have a problem, I will go and get a grant to cope with it!" "I am homeless, the Government must house me!" and so they are casting their problems on society and who is society? There is no such thing! There are individual men and women and there are families and no government can do anything except through people and people look to themselves first.'

[9]   The period in the late 1970s of Punk and New Wave music in part reflected a new start after the hippy years. In a popular television comedy of the early 1980s (*The Young Ones*) about a scruffy student house, the one long-haired hippy in the group, Neil, was sad scapegoat. By then, the word 'hippy' had clearly become an insult and long hair a joke in youth culture.

Punks celebrated their anti-social conduct publicly, with their S&M clothing, their rowdy drunken swearing and their posturing rhetoric about 'class war'. In opposition to this inchoate rebelliousness, enough of the electorate (still a minority of the population, albeit a large one) was now voting to formally legitimise a new and radical conservatism. Everyone was on the cusp of, or already enjoying, narcissistic times, with the political class, market forces and the advertising machinery of consumer capitalism encouraging selfish individualism and undermining collective solidarity and shared cultural sensibilities.

The meaning and quality of life were being defined narrowly within, and by, the experience of the successful consumer. Leaving aside those too poor to consume, this was a mirage about happiness, albeit a seductive mirage. We now know that the 'hedonic treadmill' gets us nowhere. The envy associated with a society of unequal consumers does not enhance our well-being; it does not buy us happiness but instead makes us sick.[10] The happiest countries in the world are not the most wealthy but those that have established a culture of 'post-materialist values', as a bulwark against selfish individualism.[11] In 1980, with such atomised consumerism starting to become hegemonic, some artists reacted: Costello offered a response of sorts.

Thus his work was in part a function of a particular version of rebellion in 'young-Turk' style, situated in a time when cultural coherence, for a range of reasons, was disappearing. In this world of increasingly superficial and greedy materialism, Costello offered no new clear programmatic answers about anything (he was, after all, a truculent musician not a revolutionary politician). Moreover, he held on, to a large extent, to older comforting experiences to give his life meaning as a musician. The tracks on his early records made knowing connections to a range of musical influences in his life, either in the references in his own lyrics or his devotion to the songs of others he went on to cover.

He responded to the chaos of the period by respecting rather than rejecting the old, unlike many of his generation just noted. This made him relatively unusual because he articulated some of his own generation's ethos but he also deliberately and shamelessly retained older influences. He treated the cultural legacy recalled from his earlier parental home life with considerable respect. This created the biographical conditions for nostalgia, a disavowed but blatant hallmark of Costello's lyrics and wider musical interests. We address this contradiction in Chapter 3.

Given the disintegration with Thatcher of Keynesian consensus politics, and her fetish for the individual rather than society, Costello and his fans were living in depressing times. The libertarianism of the right may have been driven by the free-market ideologues guiding her, but Thatcher disingenuously claimed to 'roll back the state'. In fact authoritarian centralisation and militarism dominated her period of rule. From the adventurism of the Falklands expedition to the use of the police as a paramilitary wing of the state, to smash faces and political power from

---

[10]   See, for example, Wilkinson (2005), Layard (2005) and James (2008).
[11]   See Inglehart et al. (2008).

beneath on the picket lines, there were good grounds for the name 'Iron Lady' (Young, 1995). Her policies were designed to punish the poor, break oppositional power (the Trade Unions) and ward off non-conformity (banning the discussion of homosexuality in schools). And of course, in case we were in any doubt, she enjoyed taking tea with a mass-murdering tyrant and torturer (General Pinochet of Chile).

This economic libertarianism of the right can be contrasted with the recurrent but vague and naive existential search for freedom common in young adults, when the developmental task of 'individuation' is always present. In the specific context of *this* young generation, authoritarianism from without was always a reference point. The historically given shadow of fascism was noted earlier, and little in the orthodoxy of the British left responded imaginatively to this cultural disaffection and suspicion of authority in the young.

During the 1970s and 1980s, the reformist leaders of the trade unions and Labour Party were often patriarchal and culturally conservative. The honourable tradition of the Campaign for Nuclear Disarmament became more and more invisible in the ranks of the Labour Party. When in power, the latter, just as much as the Tories, maintained a 'special relationship' with the USA in the Churchillian tradition.[12]

Then, as now, with either Party in power, Britain clung, without necessity, onto the trappings of militarism and it interfered, uninvited, in the business of other nations. Like the USA, Britain was a nuclear power that preached to others about limiting proliferation, with an overloaded nuclear arsenal and without a hint of irony or hypocrisy. Like the USA, finance capitalism was being favoured increasingly in Britain, as its manufacturing base was being rapidly abandoned and foreign goods flowed in. The City of London coined it in for the few, while the majority were in insecure work and the factories, shipyards and the mines, were closing.

This context was ripe material for musical agitators and Costello offered his response, though his political songs were far less numerous than other types[13] and his ideological position was never laid as bare as, say, his contemporary Billy Bragg's. Costello's lyrics were rarely in the folk tradition of linear storytelling as found, for example, in some of the early work of Bob Dylan. Any trace of agitprop present was usually offered only tangentially, even in songs like 'Tramp

---

[12]   This has been recently renamed as an 'essential relationship' by David Cameron and Barak Obama.

[13]   Costello could be described fairly as a 'political' songwriter. However, the great bulk of his songs are re-workings of the perennial emotional agendas about everyday intimacy and its loss; what the arch-conservative T.S. Eliot noted were the basic recurring human dramas surrounding 'birth and copulation and death' (*Sweeney Agonistes*). In principle, the political dimension could be ignored successfully by those liking or selectively analysing his music, though this would require willful blindness. Today at least Costello does not have the dubious honour of being adored by Tory politicians; Paul Weller has not escaped that fate ('Eton Rifles' is one of David Cameron's favourite songs).

The Dirt Down' if considered in its entirety. This is despite Costello claiming that its lyrics were too obvious in their meaning to be subversive. (We address this apparent contradiction and meaning of the word 'subversive' presently in Chapter 1.)

The politics of race and class were a shared context for Costello, his appreciative fans and his critics. However, another dimension was important: 'second wave feminism' was buoyant in the late 1970s and throughout the 1980s. In Chapter 6, we examine how Costello fared in that new context of evaluation. First though, in our first two chapters, we address very directly Costello's position as regards Thatcherism. This was a period that created the conditions of possibility for his early work, as well as its later reputation.

Chapter 1

Thatcher and Costello: Setting the Scene

Calling himself Irish was more of an act than a description, an assumption of a crest or picturesque cockade. Ireland remained for him a mystery, an unsolved problem ...

– Iris Murdoch[1]

Introduction

This opening chapter sets out some broad arguments about our topic. We begin by outlining the features of Thatcherism and exploring the reaction of Elvis Costello to that context, in both song and personal statement. 'Tramp the Dirt Down', released at the end of the 1980s, is one of a few songs of relevance, but it is probably the most transparent and pointed of his anti-Thatcher attacks in the period. We look at what Costello says about this song and unpick it to examine how it works. This establishes our intention to examine both text and context in all of our chapters.

We then move on to summarising the biographies of Thatcher and Costello, as a way into considering the divergence of ideologies they embodied in the 1980s. One, a late middle-aged conservative career politician, born before the Second World War, was in a unique position as the Prime Minister of the UK to articulate both a political programme and cultural outlook. The other a young, articulate and critical popular musician was there at the time to offer his response. Although they were seemingly like 'chalk and cheese', they also had much in common, including an appeal to Christian traditions for their authority and inspiration for radical (albeit contrasting) ideas and their conformity to the traditions of their families of origin.

This chapter is thus scene-setting. It gives the reader a broad shared context about Thatcher and Costello and is largely *descriptive*. We acknowledge, though, that even that description has entailed some interpretive judgements from us. In the next chapter we move beyond description and explore more substantively the *interpretive challenge* of examining Costello's music in the context of Thatcherism.

Thatcherism and modern British politics

On 22 November 1990, Margaret Thatcher, the UK's prime minister for 11 consecutive years, resigned. Six days later she left 10 Downing Street with eyes glistening with tears, a regal wave and a weak but defiant smile. Her party, dominated then, as now, by self-confident ex-public-schoolboys, had eventually cast her aside. She had

---

[1]   From *The Red and the Green* (1978).

become a liability to them and the class they represented. Her three governments of 1979, 1983 and 1987 had created polarised responses in the British public.

Thatcher was adored and loathed in roughly equal measure (few were indifferent to her in the 1980s).[2] By the time of her resignation, she had presided over a dramatic, far flung post-colonial war, the death of Republican hunger strikers in Northern Ireland,[3] and the significant curtailment of the British trade union movement. These political symptoms of her rule were underpinned by an economic policy of monetarism: she promoted, as far as possible within the pragmatic limits of democratic politics[4], a new emphasis on strict money control from the centre. This was at odds with the consensus left by Keynes about government stimulation of demand and growth. Stylistically, she had promoted herself in very personal and moral terms as a stout role model for British citizens, in order to encourage self-sufficiency and national pride. That combination of toughness and nationalism offended the liberal or left-of-centre sensibilities of many, especially in the artistic community.[5]

In broad terms, Thatcherism was one way that the Conservative party in the United Kingdom was seeking to adapt to post-colonial decline on the one hand and new forces of late capitalism on the other. Its multifaceted character was described by Jessop et al. (1988) in terms of a number of overlapping features, which have been emphasised more or less by commentators about 1980s UK politics. Their preferred emphasis is on her regime representing a continuity of political logic in the British Conservative Party about later capitalism. This meant an emphasis on privatization, deregulation and commercialization of the state sector as well as the promotion of the City as the centre for international financial capital. In addition to these core socio-economic emphases, Thatcher and her government reinforced

---

[2]   For example, by the end of 1981 Thatcher had the lowest endorsement of any British PM since polling began. However, that low point of a 23% approval rating soared to 51% by the end of the successful Falklands expedition in 1982. When she died in April 2013, these divided opinions were resurrected and recalled.

[3]   Northern Ireland currently is a constituent part of the United Kingdom: the term 'the Six Counties' in the north of Ireland is often preferred by Irish Republicans.

[4]   The pure free market model of the 'minimal state' and monetarism, espoused by her heroes like Milton Friedman and Friedrich Hayek, could only be applied so far within the pragmatic limits of an elected democracy, which had inherited a complex welfare state, begun in earnest in 1911. See Friedman (1970) and compare his views with Offe (1984), who noted that capitalism cannot live with the welfare state but also cannot live without it. Welfarism exists (in part) to preserve, not destroy, late capitalism but it also becomes highly costly to sustain. This is why capitalist governments tend to seek to reduce the fiscal burden of welfarism where possible, by cutting or commodifying aspects of the welfare apparatus. This imperative becomes greater when capitalism is in crisis, as recent events have shown.

[5]   We should note, though, that, like the rest of British society, many in the artistic community were in the thrall of Thatcher and her policies, which offered some of them personal advantages. Only the labour movement was the site of consistent and explicit opposition to the regime.

market forces by encouraging inward and outward investment and promoting the small business sector.

To aid and abet market efficiency Thatcher and her colleagues used new legislative means to restrain trade unionism and other policies – for example, coercive 'training' schemes, a market-oriented social security programme and a range of low-cost schemes aimed at helping business to help itself. Jessop et al. accept that, in addition to this political and economic aspect of the regime of Thatcherism, many commentators placed an emphasis on the woman's *personal* attributes, as embodying a new form of authoritarian government, within capitalist democracies in the late 20th century (Hall, 1980; Young and Sloman, 1986; Riddell, 1983).

This Conservative strategy, with Thatcher at the helm, served the interests of capital via government policies enumerated by the above range of authors. But that preservation of a British role within the global capitalist system created a number of risks for the general population. Monetarist controls would raise unemployment and the rate of bankruptcies. It would deprive money to the 'real economy' of old-fashioned manufacturing in the UK and encourage the inflow of cheap products from abroad.

By the end of the 1980s, these effects of Thatcher's policies were evident, as were other pressures on ordinary people. There were mini-crashes in the British economy, and investments went from the UK into other nations or multi-national conglomerate companies. The housing market expanded and then became depressed. With deliberate disengagement by the State, training schemes for industry were dramatically run down. This depleted the supply of trained labour and de-skilled the workforce. This compared unfavourably to competing countries in Europe, which had maintained higher skill levels. With labour flows imminent from within the EU, British workers were soon to be in competition with more-skilled workers from abroad. This would mean higher rates of unemployment and a downward pressure on wages, especially for those with few practical or academic credentials.

The encouragement of owner-occupation depleted the social housing stock and made labour migrations difficult for those seeking low-cost accommodation in areas of higher employment. This created stagnating localities of very high deprivation with unemployed people being unable to escape, a situation typified by the mining areas after Thatcher's victory over the National Union of Miners. At first this affected mostly the northern parts of the country, creating a North–South divide. But slowly its impact also moved to the South East of England, where very high housing and transport costs made daily living difficult for those on average, or below average, incomes. One result of this was an increase in homelessness. In London, un-let office space stood empty while thousands slept rough every night.

Thatcher asset-stripped nationalised industries to create short-term gains for a share-owning democracy but took no account of the longer-term implications of this policy for efficiency, safety or morale in civil society. This became most evident in the deregulation of the railway system, which split off ownership of the rolling stock from that of the rail track system.

Apart from the financial sector being boosted by these reforms, those in stable employment and with above average incomes, enjoyed new powers of consumption. However, even for this better-off group there were perverse outcomes being created. For example, Thatcher may have preached a 'count-the-pennies' prudence but her policies stimulated excessive consumption and reckless investment, which were inevitable consequences of obedience to the logic of free market capitalism. Thus, gains in wealth for those in employment during the 1980s were soon undermined by the general encouragement to consume and to use personal credit for that purpose.

A policy which controlled money within direct government jurisdiction, but gave its blessing to market forces more widely, inevitably promoted a devotion to both greed and self-centred consumerism. Eventually, in the general population new phenomena of credit debt and debt anxiety were to pervade the lives of ordinary young people, the generation whose parents had been wary of 'hire purchase'. The new 'plastic world' of credit cards was to alter norms of spending and, with it, encourage socially dysfunctional consumption for rich and poor alike.

After 1997, New Labour under Tony Blair made no decisive break from this political and economic logic of neo-liberalism. Consequently, the socially destructive impact is still with us. At the time of writing, in the wake of the recession in 2009, resonances of the 1980s are obvious but now in a moral climate of austerity, in which the State is being reduced in order to pay for the calamity created by investment banks and casino capitalism encouraged in the UK by Thatcher and the USA by Ronald Reagan ('Reaganomics'). The contradictions of unregulated capitalism were ignited and stoked up during the 1980s, and we are all still paying the price.

All of this political mixture, driven and summarised by an alleged passion to 'roll back the State' (see below), was delivered in a personal style by Thatcher that was stern, even when she was smiling. The commentators noted above, who emphasised her personal attributes, focused on her very forthright and muscular approach to her political role, whether cowing her cabinet colleagues or standing up strongly for nationalistic rights within the European Community. And this authoritarianism might be why the emblematic notion of 'Thatcherism' has persevered so powerfully. It was *embodied* and so was characterised by the visibly charismatic and sometimes frightening personal features of a single unforgettable woman. She hectored and patronised routinely, simpering and bullying as required for the purpose. As a consequence, she became an easy target for satirists. Though never physically violent, she was lampooned for whacking her enemies, and failing friends alike, with her handbag.[6]

If she was not personally violent she nonetheless unleashed violence via her government's policies on the streets, the picket lines and in the South Atlantic,

---

[6]   The satirical television show *Spitting Image* also depicted her as an overbearing wild-eyed man in a suit, smoking a cigar or shaving at her cabinet table. She was also morphed by these excoriating puppeteers into the homicidal psychopath Hannibal Lecter, mask and all. Less caustic and more nuanced (though different) views of Thatcher's balance of masculinity and femininity are offered by Campbell (1987) and Young (1995).

when defending the Falkland Islands against an Argentine invasion. And symbolic violence was evident in her policies. She and her followers punished the poor and attacked gay rights. In one form or another, violence loomed large in her political philosophy and actions. However, this violence was intended by her, from her ideological perspective, for good ends. She placed a great emphasis on the notion of 'enemies' within or without and on ensuring loyalty to her cause (see more on this below). It is this personal stylisation of the political aspects of market efficiency that created an authoritarian and moralistic dimension to her regime of power. This is why the very notion of 'Thatcherism' is open to different constructions, depending on whether political, economic or personal characteristics are emphasised by analysts of the period. Because 'Thatcherism' is still commonly held to summarise the British political regime of the 1980s, we retain it here but we also want to make clear to readers that it does mean different things to different people, depending on which aspects of it are the focus of discussion.

Costello's response to Thatcherism

On 20 February 1989, Elvis Costello provided BBC television with his views about Thatcher and her political regime. In a long interview with Tracey MacLeod, albeit with noticeable reticence, Costello clarified his position in the light of songs that had, with much force and venom, been part of a personal cultural war on Thatcher since 1979. The interview revealed the serious side of the artist, made articulate and sometimes inarticulate from indignation. He barely smiled throughout.

The young Costello was often gauche in interviews, and his performances could be unpredictable. Even on stage between numbers he was sometimes reluctant to play the crowd pleaser, depending on his mood. Despite his verbal ease when writing songs, his conversational style could be faltering, anxious, dour, nervously funny or faux-suave, depending on the context.[7] In this interview an accent of sorts was discernible. There were clear hints of 'high rising terminals' (HRTs), maybe shaped by his fascination with North America and his touring there, combined with a clear Liverpool lilt from his later childhood, softened by some southern vowels from younger experience.[8]

---

[7] Contrast the interview with MacLeod, in which Costello is unsmiling and lugubrious, with his appearance in the same year on the David Letterman show in the USA. Witty and smiling throughout, Costello fidgets constantly, touching his tie repeatedly, adjusting his glasses frantically and polishing the table in front of him vigorously with the palm of his hand.

[8] This is one aspect of several to be noted, hereon, of Costello's habitus. His childhood influences are reflected directly in his confident facility to discuss the nuances of music production and his accent reveals his cultural and geographical influences, when growing up and later.

At this point, he sounds like a polite and well-spoken Scouser.[9] Eight years earlier his London roots were far more pronounced when he was interviewed on US television by Tom Snyder; Scouse intonations and HRTs were largely missing.[10] Leaving aside his malleable verbal style and non-verbal cues, Costello makes very clear in his interview with MacLeod, albeit in a public account, his views about songwriting and production, and why he sees himself as a 'political' artist.

MacLeod begins by challenging him about how literally his listeners should take 'Tramp the Dirt Down'. She tries to hold him to account for his personalised and vindictive approach to political critique. After a long impassive pause, mimicking a common tactic of contemptible politicians, Costello simply evades the question, by arguing that analysing songs too much diminishes their impact; 'I'd rather just sing it' he insists. This begs the question, 'then why be interviewed about the songs?' However, he does go on to concede that the lyrics allude to his observations in the last general election. In particular, he endorses the bridge of the song as its core message: 'When England was the whore of the world and Margaret was her madam and the future looks as bright and as clear as the black tar macadam'.

MacLeod then picks up on a theme about Costello's songwriting, which we return to more generally in Chapter 3, his capacity to mix sentimentality with ugliness in his songs. The ethereal arrangement with its dominant Irish instrumentation contrasts with the bile of his attack on Thatcher in the lyrics. Playing the song alone on his harsh guitar, his own performance would match the brutality of the lyrics with his aggressive delivery. Indeed, in the middle of the interview he delivers such a solo performance, which contrasts significantly with the recorded and highly orchestrated version.

MacLeod notes that the latter version deflects the listener from experiencing it as a 'protest song' and in response, somewhat unusually for him, Costello directly reveals his tactics as an artist and offers us some insight into his more general approach to songwriting. The pattern of production and consumption of protest songs was now culturally shared by singers and their audiences, who now knew what to expect. To break that pattern and assert his unique style, Costello argued for the need to be 'a little more ingenious'.[11] The latter phrase, whether viewed

---

[9]   'Scouser' is a nickname for people coming from Liverpool and its surroundings. With post-Second World War urban clearance, the Scouse culture and accent extended beyond the city boundaries to Lancashire settlements like Kirkby, Skelmersdale and Huyton and so it denotes something including but also beyond 'Liverpudlian'. The name is derived from a local meat stew called 'scouse'.

[10]   The distinction readily made between his accent on the two occasions in the early then late 1980s reminds us that some aspects of habitus are not nailed down as an inexorable legacy for adulthood. They can change under social influence during adulthood. It also reminds us that Costello, as a performer, shows a persistent tendency to draw on internal resources about his origins, which include the ability to use his flexible voice with its mixed roots for rhetorical effect.

[11]   In Chapters 7 and 8 we return to Costello's egotism.

now by others as arrogance or accurate self-assessment, was telling and may explain why 'Tramp the Dirt Down' with its internal tensions about beauty and brutality was so noteworthy.

As far as the lyrics are concerned, though, Costello is adamant that the song is not subversive for the very reason that the message is direct rather than hidden. In response, and fishing for more honesty from her prickly subject, MacLeod notes that Costello does not strike her 'as being a particularly violent person' and so wonders why his attack is quite so personal. The tactic works and Costello is drawn into being a little more prosaic and direct. He notes that all of us are capable of 'monstrous violence' and that Thatcher's respectable outer appearance is deceptive. He finds her politics and violence so despicable that at this point in the interview he closes his eyes and shakes his head in disbelief. Quickly, though, he becomes inarticulate in his anger. Eventually, in an apparent cry from the heart, he exclaims: 'I'm a man. I'm thirty five years old and I'm fucking sick of it, you know, of what is going on in this country.'[12]

In this interview we can note a few themes of relevance to this book:

- *The political aspect of his work* The identification by Costello himself, and by commentators of the period, was of a disaffected and angry political songwriter. Not all of his songs are political but many have political allusions and occasionally their main thrust is one of social commentary or critique.
- *The role of his cultural background* There is some evidence of his upbringing revealed in the style of his voice and other mannerisms, as well as in his confidence in talking about music. We discuss this further below in relation to habitus.
- *The challenge of establishing authenticity in his work* The ambiguity and challenge of decoding the public declarations of a commercial artist, especially in relation to assertions about authenticity (in relation to himself and others, in this case pointedly Thatcher) is evident in the interview. This is a point picked up again in subsequent chapters but from the outset we can emphasise the problem of establishing artistic integrity in a commercial field.
- *The strategic view he adopts* He reflects on how to position his work in relation to other songwriters (especially male protest singers). For him, creativity and innovation are not just about imagination, in relation to the content of his music, but also about doing the unexpected in relation to the process of its production and performance. There is a pragmatic search for an innovatory edge in a limited field of commercial possibilities. This points us to a more extended notion of what creativity means in the music industry,

---

[12]   This particular indignant outrage may sound familiar to those who, in 1982, listened to Yosser Hughes, the tragic unemployed Scouser in Alan Bleasdale's television drama series *Boys from the Blackstuff*: 'Everything I've ever wanted and all the things I thought I had, they've all been taken away ... I'm Yosser Hughes and I can't stand it anymore!' In the MacLeod interview, the cultural influence of Bleasdale is clear.

as it includes the capacity to be different or adopt a new form of attack on a common or traditional shared task (for example, it could be about more typically writing a love song but, in this case, a protest song).

- *The co-production of his music*   We can note that the individual artist is embedded in, and relies upon, the work of others, both as reference points to position their work (the previous point) and as co-producers of a particular version of a penned song. In the latter regard, Costello worked with Irish folk musicians on this song, referring particularly to the contribution of the esteemed Donal Lunny for the album. Much of the time, though, individual artists like Costello do not mention the co-producers of their work, who are simply taken for granted.

- *His skill and confidence as a wordsmith*   Notwithstanding the criticism and self-criticism noted in the next point, his early work was noteworthy for the very reason that he was clever at playing with words. With false or true modesty, he notes in the MacLeod interview that impressing is not difficult in this regard. He describes, chopping his hand downwards to indicate their diminutive inferiority, his contemporary songwriters as being 'a race of pygmies' (*sic*).[13] He is confident or arrogant enough to know that he can play around with words for effect at will, and that this is a relatively rare skill in the music industry of the time.

- *The relationship between his inner life and the external cultural landscape of the time*   In this interview, confirmed more explicitly at another point, Costello said fairly directly what he meant in his lyrics. This was not the case in his younger days and MacLeod noted this shift in emphasis in his lyrics over time. When younger, his songs were more inward in orientation and personally inflected by a scattering of experiences and imaginings, often obscure to the listener. This interview was a long television showcase for the album *Spike* produced in 1988, and the track 'Tramp the Dirt Down' is used by us in this chapter because of its explicit personal attack on Thatcher. However, in earlier songwriting days, by his own acknowledgment, Costello was renowned for more enigmatic lyrics and habitual wordplay: definitely more Edward Lear than George Orwell.[14] Elsewhere, in the interview with MacLeod, he partially recants some of this youthful playfulness for being unnecessarily confusing and of questionable merit.

By the time he has written 'Tramp the Dirt Down' he insists that it is too blatant in its meaning to warrant a description of being 'subversive'. It is just a take-or-

---

[13]   Costello's off-the-cuff allusions to racial imagery are dealt with in Chapter 4 in relation to a more notorious incident ten years earlier.

[14]   Some random examples of Costello punning lines: 'Do I step on the gas to get out of her clutches? Do I speak double Dutch to a real double Duchess?'; 'I'm just an oil slick on the wind up world of a nervous tic'; 'Don't put your heart out on your sleeve, when your remarks are off the cuff'.

leave-it direct personal attack on Thatcher.[15] This suggests that Costello's early trajectory, in his 20s, was more of strong introversion as a songwriter. His allusions in lyrics were about his inner life and his intimate experiences and fantasies. From the outset, during that early period, macro-politics not just the politics of intimacy did concern him but they were sometimes obscured in his songs. With age, his outer allusions to political events became less obscure.

Thus, during the 1980s, this is less about a discontinuity of writing style than a change of *balance* for Costello, within his continuing biographical preoccupation about the expression of power in all of its guises. On *Spike*, along with one or two songs on *King of America*,[16] Costello did start to speak more explicitly about the larger world around him, a point made by MacLeod in the interview. Thus lyrical transparency, rather than a clear discontinuity in writing trajectory, may be the point to note here.

The workings of 'Tramp the Dirt Down'

We can deal with this song in sequence by examining its lyrics and then its musical features. In a nutshell, Costello despises Thatcher and hopes to outlive her in order to rejoice at her passing. However, when looked at in detail the lyrics are not all fully clear because they are poetic not prosaic.

Costello starts with a concrete scenario of a campaigning politician kissing a distressed baby. This may have been about an actual photograph of Thatcher or just something he imagined – how is the listener to know one way or the other? Politicians kissing babies is the stuff of voter suspicion and revulsion. Costello's allusion to compassion is thus sarcastic not literal. The baby might also be used as a symbol of the honest or artless vulnerability of the ordinary masses. This first verse hooks the listener in a state of fear and loathing about an evil force in our midst. Rhetorically, it entreats the listener from the outset, by drawing them in to the mood of a brooding lament.

The next verse reflects a culturally specific scenario of dealing with God in prayer. It is a variant of the logic of 'If I am good, then will you please, Father, give me what I want?'. This allusion could reflect Costello's ability to draw on his inner resources – in this case his Catholic past. We might speculate that Costello may well have attempted this spiritual transaction at various points in his upbringing and beyond (see later notes about his Catholic socialisation). However, the song then changes (we note this below about its musical structure); it is as if it is being

---

[15] This might be simply a semantic confusion. Costello seems to use the word 'subversive' to imply *covert* opposition to the status quo, when 'to subvert' means to oppose, upset or be destructive. Subversion can be quite transparent. He may have actually been thinking in his statement about 'subterfuge', which does have a connotation of being evasive about one's true intentions. Thus, viewed from the outside, 'Tramp the Dirt Down' *was* a subversive song. As Costello wrote it, arguably he still has the first call on how it should be described but after the event we may still call it 'subversive', with good cause.

[16] In particular, note 'Little Palaces' and 'Sleep of the Just'.

re-launched and this bridge could become a new start to the lyrics. Thus, another concrete scenario is presented at this point for the listener and is savage in its imagery: a whole nation is a prostitute and its leader is running a brothel.

This is a high-risk claim. Costello is not arguing that *some* people in the country are prostituting themselves, but a whole nation. This reflects something of the writer's contempt for England in principle and his lack of concern about offending the English. Note as well that Thatcher was the Prime Minister of the United Kingdom and yet Costello pointedly directs his ire against of *England*, the traditional target of critics of colonialism. Moreover, he presumes that Thatcher was consciously manipulative and that she set out to betray others deliberately. This view is totally at odds with those who, then and since, supported her for, amongst other things, her personal integrity – one of her unique selling points, even conceded by many of her political opponents.

Accordingly, this was a bold, melodramatic piece of gauntlet-throwing from Costello. Thatcher had and still has many defenders and so this is not analogous to sneering at someone who is universally hated. This point may explain why, when Tracey MacLeod opens her gentle questioning of Costello about the song, she says: 'How literally do you mean the song "Tramp the Dirt Down"? Perhaps you had better explain to whom it was directed and what the thought was behind the song.' She is saying to Costello 'let us get the record straight' but also: 'precisely what are you getting at in this song?' The phrase 'you had better' suggests that Costello needed to account for himself – to put up or shut up. These are fair questions and he did not answer them fully at the time, despite the opportunity being offered. He restated his anger about Thatcher in the interview but elaborated very little on its nature. (Recently at the time of writing Margaret Thatcher has died (April 8th 2013). Costello appears to have softened his stance on Thatcher.[17])

The next verse is ambiguous in a number of ways. Was the father killing his son another actual scenario played back from the period? If it was, how was Thatcher to blame personally? Was the father a victim of her contempt? Where was 'justice' to come from in this period: from Thatcher or her opponents or somewhere else? Was the allusion to 'voices in your head' and 'dreams' about psychosis? Is the 'she', allegedly angry but in denial, Thatcher or another woman? What is 'she' angry about exactly? Who are the 'they' doing the flaunting, and who is lining up for punishment? (The latter notion is a motif in Costello's lyrics.) Does the notion of 'got' in 'got the symptoms not the whole disease' an allusion to suffering under Thatcherism, or is it about *understanding* (as in to 'get' the point of something)? Do the schoolboy's hopes and aspirations being poured 'down the drain' again

---

[17]   '... I have difficulty wishing ill on people, despite having written that song. I can't celebrate. I could if it meant the death of her ideas, but they're alive and well. That's the difference here. There are few people in history you would wish death on, but there would be something pathetic, and beneath us, in celebrating the death of anyone.' At http://www.scotsman.com/the-scotsman/scotland/elvis-costello-on-his-new-tour-and-thatcher-s-death-1-2949793 (accessed 22 June 2013).

Example 1.1 Bass line from 'Tramp the Dirt Down'

symbolise Thatcher's betrayal of the future (returning us to the theme set by the baby-as-victim in the first verse)? Are the boys on both sides 'being blown to bits and beaten and maimed' a reference to Ireland or the Falklands, both or neither?

And so we have at the heart of this song a set of loosely linked imaginings juxtaposed to connote not denote (remember this is poetry not prose). Thus, by the mid-point of the song, the lyrics are not that transparent after all. There is enough loathing and contempt, though, for us to be clear about Costello's core message about Thatcher and her demise. Having looked at the lyrics, let us now turn to the structure of the song and how the music articulates and works with the words.

The prevailing mood of the song is one of unswerving political defiance, although there is a greater dynamic range than one might find in, say, a Billy Bragg song of the same era. The piece has two major textural switches – from a resolute and stirring verse/hook to a more balladic central section, and back to the opening mood.

The opening and closing sections of the piece employ obvious elements from the Irish folk tradition, featuring Donal Lunny on guitar (and Greek *bouzouki*),and Christy Moore on Bodhran. Also featured is famed Irish uilleann piper and whistle player Davy Spillane, whose misty introduction on Gaelic whistle belies the political vituperation to come. Both Lunny and Moore were members of 1970s Irish populist folk supergroup Planxty, and together with Spillane (and others) formed rock-influenced folk group Moving Hearts, noted for its politically engaged lyrics. Working with musicians of this calibre and commitment is a statement in itself.

The major melodic feature of the opening (and closing) section is the descending line implied by broken chords on the bouzouki before being played insistently by the bass (Example 1.1). Each line begins in E minor, moving through the minor III (Bm) and major II chords (A) before resolving to G major with a plagal cadence. Thus every line begins at one harmonic remove from the tonic key, hanging there for a couple of bars before the C chord which signifies the movement to the tonic. This regular slow descending movement and frequent harmonic closure gives a sombre feel to this section. Together with Costello's impassioned condemnation of Thatcher's home and foreign policies, maybe he is trying to evoke the repeated hammering of nails into a coffin, not to mention the title of the song itself.

Costello's vocal line in the first section harmonises the descending movement of the bass and emphasises that descending effect with implacable repetition and a sombre mood; Example 1.2 shows the clear downwards movement in the analysis of Costello's first vocal line, the melody of which is repeated – with very minor alterations – seven times before the refrain (itself another downwards descent, this time from the sixth degree of the scale [E] rather than the second [A]).

Example 1.2   Vocal line from 'Tramp the Dirt Down'

Voice   news - pa - per pic- ture   from the po - li - ti- cal__ cam- paign

Example 1.3   Snare drum line from 'Tramp the Dirt Down'

Snare Drum

As the cumulative effect of these reiterations builds, the texture is thickened by the addition of first a snare drum playing a typically martial rhythm (Example 1.3), and then the reintroduction of Spillane, this time doubling himself on pipes and whistle (barely audible behind the uilleann pipes, which heighten the stirring, martial nature). This was in the context of a civil war, with the IRA still active in the 1980s (see later).

After the first verse/hook, the song moves into a new texture at 01:54. The rolling snare and the Irish pipes recede and are replaced by chiming glockenspiel outlining the first two beats of each bar of 3/4, beat one in the left channel and beat two in the right, over a muted backing of harmonised violins. Instead of the previous reiterating and essentially static harmonies, we are now offered another musical perspective, to suit the lyrical change.

Costello's polemic is no less impassioned, but it is delivered in softer vocal tones (and affecting, ironic imagery) against a backdrop marked by instrumental counterpoint and a stanza-long harmonic narrative. This melody could almost be a folksy, romantic ballad or a lullaby, but there is a jarring disconnect between Costello's delicate, crooning delivery and the condemnatory irony of the line beginning 'Well I hope that she sleeps well at night …' At face value the setting is appropriate to this caring, considerate lyric. But in the context of the lines on either side this lead us unerringly to infer that Costello hopes for the exact *opposite* of what he is saying. Consider the impact this line would have had if he had explicitly stated, 'I hope she (Thatcher) is tortured by guilt and self-recrimination at night'. Costello's position would have been made clear (possibly too explicit), and there would have been a layer of irony in the juxtaposition of this highly personal judgement, with the soothing musical arrangement. However, there would not have been this gloss of sensitive consideration.

As it stands, this is *not* a casually blunt and simple attack on Thatcher. Instead we are drawn into a nightmarish vignette, where the conflicting emotions reflected by the comforting music, the caring lyric and the lurking sense of malice and betrayal congeal insidiously – and effectively – into a dawning realisation of horror. Instead of just witnessing Costello's disgust, as listeners we are invited to experience it at first hand.

Leaving aside the semantic point made earlier about what Costello meant when denying that the song was 'subversive', each listener will draw their own conclusions about his intentions in the lyrics and the performance. To our listening, a range of subtle juxtapositions create a song that is emotionally disturbing. As a consequence, it is not surprising that, in true BBC fashion, Tracey MacLeod, wanted to clarify for friends and foes of Thatcher alike, precisely what Costello was getting at in the song. She tried, but the audience was still left to draw its own conclusions by listening to the song itself. Costello denied us any post hoc explanation about his detailed intentions and evaded MacLeod's demands for detailed accountability. Instead he simply delivered a short and not very articulate rant. He just wanted to play the song and so he did.

The sense was that he (not the interviewer) was in charge of an interaction, which was going to be less about his political accountability and more about his opportunity to showcase the album *Spike*. This point about him being in charge of his public presentation of self is relevant repeatedly, as will become evident when we allude later in the book to other examples.

Costello's shouts and silences on Thatcherism

Having looked at this song and the earlier public declaration from Costello about its importance for him at the end of the 1980s, in this second part of the chapter we put this protest into a wider context of the time. Although 1980s Britain was the immediate context that provoked Elvis Costello's angry imaginings and observations, he was not galled and appalled in equal measure by all of the features of Thatcherism. Indeed, unless we have missed something – which is possible given the obscurity of some of his lyrics – Costello's songs might also be noted for their silences, not just their barks and shouts.

In his crowded and engaging *A History of Modern Britain*, the political journalist Andrew Marr devotes a whole part to what he calls 'The British Revolution' of the Thatcher years (Marr, 2007: 379–475). Much in his comprehensive description of her political regime is reflected in Costello's work. Marr describes her loved and loathed dominatrix persona ('Margaret Roberts, Superstar') and the Falklands War ('Big Hair and Bald Men'). The latter witticism was prompted by Jorge Luis Borges, the anti-authoritarian South American essayist, who described the battle for 'The Malvinas' as being like two bald men fighting over a comb.

On both sides were post-colonial reactionaries, one elected and the other not. Both were trying to exploit past imperialist claims for current domestic political advantage. The elected one won but it really could have gone either way. The victory may have played a part in ensuring Thatcher's next term in office, at a time when that outcome was in some doubt. Another point to note here (we revisit it in Chapter 5) is the ambivalent and biased way in which UK prime ministers have accommodated US interests. For example, the Falklands conflict involved a massive military effort to defend fewer than 2,000 white citizens under UK protection. Contrast this with the UK government's approach to Diego Garcia.[18]

This motif of post-colonial islands, a particular feature of the time, was to resonate for Costello and recur: his Irish identity. More generally, this period was linked to ongoing and unresolved political arguments about the Celtic fringe of the British Isles, which culminated eventually, in the Blair years, in a devolved assembly for Wales and a Scottish parliament. The 'Irish question' had always been particularly emotive, though, in British politics. Ireland was separated by sea from the centre of British imperialism and the previous two centuries had seen persistent military resistance by the Irish to the British state and its occupation of their island. Nothing on the same scale had been witnessed by Wales and Scotland; indeed Scottish settlement in the six counties of the north of Ireland had been encouraged during British colonialism, as a disruptive gambit to ward off 'home rule'.

Margaret Thatcher was nearly killed by a bomb planted by the Provisional IRA at the Conservative Party conference in Brighton, in 1984. At the time, many on the left privately confessed frustration that the assassination had been a failure and these sentiments anticipated and maybe even influenced Costello's own morbid fantasies to be found in 'Tramp the Dirt Down', four years later. Three years before Brighton, Bobby Sands and nine other IRA prisoners had died in a hunger strike, which Thatcher had implacably refused to stop by acceding to their demands for political status in prison. According to Thatcher's statement to parliament, Sands was 'a convicted criminal. He chose to take his own life. It was a choice that his organisation did not allow to many of its victims'.

The bomb attack on Thatcher was thus both very political and very personal; she survived, but one cabinet minister's wife died and the wife of another was paralysed. In all, five people perished in the rubble of the Grand Hotel, and more than thirty were seriously injured. The next day the IRA issued this press statement:

> Mrs Thatcher will now realise that Britain cannot occupy our country and torture our prisoners and shoot our people in their own streets and get away with it. Today we were unlucky, but remember we only have to be lucky once. You will have to be lucky always. Give Ireland peace and there will be no more war.

On the British left, especially among those involved with the 'Troops Out Movement', few tears were shed for these victims of a war of attrition about Irish independence.

---

[18]   In 1961 the USA invaded this tiny UK protectorate in the Indian Ocean, to create a military base, 'Camp Justice'. The UK's Labour Prime Minister, Harold Wilson, cooperated with US authorities to expel its *non-white* citizens with the specious rationale that the islanders were merely transient workers. As with the invasion of Grenada by Reagan, the UK has been highly selective about which of its far-flung citizens it bothers to protect, especially, when considering US interests.

However, as we note in Chapter 5, although Costello may have immersed himself for a time in the musical traditions of Ireland, this contemporary political commentary was muted compared to that of others, including one of his collaborators, Paul McCartney. Thus, 'mystical Ireland' may have been important to Costello (as it had been for one of his heroes, Van Morrison) but he eschewed any direct involvement with immediate questions of Irish republicanism. This silence may be linked to his pacifism, at a time when many on the left were pro-IRA. Even his involvement as a producer reflected that pacifism, with The Pogues' *Rum, Sodomy and the Lash*. He saw his role as being 'to capture them in their dilapidated glory before some more professional producer fucked them up'. It was not a recruiting call for the IRA: the album was anti-militaristic. For example, it included Eric Bogle's melancholic lament about Gallipoli, 'The Band Played Waltzing Matilda'.[19]

A third area of lyrical resonance for Costello during our period of interest was the 'special relationship' that existed between Thatcher and Reagan. This led to some of Costello's allusions being about US politics rather than UK. For reasons we explore later in Chapter 5, this touched upon a long-standing obsession of Costello's in relation to US culture – both admiring it and holding it in contempt from moment to moment.

Costello had his own special relationship with the USA, which was both cultural and financial. His records would be produced by US-based multi-nationals and his reputation on the world stage of popular music required, as for all artists, 'breaking into America'. The USA is the largest Anglophone cultural arena to play and create earnings: in popular music to 'break into America' is an important commercial goal for any artist. This possibility was bound to be attractive to Costello. However, given his oppositional and counter-dependent habits, the demands and discipline required of him to succeed in this goal also may have irritated him and evoked his ambivalence.

Let us now turn to Costello's notable silences about the period. Marr's shorthand for Thatcherism was 'The British Revolution' and his phrase was deliberately ironical. This was a revolution of the Right. Despite much puritanical agitation and indignant posturing, from the British left from the mid-1960s onwards, Britain was a country largely grudgingly reformist and culturally conservative. Costello had nothing to say about the miners' strike and the doomed cult of Scargillism, or the break-up of the Labour Party in the face of ultra-left Scottish nationalism (for a while a Scottish Labour Party was formed). He made no comment on the futile conspiratorial Trotskyist 'transitional demands' of the 'Militant Tendency' and the reactive formation of the SDP (Social Democratic Party) within Labour's leftward drift in opposition. (The SDP was subsumed eventually into the Liberal Democratic Party, which at the time of writing is in a coalition government with the Conservative Party in the UK.)

---

[19]   In 1915, Winston Churchill was responsible for the entrapped slaughter of 50,000 Australian troops in Gallipoli by the Turks. The title of *Rum, Sodomy and the Lash* ironically is a quote sometimes attributed to Churchill (when he described naval cultural history in jest).

All of this infighting on the left, which at the time was to contribute in no small part to the ongoing maintenance of Thatcherism, seemingly goes unrecorded in Costello's lyrics. His brief sojourn in the tedium of working-class life in his teens may have sensitised him to oppression in the workplace (for example, listen to 'Welcome to the Working Week') but he had no experience of sustained collective struggle or of party or trade union politics. His liberal and bohemian family life was saturated daily in the enjoyment of music, not the lived struggle or mundane oppression of the proletariat. This was a formula for rebellious individualism, not the politics of the bureaucracy and the ballot box, or elaborate macro-economic analysis.

By the time that commercial artists have broken with mainstream nine-to-five life or shift work, their concerns become hedged around by the extraordinary world of the music industry. With sustained commercial success, the masses then are pushed outwards as distant concert audiences, record buyers and fans. They are certainly accepted and actively relied upon, but warily and ambivalently. Fans might be less than benign in their preoccupations with the artist – that is one reason that burly security men are present to protect musicians. The hallowed entrances and exits from concerts, and the cosseted isolated world of backstage life, inevitably decouple artists from the daily existence of their adoring fans and the indifferent kith and kin of the latter. It takes a very strong political or religious code of humility and respect for ordinary people to resist the temptations of narcissistic isolation this 'lifestyle' brings.

In this peculiar context of the music industry, Costello was unlikely to approach Thatcherism like a writer from the *New Left Review*, a Labour Party apparatchik or a Trotskyist shop steward. Moreover, in her first term, most of Thatcher's political future was resting on the success of monetarism; and economic dogma probably inspires few song lyrics or any other art form. Monetarism was a diffuse backdrop that may have provoked a grumpy cultural fight back, from those like Costello, but no searing economic analysis was likely or was found. Thatcher's policies of punishing the poor and fetishising the free market, and so consumer power, were to stimulate no more than a few noteworthy but fleeting phrases in Costello's work.

Other important themes in the politics and zeitgeist of the 1980s that were left unmentioned by Costello were: AIDS and gay politics; North Sea oil (for a while a financial security offered from the seabed east of Scotland, but disposed of by Thatcher in an early privatisation in 1982);[20] privatisation and the ambition for a share-owning democracy; and Thatcher's systematic attack on local authorities, with one measure after another devised to centralise her own power. None of these important enough topical aspects of the period seemed to trigger Costello's interest. He did say a little about stuffy traditional elites (always in contempt of them). However, during the 'Big Bang' announced on 27 October 1986, when finance capitalism, with London at its centre, was dramatically deregulated, these traditional power bases were now being displaced by 'progress' on the right not the left. This was becoming the new world of semi-educated and ruthless 'barrow

---

[20]   In 1988, 163 oil workers died in the Piper Alpha rig explosion in the North Sea.

boy'[21] City traders, with absurd riches being enjoyed now outside of the traditional elites of the Old Etonian and Oxbridge graduate culture.

Turning to the matter of the erosion of local democracy, this loops us back to Thatcher's authoritarian persona.[22] It is an important contradiction about her ideology and all those sharing it. She was an elected right-wing politician, who insisted that personal freedom, democracy and free market principles were inextricably linked. And yet, she did not actually aim in practice to create a 'minimal state', with the removal of central government incursions into citizenship, the alleged political advantage of monetarism. This was all a rhetorical confection: in truth, she was dictatorial and controlling. As Marr notes:

> in power, Thatcher and her ministers could not trust local government, or any elected and therefore independent bodies at all. Between 1979 and 1994, an astonishing 150 Acts of Parliament were passed removing powers from local authorities, and £24 billion at 1994 prices, had been switched from them to unelected and mostly secretive gatherings. (Marr, 2007: 460)

Thatcher was a political agent of international capitalism but was ultimately unhappy with letting the hand of the market govern freely. Monetarism and dictatorship had already proved to be amenable political bedfellows in Chile, where her friend and ally General Pinochet was murdering his political opponents.[23] Being tight-fisted about the money supply and seeking to control the minutiae of life in a country seemed to be separate, and maybe even contradictory, aspects of Thatcherism but it was a unitary and compatible policy of sorts, reflecting an authoritarian personality.[24] That unity in itself exposed the lie that Thatcher was concerned primarily with the freedom of ordinary citizens. Her main concern was to protect free markets to ensure opulence for the ruling class and keep at bay socialism as an option for those governed (Jessop et al., 1988).

---

[21]   This was a common term at the time, along with 'yuppie' (young upwardly mobile professional).

[22]   Thatcher was depicted mainly as an 'Iron Lady' but other authoritarian labelling included her being called a 'headmistress' (Cole, 1987). Marr's allusion earlier to her being a 'superstar' is more ambiguous and less gendered.

[23]   In 1973, Pinochet overthrew Allende's elected Marxist government in a coup and became President in charge of a military junta. It has been estimated that more than 3,000 political opponents were murdered, up to 80,000 Chilean citizens were imprisoned and up to 30,000 were tortured. The neo-liberal economic regime now associated with Thatcher was evident in Chile during his reign.

[24]   In classical psychoanalytical theory, 'anal sadism' underpins authoritarianism and the need to control others for one's own ends. Authoritarianism became a preoccupation for psychoanalysts in the wake of fascism in the middle of the 20th century, but this attention was also directed at authoritarianism (especially Stalinism) on the left by some Marxist-influenced psychoanalytical writers (for example, Adorno et al., 1950).

Our concern here is not to argue that Costello *should* have addressed this longer and wider political agenda associated with Thatcherism during the 1980s (why should he?) but to note the meaning of the more limited way in which he engaged with the times, particularly in his political allusions. To understand his limited and focused agenda, we have to stray into his lived experience, with its particular personal and cultural legacies – our concern with habitus. This is not to turn Elvis Costello into a psychological case study for its own sake. It is to recognise that the personal does matter, if we are to develop a nuanced and specific understanding of the content and motifs of his output in the 1980s.

The themes that touched his particular heart and so stimulated his particular imagination when faced with the broad landscape of Thatcherism were gender and power, militarism, ethnocentricity, and ambivalence about the USA. We could add to this list the anachronism of miscarriages of justice about the wrongfully hanged (by the time he came to write these songs, hanging had been abolished in Britain, but Thatcher favoured capital punishment). These topics of interest to Costello were not always explored in sealed sections of his work but interwove. Nonetheless, they are discernible threads of imagination left for us, reviewable traces in his recorded performances.

Two biographical trajectories meeting in the 1980s

Having set the scene about the clash of cultural and political values between Elvis Costello and Margaret Thatcher we can now flesh out a little some matters of habitus and field that connect and separate them, when we juxtapose their lives in Britain in the 1980s. The broad facts about their lives overlapping in time are summarised in Table 1.1.

Table 1.1   Summary of Thatcher's and Costello's biographies

Margaret Thatcher	Elvis Costello
1925 Born Margaret Hilda Roberts, 13 October, Grantham, Lincolnshire, to Alfred and Beatrice (née Stephenson). Father owned two grocery shops. The family were practising Methodists.	
1930 Educated at Huntingtower Road Primary School Grantham and goes on to win a scholarship to Kesteven and Grantham Girls School.	

Margaret Thatcher	Elvis Costello
1943 Goes to Somerville College Oxford to read Natural Sciences and specialises in Chemistry.	
1946 Becomes President of the Oxford University Conservative Association	
1948 Works as a research chemist and becomes active in the Conservative Party	
1949 Is adopted as the Conservative parliamentary candidate for Dartford. She is the youngest Conservative candidate of the time and loses to Labour in 1950 and 1951.	
1951 Marries Dennis Thatcher an Anglican divorcee and wealthy businessman. He funds her studies at the Bar.	
1953 Qualifies as a barrister and begins to specialise in taxation. Her twins Mark and Carol are born.	**1954** Born Declan Patrick MacManus, 25 August, London to Ross MacManus (stage name Day Costello) and Lilian (previously Ablett). Father was a professional musician and mother worked in a retail record store.
1958 Is selected as Conservative candidate for Finchley and wins the seat in the General Election of the following year.	
1961 Against her own front bench position, she votes in favour of the return of corporal punishment for petty criminals (birching).	**1959** Attended St Mary's Catholic Primary School in Twickenham and then St Mark's Secondary School in neighbouring Hounslow.
1962 Is promoted to Undersecretary for State in the Department of Pensions and National Insurance. Loses position in 1964 when Macmillan's government is replaced by the Labour administration led by Harold Wilson. Votes for the	

Margaret Thatcher	Elvis Costello
de-criminalisation of homosexuality and abortion, but also for the retention of capital punishment.	
1970 Appointed as Secretary of State for Education in Ted Heath's new government. Begins a programme of cuts in education, including the ending of free school milk for 7- to 11-year-olds. She is dubbed 'Thatcher the milk snatcher' by the beginnings of the burgeoning response from her political critics.	**1971** Moves to Birkenhead Merseyside with his (Liverpool-born) mother and completes his formal education at St Francis Xavier Comprehensive School. He does not apply for university. Forms folk duo, Rusty, with Allan Mayes.
	1974 Returns to London. Forms the Pub Rock band Flip City and adopts his first stage name of 'DP Costello' (his father had used 'Day Costello' as a stage name). Works in the Elizabeth Arden cosmetics factory and then becomes a computer operator at the Midland Bank back on Merseyside (Bootle).
1975 After the defeat of the Heath government at the General Election of 1974 she successfully challenges him for leadership of the Conservative Party, becoming its first ever female leader. Becomes a contributor to the right-wing think tank the *Institute for Economic Affairs*. This establishes her ideological position: opposed to both welfarism and Kenynesian economics; and for less state investment (to allow for lower taxes) and more free market principles (to stimulate business activity and consumerism).	**1977** Is signed to Stiff Records and his first manager, Jake Riviera, suggests his next stage name of 'Elvis Costello'. His first single ('Less than Zero') and album (*My Aim is True*) are released. Is arrested for busking in protest outside a meeting of CBS executives because of their distribution policy about his work with Stiff Records. A few months later is signed by CBS's Columbia Records. Initially he works with Clover, a US West Coast band, but presently creates his own British band, The Attractions, with Pete Thomas on drums, Bruce Thomas (not related) on bass and Steve Nieve (born 'Nason') on keyboards. Appears with George Jones on the duet album *My Very Special Guests*, singing 'Stranger in the House'.

Margaret Thatcher	Elvis Costello
	1978 Releases *This Year's Model* with The Attractions. Causes a riot at a Sydney concert venue: on stage for only 35 minutes and then refuses to play an encore.
1979 At the General Election she becomes Britain's first female prime minister and reads her mission on the steps of 10 Downing Street: 'Where there is discord, may we bring harmony. Where there is error, may we bring truth. Where there is doubt, may we bring faith. And where there is despair, may we bring hope.' Forms close ideological alliance and personal friendship with Ronald Reagan who was elected as US President in the following year.	**1979** With The Attractions he releases *Armed Forces* (originally called 'Emotional Fascism'), which goes to no. 2 in the album charts, the same position as his single 'Oliver's Army'. He produces the first album for the Ska band The Specials. Has to face the music at a public press conference in New York about a drunken outburst in a bar in which he called James Brown and Ray Charles 'niggers'.
1981 A hunger strike by Republican prisoners in Northern Ireland demanding civilian clothing is met with total refusal by her. Ten prisoners starved themselves to death.	**1981** *Trust* and *Almost Blue* are released. The latter is a set of Country & Western covers, the making of which is a focus of a *South Bank Show* documentary.
1982 On 2 April, Argentina invade the Falkland Islands claiming them as its own territory (the 'Malvinas'). The next day she sends a task force to the South Atlantic to recapture them. Casualties included the deaths of 255 British military personnel, 3 Falklanders and 649 Argentineans. Half of the latter fatalities were on the *General Belgrano*, which was retreating when torpedoed. Its sinking was met with the headline 'Gotcha' in the pro-Tory tabloid *The Sun* and remains a focus of accusation against British forces. Thatcher's popularity was boosted by military victory (the Argentineans surrendered on 14 June). After a memorial service at St Paul's cathedral (26 July)	**1982** *Imperial Bedroom* is produced by Geoff Emerick (who had worked as engineer with The Beatles on *Sgt. Pepper's Lonely Hearts Club Band*). The song 'Shipbuilding' (co-written with Clive Langer) charts for Robert Wyatt.

Margaret Thatcher	Elvis Costello
she expressed disapproval about the Archbishop of Canterbury's sermon, which called for prayers for the Argentinean fallen as well as the British. The same year she commits £10 billion to the bolstering of the Trident nuclear weapons programme.	
1983 She wins the General Election and accelerates the privatisation of state utilities. One of these, British Shipbuilders, was broken up and the industry in England soon declined rapidly in the face of foreign competition. Wealth accumulation is encouraged by her, via finance capital exchanges not traditional manufacturing (a new ethos of 'casino capitalism'). Hereafter, an escalating attack on the trade unions is also evident.	**1983** *Punch the Clock* appears, with a female backing vocal duo (Afrodiziak) and a four-piece brass section (the TKO Horns) playing alongside The Attractions. Costello as 'The Imposter' releases the single 'Pills and Soap' in the run-up to the General Election, a period in which it was banned from the BBC. Plays at anti-Cruise missile benefit concert (The Big One). 'Every Day I Write the Book' becomes his first US Top 40 hit.
1984 As part of the break-up of nationalised industries, the National Coal Board announces the closure of 20 pits and the loss of 20,000 jobs. The National Union of Mineworkers calls a strike of its members, with violent confrontations with the police ensuing on the picket lines. On 12 October an IRA bomb explodes in the hotel in Brighton where she is staying for the Conservative Party conference. She escapes unharmed but there are five fatalities, including the wife of a cabinet minister. She insists on business as usual at the conference.	**1984** *Goodbye Cruel World!* is released, as well as *Elvis Costello: The Man* and *The Best of Elvis Costello and the Attractions* – conveying the impression of a stock taking or the end of an era of production. A split with The Attractions looks imminent but the relationship perseveres episodically until 1987.
1985 The miners' strike ends without a deal being struck. Subsequently, 97 not 20 pits were closed down.	**1985** Is the producer of *Rum Sodomy and the Lash* for The Pogues. Alone he sings 'All You Need is Love' at Live Aid.

Margaret Thatcher	Elvis Costello
	1986 Releases *King of America*, with some input from The Attractions but also involving a range of US musicians. Reverts to a version of earlier name (now 'Declan Aloysious MacManus'). Performs in a concert for Self Aid, an Irish charity for the unemployed. Later this year returns to work with The Attractions and releases *Blood & Chocolate* produced by Nick Lowe (after a gap in collaboration with him). For this album Costello adopted the name 'Napoleon Dynamite' (also used fleetingly in 1982) and 'Eamonn Singer' when supplying the artwork for the album sleeve. No single hits from it but contains the song 'I Want You', which will become the central audio motif for the film of the same name (to be directed by Michael Winterbottom in 1998, starring Rachel Weiss).
1990 She resigns and is replaced, as prime minister and leader of the Conservative Party, by John Major in the wake of the 'Poll Tax' riots in London and other towns (earlier during March). Major withdraws the tax proposal in his first parliamentary speech.	**1989** *Spike* is released on the Warner Bros label. 'Tramp the Dirt Down' and 'Let Him Dangle' are notable direct protest songs. The album leads to a hit for the single 'Veronica' with Paul McCartney). Costello discusses *Spike* and music production more generally with Tracey MacLeod in interview for BBC television (the launch source for this chapter).
1992 She resigns as an elected MP and enters the House of Lords as 'Baroness Thatcher of Kesteven'.	

The above table offers an overview of the comparisons of the two biographical trajectories that overlapped, for our purposes, in the 1980s. Some particular dimensions to this comparison are highlighted below.

Age

Thatcher was born pre-Second World War and was old enough to be Costello's mother (indeed her own children were born roughly at the same time as him). This generational gap may be important as one factor in understanding their differing world views. Whereas Thatcher lived through the war (but was a student and so not in active service) Costello, like many born shortly afterwards was affected by its immediate cultural and economic legacy. The spectre of fascism, aspirations for a better life in its wake, militarism and the trauma of war, austerity and hopes of luxury beyond it, US cultural imperialism, the precarious nature of peace and its temporary opportunity for artistic expression and enjoyment – all these were part of British culture in the 1950s and 1960s, when Costello grew up. They formed a landscape for his imagination.

By these decades, in comparison, Thatcher was concerned with the *realpolitik* of the period. Her imagination was limited to developing and refining a particular conservative political philosophy based on economic rationalism and individualism. She wanted to put into reverse the social democratic health and welfare reforms created by the post-war Labour government in 1945 and after.

Ethnicity and class

Thatcher was born and bred in small-town 'Middle England'. Costello grew up in London and on Merseyside and, more importantly, he had no clear English identity. Whereas Thatcher had a confident sense of place as a middle-class English girl from Middle England, Costello was mindful from a young age of his Anglo-Irish background and that, living on mainland Britain, his class position was unclear.

Both his parents were children of Irish émigrés, born on Merseyside but marrying and raising their son in London. He never achieved the cultural capital that comes with university education (let alone that from Oxbridge) but the occupational background of his parents was not traditionally working class either (see later). His lack of higher education was compensated for by Costello becoming a dedicated and accomplished autodidact. However, his intelligent reflection on his particular ancestry demonstrates his ability to see the connection between working-class life in previous generations and his current privileged existence. In a recent interview about 'Shipbuilding' for BBC Radio 2 (25 June 2012), a song we explore further in Chapter 4, Costello makes the following autobiographical points:[25]

---

[25]   This quote contains elements we explore later, but here note his family script of musicianship and his pride in honouring those in the past, who gave him his current benefits. Like Bruce Springsteen, who we compare him with at times, the working class was his self-attributed original place of origin but he has to live with the actual situation of now being rich and famous; hence his caution not to be 'arrogant' about a false claim. The nobility of manual work is a common theme in both Costello's and Springsteen's narratives, though this is more transparent in the *lyrics* of the latter.

I am blessed in that I've had a very lucky life, where nothing has been hard. The freedom that I have had to do what I do is on the foundation of the work that my parents and grand-parents did. And I'm not telling a sad story about 'I used to live in a shoebox', cos I never did. But I am aware of exactly the relationship to the sea. My great-grandfather was killed on the docks in Birkenhead. The travelling in music was set in train on my father's side of our family due to that – my grandfather was an orphan and became a boy soldier, then later a ship's musician. My father became a musician. Then I became a musician. We are [*sic*] all in a sense in an occupation. It would be arrogant to call yourself a 'working class' person, but I am a working man.

If Costello was sensitive about his rootedness in the oppression of the Anglo-Irish working class, Thatcher's image instead was of a modern day Boadicea;[26] a militant British nationalist, who was proud to be photographed at the controls of a tank. Costello's self-image was far removed from this. He held militarism in general, but British militarism in particular, in contempt. He had a historical sense of the contradictions of the Irish, who were colonised by the British, as being both co-opted by the military machine and being its victims.[27] Anglo-Irish identities, like other post-colonial ones, are then full of contradictions, with emotional ties being both in the place of birth (of an oppressive coloniser) and in an imagined, maybe idealised, historical alternative. The first of these may give both security and insecurity, creating the conditions for personally experienced confusion, anxiety and anger, which might be expressed creatively in some.[28]

Gender

This is so obvious that it could be missed and it will be discussed more in Chapter 6. But here we can note that the matters of masculinity and femininity as well as the relationship between the sexes were important, albeit for somewhat different reasons in the lives of Thatcher and Costello during the 1980s. If Costello was to be taken to task for his alleged misogyny, then Thatcher was under the scrutiny of feminist critics for different reasons. Campbell (1987) depicts Thatcher as a middle class girl who adored her father and took her mother for granted. Moreover, a contradiction of Thatcher's pro-family ideology was that she considered that

---

[26] Latterly renamed 'Boudica', she has come to symbolise the female form of warring British resistance to foreign oppression, even though she was a Celtic, not an Anglo-Saxon, heroine; a case of English imperialism appropriating images from its own colonised Celtic fringe of the British Isles.

[27] The song 'King's Shilling' on *Spike* is an allusion to his Irish grandfather in the British army.

[28] In the 1950s, by repute, boarding houses displayed notices saying 'No Irish, no blacks, no dogs'. This was the sub-title of the biography of another Anglo-Irish contemporary of Costello's, 'Johnny Rotten' (John Lydon), the lead singer of The Sex Pistols.

mothers should work, as well as running a good house. In her case, being married to a man rich enough to pay for a nanny for her own children meant that she could have it both ways (first working as a barrister and then an MP, when her children were young). Moreover, Campbell's account of Thatcher's upbringing is one of emotional distance and an austere outlook on life ('not poor but frugal'). The outcome, then, was not of a powerful female leader, now softening and humanising politics, but the opposite:

> Thatcher has never brought to bear her own experience as a critique of the patriarchal family and of the conditions of most women's existence. She hasn't taken her mother's side and she hasn't taken other women's side. If anything she has annihilated her mother from her own biography, as if assimilating her mother would have assimilated her mother's and every other mother's pain and anger. (Campbell, 1987: 241)

We argue in Chapter 6 that Costello did not hate women in general, even if he hated Thatcher as a particular woman. Moreover, he, like other men, was *expected* to evince patriarchal values and actions (that is what patriarchy is about if it has any meaning as a sociological description). And, interestingly, his voluble critics were men not women. Possibly Thatcher became a larger target than male artists like Costello in the eyes of women feminist writers because she let the side down so very badly in their eyes. She was not a 'sister' to be respected. As Campbell put it in a summary dismissal, 'she wants to be a women who does what men do' (Campbell, 1987, 241).

Radicalism

This is another dimension of comparison which connects these two people. For Thatcher, this meant stepping out of line with her own parliamentary political culture (for example, in voting for capital punishment or challenging Ted Heath for her Party's leadership in 1974; which, for his supporters, was a form of unforgivable treachery). She was a Conservative but not always conservative. Much of her image is of her cruel authoritarianism (the 'Iron Lady' who craved the return of the birch and rejoiced at the sinking of the *General Belgrano*) but she could break rank over some causes about individual liberty (such as her early voting on homosexuality and abortion).

On the latter point, some biographers of Costello (for example, Thomson, 2004) have suggested that he may have been opposed to abortion, which would be consistent with his Catholicism (if so, a point about conformity not rebellion). More generally, though, Costello's radicalism was a version of adolescent rebelliousness, which gave way, eventually, to more a calmly expressed anger on behalf of left-wing causes. The 'anti' legacy of being part of the Irish diaspora was noted above.

Faith and morality

Both were brought up in Christian households and, in the case of Costello, this was reinforced in his Catholic schooling. Christian imagery was to become a touchstone for both, even if used in different ways. For example, we have the staged and sanctimonious reading from St Francis of Assisi (with Thatcher glancing down at her notes on a prompt card in her hand). For this reading, the steps of 10 Downing Street were used as a pulpit by the new Prime Minister on 4 May 1979, her day of electoral victory, to indicate that she was going to now heal the social divisions and societal inefficiencies created by the mess of Labour governments.[29]

Thatcher retained all of the righteous indignation that religious belief and rhetoric can create and sustain. For example, in an early speech she declared, 'I am in politics because of the conflict between good and evil, and I believe that in the end good will triumph.' This binary reasoning would cast any opponent in an evil role. Anyone opposing her would be denied a legitimate voice, pre-emptively, including that of Elvis Costello (if she knew of his existence), because it would be an evil voice. That is what religious righteousness does – it creates moral certainty and prevents dialogue for those who opt for the authority of faith rather than its experiential offerings of spiritual exploration and liberating uncertainty (what Keats called 'negative capability').

Thatcher's hectoring style and desire to convert biblical messages into support for her Conservative secular political aims continued to create a problem for her in Scotland after nearly ten years of the impact of her policies. For example:

> I believe that by taking together these key elements from the Old and New Testaments, we gain: a view of the universe, a proper attitude to work, and principles to shape economic and social life. We are told we must work and use our talents to create wealth. 'If a man will not work he shall not eat' wrote St Paul to the Thessalonians. Indeed, abundance rather than poverty has a legitimacy which derives from the very nature of Creation. (Margaret Thatcher at the Assembly of the Church of Scotland, May 1988)

This speech was not received well at the time by her Scottish audience, and it is noteworthy that Conservatism all but disappeared north of the border thereafter. Whether these offensive sentiments were the sole reason for this is unlikely. Another salient factor was Thatcher's calculated experiment with the deeply unpopular Poll Tax. She used Scottish householders first as a test population, before imposing it on the rest of the UK.

---

[29]   Thatcher's use of Old Testament justifications for Conservative thought was joined by a close Cabinet ally who was Jewish. Nigel Lawson argued in his *New Conservatism* (1980) that socialism was in principle at odds with the concept of 'original sin' and thus the imperfectability of human nature.

Thatcher was a strict Methodist (under instruction from her father as a girl) and only converted to Anglicanism when she married. In her autobiographical account *The Path To Power* (1996), Thatcher recalls that the Sabbath was adhered to strictly, with repeated prayers, and no newspapers, entertainment or frivolity permitted. The Roberts were 'teetotallers' as well, and so she recalls a strict non-conformist household of sobriety, probity and frugality. The legitimacy of the lay preacher tradition, as embodied by the work of her father in the Church, was familiar to her as a child.[30] It became an inner resource for preaching of a different type in her later life. She became the self-righteous lady who was 'not for turning', when faced with the demands of European Union and she made her views clear about why, both to her contemptuous opponents and to delighted Conservative devotees. This preachy authoritarian style of leadership came to define 'Thatcherism' for some analysts. For example:

> Thatcherism is essentially an instinct, *a sense of moral values* and an approach to leadership rather than an ideology. It is an expression of Mrs Thatcher's upbringing in Grantham, her background of hard work and family responsibility, ambition and postponed satisfaction, duty and patriotism. (Riddell, 1983: 5, emphasis added)

Thatcher's original adherence to Methodism was modified later in her life, when seeking particular religious rationalisations for her political ideology (for example, from the conservative Anglo-Catholic wing of Anglicanism).

This political pragmatism about supportive religious ideology even went beyond the Christian faith. Her constituency of Finchley in North London had about 20% Jewish voters and she soon discovered that the Chief Rabbi at the time, Immanuel Jakobovits, was markedly socially conservative. The two soon became friendly and mutually supportive. Thatcher ensured that he was knighted in 1981 and elevated to the House of Lords in 1988. He could be relied on to attack the Church of England's reaction against Thatcher's social policies. For example, he responded critically to the Church's report *Faith in the City* (1985),[31] which focused on the Thatcher government's causes of urban poverty (Young, 1995).[32]

---

[30]   Note, however, an important theological and ideological reversal in her life. Her father argued that the main challenge to Christian piety was the pitfall of wealth (he considered the challenge of poverty already solved, with the emergence of the Welfare State). By contrast, his daughter venerated wealth.

[31]   Jakobovits issued a response called *From Doom to Hope: A Jewish View of Faith in the City* (1986).

[32]   During the 1960s, the Church of England was dubbed the 'Tory Party at prayer'. All this changed in the 1980s: for example, in 1981 the Church came out in favour of unilateral nuclear disarmament, a policy linked very much to the political left in UK culture. For further reading on Thatcherism and religion, see Nunn (2002) .

None of this discussion of moral righteousness implies that a shared Christian background meant that common influences or sympathies were apparent between Thatcher and Costello, but it does give them a broad and shared reference point for both of their value systems.[33] Beyond this shared world, we could caution that the Bible and other religious texts have been used at various times to justify virtually any and every political stance or action. The ideological divergence between Costello and Thatcher exemplifies this point, as does Thatcher's selective attention to differing conservative religious allies noted above.

Also, note that the culture of Methodism is not the same as Catholicism, with the former being simple and unadorned in its approach to practical moral priorities and even styles of prayer. By contrast, Catholicism is more ornate and mystical in its devotions: the world of 'bells and smells', dressing up in elaborate bright clothes and claims to a long and unique historical spiritual authority in Rome. Catholic rituals are grand, priest-focused and dramatic, whereas those in Methodism are low-key, sparse and far less determined by a system of clerical hierarchy (for example, in the explicit valuing of lay preaching, which, we might deduce, influenced Thatcher's public style). And if lay preaching and non-conformity were resources to draw upon from within Thatcher's early life, then a childhood exposure to Catholic showmanship, grandeur and grandiosity may well have helped Costello in his professional life. (Their different and particular *paternal role models* must also be put into this mix though, when understanding their special performative capability in their separate fields of operation – see later.)

On the matter of capital punishment, which they approached from diametrically opposed positions, Thatcher and Costello could both draw upon Judaeo-Christian reference points: in her case, the Old Testament dictum 'an eye for an eye, a tooth for a tooth', when demanding capital punishment; in his songs, the New Testament emphasis upon love of one's enemies, the sanctity of life and the older acknowledged sin of killing. Costello's pacifism, which we return to in later chapters, is noteworthy, despite his reputation for being aggressive, and his preoccupation with violence at times in his songs.

To conclude this section on religion and morality, it would seem that, despite these differences between Costello and Thatcher, what they had in common during the 1980s was a preachy tendency: they both stylised versions of righteous rhetoric for their audiences.

---

[33]   A direct comparator though is Bruce Springsteen, who was from an Italian Catholic background and whose concern for social justice is close to that of Costello's. However, this obvious comparison is not made by any of the contributors to a recent collection of essays on Springsteen (Womack et al., 2012). (This may reflect the limited relevance Costello has had for US musicology and cultural studies.) Christian references are even commoner in Springsteen's lyrics and he has made an explicit allusion to those of Italian and Irish backgrounds being distinct from the Anglo-Saxon cultural tradition in their emotional expressiveness. According to Springsteen, the diaspora of these Catholic nations 'come through the door fists and hearts first' (cited in Pardini, 2012).

Family scripts and cultural capital[34]

Both Thatcher and Costello were set on a likely trajectory by their families of origin, and, despite their radicalism, both were arguably conformist in this sense. Thatcher's father was a local politician (albeit an Independent not a Conservative). Her Methodism provided the basis for her sense of individual responsibility, directness and moral propriety in life according to both her biographers and in the statements she made at times in interviews with journalists (see above). The embodied legacy of frugal probity and industriousness from her upbringing was reflected in her gait and gestures. She was famous for her taut posture and walk. Her upper body was stiff and upright but on the move she tilted forward slightly in a brisk walk, communicating a no-nonsense spirit of 'we need to get on with it – there is a job to be done!'[35]

In her oft-recorded public dealings with politicians and citizens, she might, when speaking, tilt her head back to indicate haughty superiority or at times turn it gently to one side while smiling in a feminine tactic of entreaty. Her posture was thus largely about rhetorical power – it was part of a learned bodily apparatus of political persuasion. After her political demise, ex-cabinet members confessed their sense of intimidation in her presence, with images at the time of quaking schoolboys in the presence of a scolding headmistress. The latter was an image invoked by the BBC's political journalist John Cole (see Cole (1987), ch. 2: 'The Headmistress Takes Over').

Given that her family of origin was middle class but not particularly wealthy, the meritocratic path was important; Thatcher used her brains and scholastic effort to attain status as she grew up. She was in the presence of Tory 'grandees', who were typically from very wealthy families and top public schools, like Eton and Harrow. The class divisions in British culture might typically overawe any person outside of traditional elites, but especially a woman, who was not from a public school background.[36]

---

[34]   The term 'family script' is traceable to transactional analysis ('life script' or 'childhood script') and describes the provision of models of action during childhood from our families of origin; it is one aspect of habitus (Berne, 1964). For Berne, this was not simply a mechanistic imposition of external rewards on the child, to act in this or that way, but included his or her own experience, interpretation of and reaction to the role being encouraged. 'Family script' is now a common notion in family therapy and so has been adopted by those not narrowly committed to Berne's model. The term 'cultural capital' is explained more fully in Bourdieu (1977). It refers to the inheritance from our *particular* families and social networks, as we mature, of our scholastic knowledge, personal contacts, accent, vocabulary and possessions, which together afford us fewer or more life chances than our contemporaries.

[35]   However, note that her slight stoop of the period may also have signalled the onset of osteoporosis and an early 'dowager's hump', a condition which affected her clearly in her very old age.

[36]   For North American readers, the term 'public school' in the UK refers to expensive fee-paying residential educational establishments for children from 5 to 18 years of age ('boarding schools').

Thatcher had to draw upon her own personal cultural resources to maintain authority in that traditional setting of Conservative Party politics. She was a scholarship girl and her family had not bought her particular privilege. Her gender and meritocratic status made her very unusual in Conservative governments of the 20th century and obviously unique as a leader and premier. She suffered a double marginalisation in Tory ranks: she was not a man and she had not attended a top public school (though she was an Oxbridge graduate). This reinforced the need for her to be stern and resolute with anyone, including, if required, her own senior Party colleagues.

This unusual 'out group' scenario probably shaped her body language (stiff, energetic and uncompromising) and her bullish and forthright individualism. And, given this sensibility about 'belonging' in a patriarchal Conservative Party culture, it is noteworthy that many of her most famous allusions are about in-group and out-group membership. For example, she described the striking coal miners of 1984 as 'the enemy within' and General Galtieri of Argentina as 'the enemy without', in relation to the Falklands conflict. She often wanted to know whether a person was 'one of us' (or not) and so this became an obvious title for Hugo Young's biography of her (Young, 1995). This returns us to the point made earlier about her binary reasoning about 'good and evil' (friend=good, enemy=evil).

Young notes as well that the notion of 'one of us' connoted a cultural feel for being English and so was not only about Thatcher being ethnocentric but also Anglo-centric; the polar opposite of Costello's pointed antipathy towards England in 'Tramp the Dirt Down'. (In Chapters 5 and 9 we dismiss charges of racism against Costello but his contempt for the English may have channeled some feelings of this sort in him and his artistic expression.)

The dichotomous reasoning of Thatcher (for or against me? in my group or out of it? friend or foe? good or evil?) reflects a lack of tolerance of ambiguity and is a recurring feature of irritable authoritarianism. Thatcher in power was a good example of this political trend. But her marginal and insecure status then took on a particular visible poignancy, spotted even by those not liking her, when the Party patriarchs eventually dumped her. Her glassy-eyed departure from Downing Street reflected a return to a state of personal vulnerability in her political culture, which the years in power had temporarily disguised.

Turning to Costello, he was clearly his father's son, given that he followed in his footsteps as a talented and versatile commercial musician. Costello's relationship with his mother is less evident in relation to his public role, except for her knowledge and supply of records of popular music during his upbringing. And his intense privacy and tendency to obscure his off-stage identity from public gaze leaves us speculating about the nuances of his parental influences. In his early career, despite his masculine persona, which mixed slightly pathetic and gawky masochism with aggressive bravado, the content of his lyrics implied a very emotionally driven and practised imagination. This was not the stereotype of modern man but closer to a common attribution of femininity. His early learning was not bookish; instead, recorded music and his direct learning about life on stage were highly influential.

Thus schooling, the usual meritocratic vehicle for ensuring status maintenance or advancement in middle-class life, exemplified by Thatcher's career trajectory, did not figure. Although Costello is clearly a very intelligent man, he did not go to university and his school achievement record was very average – just the one A level in English. His family's socio-economic position was comfortable not poor (his parents were owner-occupiers and both wage earners) and the value system of the family was of liberal or leftish character. Resonances of Irish rebelliousness had rippled through three generations and so to be 'anti' was a family tradition.[37]

Costello showed all three of Bourdieu's connotations of cultural capital. First, it was *embodied*: from a very early age Costello learned and sang popular songs. He was a budding performer from being tiny. Second, it was reflected in *concrete objects* in the family: his mother and father ensured that the home contained many records, in excess of the norms of other households. As a child he was exposed disproportionately to recordings of popular music, much of which would have been simply unknown to his peers (Thomson, 2004). Third, his learning was *rewarded and encouraged in its expression*: he went on to perform successfully and had learned the 'tricks of the trade' by direct involvement in musical performance, when working with his father. By his teenage years, he already possessed what Bourdieu calls a 'feel for the game'.

At the end of all of this, his posture was adaptable, cocky and playful, when performing on stage or in music videos. When he was playing music he was accomplished and confident; he knew how to handle himself on stage. The totality of his performances could draw on both sets of learned competencies, as an actor *and* a musician. Early music videos show clever and unscripted versatility. He communicated a wide range of performance messages, from anger to jokiness and from earnestness to anxiety.[38] His knock-kneed, pigeon-toed, faux-Buddy Holly persona is well known from this early period, by which time, in his twenties, he was already a 'natural' performer. However, then, as now, some performance anxiety peeks through, to such an extent that we might speculate that, had he born into another family context, he might have become quite a shy person.

Conclusion

This first chapter has provided a description of Thatcherism, and of Costello's personal reaction to that context. The lives of these two people have been compared and contrasted. Some salient features of Costello's production of music have been introduced. In the next chapter we explain more fully the challenge of interpreting Costello's work from the 1980s.

---

[37]   See the first chapter of Thomson (2004) for a detailed summary of Costello's early family life.

[38]   See, for example, the 1979 video version of *Oliver's Army*.

Chapter 2
Interpreting Costello's Early Music

Music is your own experience, your thoughts, your wisdom. If you don't live it, it won't come out of your horn.

– Charlie Parker[1]

Introduction

The first chapter introduced the time and place of our interest and the two key players for our focus. Something was said about their characters and the ideologies expressed. In particular a cultural product, the song 'Tramp the Dirt Down' was adopted as an initial illustration of some of these points. The period in Britain from the late 1970s to the resignation of Margaret Thatcher in 1990 sets the wider context of time and place for understanding the tension between Costello's musical production and Thatcherism. *In part* it explains the artist's motivation to write, what he wrote and how he performed his song. In the introduction to the book we mentioned something about our interpretive premises and in this chapter we revisit and extend them here for clarity for the reader.

Time, place and situated experience

The biographical summaries of Thatcher and Costello we offered in Chapter 1 came together in the specific context of the 1980s in Britain. Although we could be tempted to go into their personalities and lives of the time in further depth, as an end in and of itself, we are mindful that *situating* these personal details is important. The objective fields that existed beyond these – or any other – individuals need due consideration.

Biographies as individual stories are interesting and can provide degrees of voyeuristic pleasure for their readers but they can also readily become narrow hagiographies or prurient character assassinations. These personalistic outcomes divert us from a fuller picture, when they overstate the agency of the individual, as a hero or villain and generate de-contextualised, and so partial, accounts. However, to only explore the *objective context* means that we might fall into the trap of crude and mechanistic social determinism, where the unique lived experience and action of people is rendered irrelevant. In our case, aspects of Costello (and for that matter Thatcher, though for our purpose the artist and his work is our main focus) would be epiphenomena of deeper social forces and hardly worth examination.

---

[1]   Cited by R.G. Reisner, *Bird: The Legend Of Charlie Parker* (1977): 27.

With a strongly objectivist analysis, they would be like tiny bursting speckles of froth on the surf of large waves.

With these risks of imbalance in mind, if we want to understand the contextualised relationship between social causes and personal meanings, then in some fashion or other, *both* the subjective, and unique, *and* the objective, and general, will need to be examined in tandem or interaction. This is a large challenge to all human scientists and there is no single magic formula.[2] In our case, we are faced with two common problems in the study of popular music. The first challenge relates to the question of the *authenticity* of the artist. We exist in a culture in which, to various degrees, we have become fascinated by, or search for, the 'true' and private 'nature' or 'character' of icons and stars, as if in private there resides an authentic person untouched by audiences or other social forces.[3] In this case, we could ask 'who is the real Elvis Costello?' but we will never get a definitive or persuasive answer for ourselves. There is simply too much ambiguity about the artist (see Chapter 9).

The second challenge facing us overlaps with the first, especially when the artist also writes and performs their own material, and relates to the *meaning* of their songs at all stages of their production. What are they getting at in their writing and performance (and do they know)? When we listen, are we grasping what was intended (if it was)? Are we projecting our own needs and search for meaning onto the outpourings of a stranger, who appears to offer us intimacy, rendering the writer's intentions irrelevant? How much attention should we pay to the technical determinants of the music and the role of other musicians and technicians (especially producers and engineers)? Does this practical process of co-production diminish the role of the artist or even render them irrelevant? Should we limit our empirical attention to the experience of *listener*s rather than the performers they venerate or should we dwell only on the content of the musical text? When we look at the interpretation of music we are reminded of the old adage that a fool can ask more questions than ten wise men can answer.

Answering these fair questions is beset on all sides by risks of reductionism and mystification. For example, the field of commercialism ensures that all public

---

[2]   Foucault (1973) noted fairly that human science is condemned to contestation about what exists (ontology), what is legitimate knowledge-claiming (epistemology) and how we should study people (methodology). Human science exists in the ambiguous spaces between the *a priori* sciences (like maths and physics), the *a posteriori* sciences (like biology or geology) and philosophical reflection. Accordingly, it invites perennial controversy and diverse approaches to work in the academy.

[3]   All sociological rationales that take roles, norms and mores seriously demonstrate that we are all actors, whose conduct and inner worlds are bound up with others. However, commercial artists are under particular scrutiny and so the requirement for them to 'act the part' is more evident and pressing than in the lives of the ordinary citizen. They, more than others, are prone to develop contrived personas to hide behind and promote their particular interests at a moment in time.

performances encourage impression management[4] and rhetorically-saturated posturing. This refers to the manner in which the artist will present himself or herself in a particular context to persuade their audiences about the merit or worthiness of his or her talents and products. This is the very scenario in which potentially people are at their most *inauthentic*. This is not to say that artists do not have sincere intentions or real enough artistic competencies to express them. The problem is that it then becomes difficult to sort the wheat from the chaff.

Similarly, how might we set about understanding the meaning of songs, when the commercial field and its current technological character immediately intrude upon or 'mediate' the artist's original concept? In the case of 'Tramp the Dirt Down', for example, Costello in the interview acknowledged that the song could be performed on his harsh 'clanky' guitar in a stripped-down version that allowed his own angry performance to be foregrounded. (At the time of writing, the interview we utilise from *Youtube* has the latter as part of the programme watched.) This direct and angry performance from Costello reminds us of Van Morrison's assumption that 'it's not the words one uses but the force of conviction behind those words that matters'.[5]

However, once he began to work with other artists in the studio, we find that the song immediately becomes more a mournful lament and far less of a rant (a point he wants to impress upon MacLeod in the interview), even though the lyrics inherently can never escape the persistent feel of the latter. Fantasising about gratefully stamping on someone's grave is a fairly unambiguous image, whatever the style of presentation. It reflects a variation on Bob Dylan's final verse of 'Masters of War', which finishes with the line, 'And I'll stand over your grave 'til I'm sure that you're dead'.[6]

Dylan wanted his political targets to die as soon as possible. By contrast, Costello did not want Thatcher to depart imminently, but wanted her to 'live long'. Also, he did want to do a little more than merely check that she was dead, yet this connecting motif from Dylan suggests that another 'mediation' to consider is the work of *others that go before* in the field of popular music. And if Costello followed in Dylan's footsteps in wishing death on those he held in political contempt, he let that thread that connects him to another musician be changed further by other

---

[4]   The term 'impression management' was coined by Erving Goffman in his book *The Presentation of Self in Everyday Life* (1959). His 'dramaturgical model' was an example of a wider sociological tradition in the 'Chicago School' of the 20th century.

[5]   See Fricke (1983). Resonances of Morrison's emphasis on the emotive use of voice can be found in Costello's live and recorded performances. They have performed together occasionally and both were involved in Self Aid. During the time that *Spike* was emerging, they sang together in London (28 January 1987). Costello considers Morrison's *Astral Weeks* to be one of the greatest albums of all time.

[6]   Revenge killings in the face of social injustice are a shared motif in Bruce Springsteen's recent anti-banker album *Wrecking Ball* in which he sends the 'robber-barons' straight to hell. In the song 'Jack of All Trades', he finishes with this sentiment: 'If I had me a gun, I'd find the bastards and shoot 'em on sight'.

artists. As we noted in the previous chapter, it is the lament version, with some of the vocal spite taken out by the softening impact of Donal Lunny's bouzouki and Davy Spillane's uilleann pipes and tin whistle, which the record-buying, radio-listening public would be aware of from *Spike*. All of this means that 'Tramp the Dirt Down' is Costello's song but it is not clear how much we should provide due credit to its co-producers in practice.

The example of 'Alison'

Let us now look at another one of Costello's early songs, as it also contained much ambiguity, and was one well known because it was commercially successful. 'Alison' appeared in 1977 on his debut album *My Aim is True*. It begins with an encounter with a past lover who looks at him in contempt. He reflects then on being cuckolded by her and his friend. He denies feeling sentimental about her. The chorus is superficially simple but hints at darker thoughts: 'Alison, I know this world is killing you. Oh, Alison, my aim is true.'

It moves on. She has been married but did her ex-husband 'leave her pretty fingers lying in the wedding cake?' Does Costello mean lying, as in deceiving, or lying as in the vernacular corruption of the word 'laying'? The chorus repeats and ends with the line 'my aim is true' repeated. Just before that, desperation is felt by the singer who wants to 'put out the big light' because he cannot abide seeing Alison in her current state. That is it: a short sharp shock of a song, light on lyrics but replete with horror. It is certainly not a hopeful or wholesome song, despite its faux-sentimentality.

On an album mostly comprised of vigorous Rock and Roll/R&B/Soul pastiches, 'Alison' stands out for its walking pace and relatively cool, detached delivery. The lyrics are an example, like 'Tramp the Dirt Down' (see Chapter 1), of sentiments which are seemingly obvious but are deceptive in their apparent transparency. If the surface meaning of the words is not scratched it is possible to play the song over and over again, as if it is no more than a nostalgic lament for lost love.[7] This expectation is certainly set in the first verse. However, there are more sinister undertones in the chorus and the second verse, which connote betrayal and death. Whether the singer's aim is intent upon murder is left as an open question in the final line and the metaphor of putting out 'the big light' might hint at either homicide or suicide. The listener can make their own judgement from the words.

---

[7]   It is not uncommon for seemingly soft love songs to contain sinister meanings, which might be missed by superficial listening. A comparable example to 'Alison' with dark undertones is Sting's 'Every Breath You Take'. These can be compared with a benign 'what you hear is what you get' type of song, of loss, and moving on, as in the maudlin ballad 'Someone Like You' (2011) emotively voiced by Adele (and written with Don Wilson). Adele has been transparent about the sentiments in the song referring to an actual relationship break-up and its impact upon her.

At first listening, the most striking feature of the song is the tired and anodyne backing by members of US country band Clover. This lacklustre performance smacks of function bands but presumably is intentional, judging by the rest of the album, where considerable musical flair is demonstrated. In this song instrumentally everything is performed within a very restrained dynamic and textural range; even at the obvious moments of climax, the band barely warms up enough to offer us these signposts. The only ornamentation is provided by a warm-toned, chiming guitar that reveals Country and Soul influences.

In the first chorus, and later solely on the word 'Alison', Costello harmonises with himself on a separate track, dropping back to a single voice to give clarity and weight to the punch line 'my aim is true'. True to their detached aesthetic, the backing band maintains its steady, cool groove. Over a measured drum pattern of hi-hat, bass drum and rim-clicks (the full snare sound is employed occasionally to create a more forceful sound, but toms are noticeably absent), the bass lays down a workmanlike platform of root notes with a fat, round sound throughout; until the second verse the bassist is locked in with the bass drum. From the second verse there is a little more leeway with pairs of semiquavers replacing the quaver anticipation of the third beat and, in the play-out, the bassist further accents that fourth quaver with a line that harks back to Smokey Robinson.

From the beginning of the second verse there is some increase in rhythmic accentuation from the band; on the line 'In the wedding cake', the bassist plays staccato crotchets on the last two beats of the bar that hint at the word 'stop' later on in the verse, where the whole band hit on beat one and return in the back half of the bar, standard devices from soul ballads. The drummer plays more off-beat accents on the bass drum and hints at another level of time in the play-out with brief bursts of semiquavers, but none of this is played with any conviction, in the sense of the usual drumming aesthetic of building excitement.

The drummer's articulation and phrasing is 'correct' but no weight is put behind any of the moves. Contrast this with the previous track from the album, 'Blame It on Cain', where the drummer drives the whole band forward with his placement of the groove. Given this capacity for engagement on the drummer's part we seem to be listening to a detached drummer in a function band on 'Alison', but we are really hearing an alert, highly competent and conscientious drummer pulling his punches to produce a specific effect. This 'underplayed' characteristic of the band's performance adds to the downbeat experience and the bitter, jilted effect of the vocal.

The most musically interesting moment of the song comes at the juncture of the first chorus and the second verse: the band resolves on the tonic chord (I) as Costello delivers the last word 'true', and the guitar chimes in with a fill that resolves on the next chord (IV). This I–IV movement is a standard harmonic filler/vamp from the era Costello references, and the listener expects the second verse to begin on a tonic I chord after this little insert has concluded, whether it be repeated or not. However, the listener has possibly forgotten by this point that the verse begins on the IV chord, and Costello delays his delivery of the first line of the second verse till halfway through beat three of this bar of IV, cramming two bars of lyric into the space of four beats.

In hindsight, what has actually happened is that one measure (necessary for symmetry in a song so far steadily moving in phrases of two bars) has been lopped off the end of the chorus, facilitating the movement from I (termination of the chorus) to IV (commencement of second verse) without the obstacle of an extra measure of I to overcome. By removing this harmonic deadwood, Costello achieves two aims – he maintains pace in what is otherwise a deliberately mundane performance and he grants us a brief, illusory, instrumental interlude – the guitar is there, granted, but the elision between chorus-interlude-and-verse is such that we hear a two-bar space between chorus and verse that doesn't actually exist. It's a neat manoeuvre.

Costello's trademark vocal delivery is evident: a narrow mid-range tessitura and a nasalised tone, complete with Americanised vowels, slurred consonants and clipped-off words that pastiche mannered, stagey soul balladry. All of this adds a layer of irony to the performance. Without these vocal clues, the intention of the frequently misunderstood lyric would be yet more opaque.[8] Costello's ruse worked very successfully, as Linda Ronstadt then covered the song without Costello's sardonic edge and it became a hit for her in 1978.

If Costello's original intentions were caustic, by the time Ronstadt reworks the lyric, the listener is being drizzled in golden syrup. Because it is sung by a woman it could have implied lesbian desire if expressed verbatim.[9] However, the slight but crucial modifications now position the singer as a female friend (not a male ex-lover), who is betrayed by Alison. To signal this, Costello's original lines 'loving somebody, I only hope it isn't mine' becomes 'loving somebody, I only hope he wasn't mine', implying anxiously that it is her boyfriend that might have been involved in the betrayal.[10] (Strictly, the original lyric should have read 'some body' rather than 'somebody' for the pun to work at the end of the line, but that type of ambiguity is not unusual in Costello's wordplay.)

This simple switch of lyrics and the song's cloying treatment seem to lead the listener well away from the originally produced sinister undertones about revenge and regret and possibly even (his) homicidal or (her) suicidal impulses. Instead Ronstadt establishes a completely new overall sentiment for the song: a clichéd soap opera concern that boyfriends do not cheat on their women and that female friends do not betray one another. And just as 'Tramp the Dirt Down' can

---

[8]   In Chapter 6 we discuss the significance of the 'grain' of Costello's voice more.

[9]   By 1992, on the EP *Covers* by Everything But the Girl, Tracey Thorn's rendition is of the original Costello lyrics and any commercial risk of confusion of sexuality no longer seems to be affecting marketing decisions. In the late 1970s Ronstadt was a heterosexual sweetheart not a champion of recent second-wave feminism, straight or lesbian; it was a different commercial scenario. Costello donated the royalties from the Ronstadt version of Alison to the African National Congress, on hearing that she had performed at Sun City in South Africa.

[10]   The identity implications for gender and sexuality, when female artists cover the material of male writers, are discussed in Griffiths (2002).

be situated in relation to 'Masters of War', by Costello's own admission 'Alison' is modelled in part on 'Ghetto Child' by the Detroit Spinners from 1973. Hence, both its origins and its destination in the USA separate it from its singular identification with Costello as the author.

The challenge of interpreting popular songs

This lyrically compact and musically unremarkable song (despite its commercial success) and its immediate transformation by another singer, exemplifies the challenge of song interpretation. Interpretations of songs are not easy and can only ever be provisional because the intention of the artist is part of a longer process of inheritance and current modifications of that legacy, which implicate others.

To ward off the sense of futility this challenge of interpretation creates for us, we can try to explain our interpretations in ways that go beyond a bald expression of personal taste or idiosyncratic meaning for the listener. For example, here are a couple of listeners to 'Alison' posting their views on Youtube: 'I love this song. It's one of my all time favourites. Elvis Costello rocks!' and 'I like this song a little but my name is Alison and its annoying that most Alisons are spelled with 2 lls'.[11] However, interpretations, even when their rationales are elaborated beyond this type of cursory empty account, are still inevitably subjective. Here we use the metaphor of the 'Bermuda Triangle'[12] to outline this methodological dilemma more.

Authenticity, meaning and the Bermuda Triangle of interpretation

Students of popular music may have already come across a relevant aphorism to start this discussion, the source of which is attributed at times to Costello himself: 'writing about music is like dancing about architecture'. At this stage, we might all simply give up and just enjoy playing or listening to music; a legitimate option in life. Alternatively, we might plod on in our interpretive efforts. In this book, when plodding on, we are aware of three broad constraints, but also opportunities, for our inquiry: the stated intention of the artist; the musical text ('on the record'); and the context of production and consumption.

On the last of these, this book is not an empirical investigation of the myriad ways in which Costello's songs have been listened to and appreciated by his fans

---

[11] This sort of short personalised comment is commonly posted. It is what is known in social psychological research into ordinary explanations as an 'empty account', as undefended opinion or idiosyncratic experience with the implicit rhetorical plea: 'you must believe this to be particularly true and relevant because it is from my special and unique experience'. The banality of this sort of narcissistic epistemological privileging typifies online fan discussions of popular music.

[12] This is an area of sea between Florida, Bermuda and Puerto Rico, where, it is alleged, a disproportionate number of aircraft crash or disappear without trace.

or dismissed by those disliking his offerings.[13] However, as was apparent earlier in the chapter, we are doing our best to recapture the context he played in during the 1980s and discuss this in particular in Chapter 7.

When we turn to the second side of our triangle we can examine his songs and how they work both as musical texts and as particular performances bound up with the writer himself (his voice, singing inflections and non-verbal aspects of his stage performance). On the first side of the triangle, we could, with various degrees of caution, listen to what Costello has to say about writing about a particular song (if that information is available to us). We need to be mindful of our point above about scepticism in a field of commercial constraints, with the artist constantly searching for marketing opportunities.

The true intention in any personal account is open to question in all public statements. The best that any of us can do is test the credibility of statements by seeking confirmatory evidence elsewhere or by making a personal judgement about the veracity of an account in a particular context. This is a reasonable middle path between naive gullibility and an insistent stance of disbelief about all of the statements of all commercial artists.

For example, in the interview we examined in Chapter 1, Costello was in a showcase for the BBC but it was also in his interests to put on clear record what he thought about Thatcherism. Paradoxically, by the end of his statement, when he gets a bit tongue tied and resorts to the 'F word', he is more likely to be speaking from the heart than in his calmer earlier statements, which might well have been rehearsed for the occasion. Yes he was marketing *Spike*, but watching the interview reveals a plausible account, including his sincere views about the political context of his time and place. His voluntary role in political action over the years has reinforced this credibility and the veracity of much of what he articulates. On the other hand, suppose his tongue-tied indignation was still part of a performance; we will never know for certain and so we still have to make our best judgement about his sincerity.

Thus, we need to keep on our toes, particularly in relation to Costello, whose dramatic versatility and capacity to change moods and messages from audience to audience has been noted by those chronicling his climb to fame in the 1980s. If Costello is not a chameleon, he is certainly a slippery fish. Griffiths (2007) cites Frith (1988) and his dismantling of Bruce Springsteen's authenticity (as an ultra-rich working-class hero, dressing the part to persuade) and looks for similar fracture lines in Costello's credibility. The ones he finds, in the critical writings about Costello, are: the variability in his personal accounts (Marcus, 1993); his innumerable mystifying personas (Reese, 1981); the marketing challenge posed

---

[13]   Some sociologists argue that performance and listening in *specific lived contexts* should be our main legitimate focus when studying popular music (for example, Frith, 1996; Martin, 2006) assuming the musical text to be of secondary importance or irrelevant. For a musicological defence of studying the musical text, see Moore (1993). For a sociological defence of studying the aesthetic autonomy of the music itself, see Marshall (2011).

by his highly variegated presentation (Hepworth, 2003); the mixed emotional and ideological messages in his lyrics – for example, in his fascination with, but contempt for, the USA (Hoskyns, 1991); his disdain for, but participation in, a culture of consumerism (Thurschwell, 1999); and the confusing extensive eclecticism in his musical output (Perone, 1998). We could add to this list his ability to adopt a different accent from one interview to the other, or to be deadly earnest at one moment and play the joker at another. This makes it difficult for any of us to spot when he is saying what he truly means in his ordinary voice. Indeed, in the case of Costello, the latter may now beyond the reach of any of us, a conclusion we elaborate in Chapter 9.

In the light of the problems all of this creates for onlookers trying to 'decode' Costello and his music, Griffiths concludes on a highly critical note (to which we return in the final section of the chapter) about the artist's hypocrisy:

> Costello is a self-styled enemy of the music industry but also a textbook case of commodity fetishism ... Costello grants his listeners total autonomy but keeps telling them what to think. (Griffiths, 2007: 9)

Thus, when we come to understand Costello and his music, the intentions of the artist are clouded by the doubts Griffiths summarises from a range of writings about him. We would certainly be naive in taking, at face value, what the artist says about his own work. However, it would be unwise not to *listen* to those accounts, in order to discern when he is 'crying wolf' or indulging in rhetorical excess and when he is telling us something more trustworthy, important and illuminating.

The sceptic about Costello's public presentations does not *have* to be a nihilist. We are not obliged to disbelieve *everything* he says, but merely to listen to him, even if very cautiously, and place his accounts in a wider social context and the situated settings in which he spoke. For example, we might evaluate his contrasting performances on US television's light entertainment shows and the more serious cultural reflections of BBC2 television. We may also glean some insights into his credibility by listening to those who were close to him, even if those accounts are inherently bound up with the politics of their relationship (for example, Thomas, 2003).

Assessing the merit of Costello's work

Extending the above considerations about interpreting Costello's music in context, we move now to consider its merit. Musicologists, sociologists and music journalists offer us no fixed template or consensus for this task. Griffiths (2007: appendix 4.3) overviewed a range of opinions from those who have written about the artist and we can note some points relevant to the 1980s. St Michael (1986) considered that *Imperial Bedroom* was inferior as an album compared to *Punch the Clock* and *Goodbye Cruel World*. Gouldstone (1989) ranked *Trust and*

Imperial Bedroom at the top and considered that *Goodbye Cruel World* and *Blood & Chocolate* 'definitely failed to make the grade'. Smith (2004) liked *Trust* and *Spike* but was damning of *Punch The Clock* and *Blood & Chocolate*. Thomson (2004) extols the virtues of *Imperial Bedroom* but damns *Goodbye Cruel World*; and against the trend of other opinions, he was not that keen on *Spike*.

Thus we are not faced with a clear consensus, though some views overlap. Earlier we noted the dilemma of epistemological privileging: should we warrant the subjective views of some but not others and if so why? This invites us to ask why 'experts' should themselves be given any privileged view. To take as an example of our dilemma in summarising the merit of *Spike*, Thomson (2004), whose book is a detailed and well-written chronicle of Costello's work in the studio and on the road, says this of the album:

> a strange, oddly aloof record, easy to admire but difficult to love. It was only possible to be 'an angry young man' for so long without descending into self-parody ... there was a distance, a coolness at the heart of the record. The changing personas and lack of musical coherence from track to track meant that *Spike* was often more technically impressive than emotionally resonant, almost a sampler rather than a unified album ... (Thomson, 2004: 265)

In this aesthetic assessment, there is an elision between ontological claims (factual statements about what exists, such as 'it *was* only possible' or 'there *was* a distance') and subjective emotional apprehension ('difficult to love') in order to create a hybrid judgement of fact and feeling ('more technically impressive than emotionally resonant'). Thus eventually the judgement about musical technique and production on *Spike* and its eventual impact on *this particular* listener become an amalgam, the elements of which we cannot discern separately and clearly. As with all music critics, the author claims an epistemological privilege by becoming 'everyman': Thomson's individual judgment stands in boldly or arrogantly for us all.[14]

For example, when he says that the record is 'difficult to love' (seemingly an ontological or factual claim) he can only *really* vouch for the subjectively experienced lack of affection on his own part, because affection is a subjective and relational emotion not one that resides objectively in things and people. To state the obvious, others may or may not share the same emotional reaction to the album. Moreover, even within an individual there may be a change over time about the emotional impact of the same piece of performed music.

---

[14] *Whose* subjective view warrants a privilege is decided by power and ideology, in good part at least. Marxists would privilege the views of the proletariat, feminists of women, disability activists of disabled people, and so on. Also (and students encouraged to use their personal experience can get into a tangle here), simply because one has a unique *experience* does not necessarily make the particular *opinion* arising from it inherently superior to another person's viewpoint. An opinion can still be critically appraised for its logical cogency and empirical legitimacy.

Our point here about epistemological privileging is not to endorse or challenge Thomson's view but merely to point out that it is ultimately a view and it is his. Certainly it goes beyond the 'empty accounts' we noted earlier because there is a *plausible justification* offered for the view. But, at the end of it all, it is still Thomson's opinion. Thus, there is an irreducible aspect to musical appreciation; like taste in our appreciation of a cooked meal (to revisit the metaphor used in our introduction). We could resolve the different views of academic or journalistic analysts by appealing to other seemingly measurable criteria. For example, Griffiths (2007: appendix 4.1) tables when Costello's music was recorded in journalistic rolls of honour, such as the *NME*'s 'best hundred albums' – where his work is represented in 1985, 1993 and 2006, but not in 2003. Turning to *The Wire*'s '100 records that set the world on fire', Costello's name is absent. These mixed messages move us little further on but they are interesting seminar material. What is being measured in these estimates and what do we do when or if measures are incommensurable?

Text, context and artist

From our perspective, in the light of the previous section, there are two particular interpretive challenges, when assessing the merit of Costello's music, or any other commercial artist. First there is the tension about the text (Costello's songs and performances) and the social context of their production (Thatcherism) and we try to steer a middle way, by taking both seriously. The second is the tension between the text and the artist.

Some commentators, who we do not agree with fully but mention as part of the dilemma for us all about aesthetic appreciation, have argued that the text is the *only* remaining object of our legitimate inquiry, at least as far as artistic criticism is concerned. It is deemed to stand alone and whatever meaning there is to understand in a song, painting or poem resides *singularly* in the product to be examined and its context of production. Considering the artist and his or her intentions (the argument goes) leads us astray from this preferred focus and must be discounted. This leads some like Barthes (1967) to announce 'the death of the author' but, as a consequence, creating the birth of readers, who variably construct the meaning a song *after* its production.

Similarly, Derrida (1974) argued that 'nothing exists outside the text', which (confusingly) did not mean that the text had no context but the reverse: he meant that there are no *objective* criteria to judge meaning only a multiplicity of other surrounding, and mutually reliant, texts as sources of interpretive authority. Thus the stance of obscurantist and nihilistic poststructuralist critics, like Derrida, is all for context but completely against the possibility of describing its *objective* ontological status. We return to a reading of Costello's work according to poststructuralist criteria in Chapter 8, as well as addressing 'inter-textuality' and its problems. A contrasting view, which we also consider an overstatement in the other direction, emphasises the centrality of the 'auteur': the contention that the individual creative artist will place their *particular* stamp on *their* product. This stamp will heroically survive the constraints and demands of the commercial field of the time, with its technical possibilities and fads and fashions. Costello's reputation in his twenties and thirties as a sometimes controversial and larger-than-life figure who ploughed his own idiosyncratic furrow with an encyclopaedic musical knowledge, might encourage us to see him as an archetypal 'auteur'. The danger of this perspective is that it leads to a form of psychological reductionism, in which we would *simply and only* understand Costello's songs as a direct read out of his brilliant mind and particular talents.

Here we note the risks linked to competing interpretive positions of *both* the 'intentional fallacy'[15] *and* the assumptions about the heroic auteur and below we offer a middle way. Costello's own ambivalence about privileging a named source for creativity is expressed here in his interview with David Hepworth for *Word* magazine in February 2008:

> DH: They're saying that the people who perform on songs but don't write them should participate in the revenue for as long as the person who writes it. Some people see it as just the record companies trying to hang on to their revenue stream as long as they possibly can.

> EC: Yeah. Well, I suppose if they're benefiting and *not the people who actually created it,* yeah, they've got a point, you know. And *there's always an argument between,* there's players that have lit up records and the thing that you actually remember. Wasn't there a case of Herbie Flowers a few years ago about the bass line of 'Walk On The Wild Side'? Because the bass line is as much a hook as some other things on that record are, *though, you'd have to say that none of them could have started to do any of those things unless Lou Reed had written the song, so which comes first?* (Emphasis added to highlight Costello's uncertainty)

The risks associated with the intentional fallacy are worth noting but can also be challenged. Our view is that this vulnerability of interpretation can be productively converted from being a directive prohibition (that is, we must at all times discount the intentions of the artist) to a caution (that is, we could examine their intentions seriously but sceptically). After all, from our viewpoint, Costello's work, like that of any creative artist, undoubtedly was *in part* a product of his, rather than someone else's, *particular* imagination and industry. When inside this inspiration and effort, Costello, like any artist, may overstate this point, to aid self-promotion. But rhetorical overstatement does not negate the presence, in principle, of personal creativity; we are all, to some degree, imaginative but some of us are

---

[15]   Wimsatt and Beardsley (1946) discounted authorial intentionality as worthy material in literary criticism, prompting a debate since then about how to understand creative products. This point reappears in a modified guise in postmodern approaches to texts (see Chapter 8). For these critics, the role of the artist is only of incidental biographical interest and does not warrant investigation.

more so than others. We also all vary as to how motivated and competent we are at translating our imagination into some form of practice. Musical imagination has an expressive not just an inventive aspect, which implicates nuances of practical style and degrees of individual competence, as well as varying degrees of confidence in offering regular performances, considered to be attractive by mass audiences.[16]

Not to recognise this point is disrespectful to the artist and a potential source of empirical inaccuracy and premature methodological closure about their work and its social position.[17] However, our recognition of this point about the agency of the artist should still be placed in relation to the salience of the other factors to consider about important matters, such as the time and place of Costello's work and the presence of others as co-producers of his music, whatever role is conceded on the record about them. Put simply, we do not want to get paralysed by the risk of the intentional fallacy but, instead, we want to put the views of the artist in context and take his products seriously, without taking them naively at face value.

In this light, we wish to avoid the psychological reductionism of the auteur emphasis, while still taking Costello's unique characteristics and achievements seriously, especially as we now live in a context in which media populism fetishises celebrity. Also, the radical relativism of our postmodern times means that strong or definitive value judgements may now be seen as inherently risky or even futile but we offer a view nonetheless.[18]

It will be clear as we offer interpretations of Costello's songs that we are not naive about assuming a simple 'read off' from his claimed intentions or the surface meaning of his lyrics. The discussion of 'Alison' above illustrates this point. At the same time, we are not dismissive of the idea that Costello *had* intentions in his songwriting. For example, we spell out to the reader what we believe that he was getting at when writing the lyrics for the song 'Shipbuilding' (to be discussed in Chapter 4).

Ambiguity is certainly there but that does not divert us from pursuing what we consider to be legitimate and useful understandings of the songs we cite in the book. 'Shipbuilding' is clear in its intentions. This is also the case with 'Tramp the Dirt Down' (though his obvious bile about Thatcher is not carried through in a totally

---

[16]   Some highly respected musicians have struggled in the last of these and 'underperformed' and so arguably they 'underachieved' commercially (for example, Nick Drake and Steely Dan).

[17]   It is also disrespectful to others internalised in the habitus of Costello (in this case). His musical collaborators helped to create unique products and performances, and his confidence and competence were bound up with the love and encouragement of his parents during his childhood.

[18]   This reflects 'the undecidability of propositions' for postmodernists. But although truth claims are indeed contestable, we can still discuss reality, albeit with caution, especially in the human sciences (Bhaskar, 1991). Scepticism does not have to become nihilism and solipsism; the slippery transitive world of language is not the same as the real intransitive world. Postmodernists like the rest of us bleed when they are cut and will all die. Reality ultimately rules, not language.

transparent way verse by verse, as we noted in the previous chapter). Similarly 'Peace in Our Time' (to be discussed in Chapter 5) is broadly an obvious protest song about militarism but there are some ambiguities in the lyrics, which mean we have to make some interpretive leaps, albeit ones that we consider safe and legitimate.

By the time we get to 'Battered Old Bird' in Chapter 8 we have to deal with a central interpretive challenge: Costello claims (somewhat shockingly) that it is based upon *actual biographical material* from his pre-school years, when it reads like a sinister Gothic tale. Thus we are not claiming that song interpretation is always easy but we are claiming that it is worth the effort and risk.

The matter of intention and meaning is one aspect of taking songwriters seriously, while being cautious about the endorsement of the role of the 'auteur'. This interpretive restraint is also required when we try to assess Costello's particular *talents* as a musician. An over-reliance on the concession to the role of personal creativity, even if we abandon a *strong* 'auteur' position in our analysis (as we do about Costello), could contribute to the illusion that individual talent and public recognition of its merit are directly correlated, when this is not inevitable. Lots of very talented people go unrecognised and, conversely, the music industry can at times generate famous individuals whose merit is in legitimate doubt. Reality television, particularly recent shows like the 'X Factor', have encouraged a popular 'Warholian' discourse about fame for fame's sake[19] and the spurious and unwarranted conflation of artistic merit with the achievement of ephemeral celebrity.

None emerging from this new television-driven system are writers. They are all *performers* – that is, young attractive technicians who look the part on stage, judged at a point in time. They are reliant wholly on the musical imagination of others for their initial success. They only cover the already successful songs of others and, in later heats, they are provided with arrangers and singing coaches. Reaching the finals, most ambitiously they might, in the future, become successful *vocalists*,[20] even if, more typically, they are likely to vanish from public awareness as quickly as they came.

In this recent media context, which positions the performance of popular music, we are drawn to the fair conclusion that singer-songwriters, particularly those who, like Costello, can sustain public recognition and commercial success over many years, are probably worthy talents, by any standard, even if their form of music is not to our particular taste. A caution against this broad conclusion is the evident demographic bias in the music industry. The industry, like most other fields, is characterised by age, gender, race and place. Successful talent tends to be overwhelmingly recognised in young adults in popular music. Men are generally commercially promoted and recognised more than women, and the

---

[19]   Andy Warhol predicted that 'In the future everyone will be world-famous for 15 minutes'.

[20]   Note the veneration of vocalists in popular music from Frank Sinatra to Madonna (most of these are female).

rootless, hedonistic lifestyle of being on the road maybe is less attractive to the latter, especially if they are mothers.

Also, as well as our gender our locality increases or decreases our luck about our talent being recognised and the language we sing in is also a factor to consider.[21] With these sorts of necessary caution about demographic bias in mind, we are of the view that commercial success is not a necessary and sufficient condition to define merit. Moreover, as we noted above, conversely merit does not always generate commercial success. However *sustained success*, for example achieved by those like Costello, is a reasonable indicator of aesthetic merit, when and if we accept popular music as a legitimate art form. With sustained success we encounter *reputation* and can use that as a good enough, if rough, guide to merit. We are mindful though, and note again for emphasis, that being an Anglophone male played its role in increasing Costello's luck in the business.

Assessing Costello's political credibility

The above sections have restated and elaborated our starting assumptions about the focus of this book and explained the interpretive challenge facing us. They followed our first outline of Thatcherism in the previous chapter and the contrasting ideological position of those like Costello in the 1980s, who offered their version of a cultural riposte. In the following chapters we will apply our analysis to this topic in more detail. To close this chapter though we will offer a view about a more fundamental question: if Costello was part of the cultural-political field of Thatcherism, was his personal response worthy and credible?

Griffiths (2007) casts doubt on the latter by highlighting two main problems with his actions as an artist. The first relates to Costello's unrelenting negativism and the second to his dubious interpersonal politics. With regard to his negativism, Griffiths notes that Costello only produces lyrics of complaint and seems to show no ability to sing affirmative songs, which celebrate human progress. For example, in 1995 Costello was appointed as Curator of the Meltdown Festival[22] and he worked enthusiastically to encourage its success (Thomson, 2004). Griffiths wonders why such formal engagement with practical politics generated no creative outputs:

> What's interesting is that the project inspired no songs, no titles like 'Public Funding Gets a Good Job Done' or 'Tax and Spend Gotta Be A Good Thing Babe'. Why not '(Nothing Funny Bout) A Minimum Wage' after Labour's

---

[21]   In the post-Second World War music industry more male than female singer-songwriters (not vocalists – see previous footnote) have enjoyed prolonged success. Also note that these are all overwhelmingly Anglophone artists from the *northern* hemisphere. For example, probably few music fans in the north know of Paul Kelly from Australia, who has been feted there for the past thirty years.

[22]   An annual invited leadership role from the Southbank arts festival in London.

election in 1997? If Irishness could serve Costello's purpose as lament, what's to stop it appearing at, well, better times: reconciliation, compromise, 'Peace In Our Time: The Ulster Mix', however precarious? What's with these bitter left wing guys? (Griffiths, 2007: 124, emphasis in the original)

Although this is fair comment from Griffiths, it is also true that, in the field of left-of-centre politics, negativism 'rules' and critique is constantly rewarded and celebrated. We might speculate, as well, about whether any listener would be seriously interested in the titles imagined by Griffiths. The last one might have got off the ground but the others sound more like titles for discussion papers generated by a young internee for the consideration of a Labour Party policy committee.[23]

Generally, the whole point of the left is to complain perpetually as part of a project of political opposition. It is difficult to find any artist coming out of that stable who does *not* focus on attacking the current state of affairs. To develop a sustained enjoyment or celebration of evidence of progress ('reformism') is held in suspicion, as a 'slippery slope' to acceptance of the status quo and even treachery. The left is prone to constant critique, whether the latter is expressed poetically and emotively (as in Costello's episodic laments and rants) or prosaically and analytically, as in more formal social commentary from other writers. Costello is part of the angry and dour norm of that left political field, both complying with that norm and appealing to its sympathies in his receptive listeners.

Moreover, being angry and critical might well have been the *main way* that Costello expressed his creativity during the period we are considering. If this is the case, then any appeal to him to write celebratory joyful songs would have probably been futile and might even have signalled the end of his creative source.[24] This raises a much deeper psychodynamic question about how some artists turn aggression into creativity; Costello is by no means unique in this regard, especially on the musical left.[25] Put differently, if he were not angry and critical to start with, no songs may emerge or, if they did, their content might be bland and unremarkable. Thus, this first criticism from Griffiths is well worth discussing, but critically: people on the left do constantly whinge and protest and they can at

---

[23] There are examples though of some agitprop-influenced songwriters being successful commercially. An example is some of the work of Lionel Bart, with the British workerist lyrics of his musical *Maggie May*, which were recorded, somewhat anomalously, by the US diva Judy Garland, who was a friend of the writer.

[24] The poet Rilke's warning is relevant here: 'Take away my demons and you take away my angels.'

[25] A brutal example of this is the renowned single 'Killing in the Name' (successful in both 1993 and 2009), from *Rage Against the Machine*, which finishes with the line 'Fuck you, I won't do what you tell me!' repeated no less than sixteen times before signing off with 'Motherfucker, ugh!' which makes Costello's lyrics and performance of 'Tramp the Dirt Down' sound rather delicate in comparison.

times turn this disaffection into an art form. Whether this should be a matter itself of complaint is open to discussion and not a foregone judgment.

Griffiths' second – and for us more telling – criticism relates to Costello's political hypocrisy, drawn from the artist's own description of his behaviour, written in the liner notes of the 1995 album *Kojak Variety*. At the start of the notes, Costello describes a meeting with Larry Adler and George Martin in which he indicates a cool, no pressure approach to his professional relationships: 'there is no real rush with music'. By the end of the notes, Costello relates a contrasting memory, of a recording engineer clowning around in the studio; 'I fired him on the spot', he recalls proudly. For Griffiths, understandably, this apparent double standard 'rankles'.

Elitism and individualism in the field of popular music

Here we encounter a more general problem of elevating pop icons to political idols: their field of action (the division of labour and power relationships involved in recorded and performed music) militates against fairness and empathy for those with less status and power.[26] But in a post-feminist world since the 1970s, where 'the personal is political', those with confidence drawn from their status are particularly vulnerable to charges of being gods with feet of clay, when and if they lose a sense of common decency. Whether we call a successful commercial artist a 'star', 'celebrity', 'idol' or 'icon', what is not in doubt is that at any point of music production or performance, which places them at the centre, they can exercise arbitrary authority derived from their peculiar status. They may choose to be respectful, fair-minded and gracious or haughty, mean and spiteful, or all shades of courtesy in between. But the point is that it is *their choice*.

The organisation of the field of popular music production is inherently elitist and radically individualistic because the artist at the centre can always 'call the shots'.[27] The fact that Costello also chose to turn his whimsical firing of the engineer into a publicly declared boast (in the liner notes that Griffiths draws our attention to) might confirm our worst fears about the artist's arrogance and insensitivity to the rights of others (in this case the right to work). But the incident certainly also reveals something about the field of popular music in practice: the normal rules of employment do not apply and a regime of grace and favour is commonplace. There are no organisational policies and procedures 'in place' that are common in other places of work, to ensure individual justice or their rights and responsibilities. Accordingly, those surrounding the artist have to be careful to be inoffensive and to 'know their place'.

---

[26]   This reminds us of the oft-quoted cynical aphorism from Hunter S. Thompson: 'The music business is a cruel and shallow money trench, a long plastic hallway where thieves and pimps run free, and good men die like dogs. There's also a negative side.'

[27]   Traditionally their main grievances have been directed at the constraints placed upon that power by the record companies (see Chapter 7).

The problem for Costello is that his protests about social injustice, in his rhetorically-saturated[28] interviews and in the themes of some of his lyrics, make him particularly vulnerable to legitimate personal scrutiny. Nowadays, the concept of a 'political artist' has become a broader one than defined solely by their lyrical content. Now it has also become part of a moralistic discourse about the micro-politics of their personal relationships. Now we *do* judge artists by their actions, not just their music, and we *will* tend to check the credibility of the latter against the integrity of the former. And this is where the attack on Costello for his political (not artistic) integrity by Griffiths is highly pertinent. The extent to which this should, or will, affect our evaluation of his music will remain a personal judgement for any of us. In the case of the political rhetoric, of say 'Tramp the Dirt Down', we will all then take from it what we wish.

The music industry certainly encourages preciousness and arrogance. This field of action is a sort of 'opportunity structure'[29] to enjoy, play out and boast about personal power over others, often at the hands of those who have known hunger and lowly powerlessness themselves. The business stimulates a form of 'ego inflation' or grandiosity. Commercially successful artists are surrounded, not just by adoring fans, but also by a whole supportive workforce, which depends upon them. Prospects of status and high earnings shape norms of competitiveness and egotism in those who succeed, especially when they look back over their shoulder to the mundane, unrecognised world they have left behind and might fear returning to.

In the case of the incident of Costello boastfully sacking his engineer, the explanation may be simple: he did it 'because he could'. 'Policies, procedures and protocols' in mundane corporate working life (in the private or public sector) exist to protect employees against such arbitrary personal power.[30] The sub-culture of popular music, at least at the end point of production and performance, is exempted from this protective norm.

This point about artistic narcissism situated in the idiosyncratic field of popular music is a good one to end this first chapter, as maybe it is *both* a source of Costello's claim to a political mandate *and* grounds for him and his work to be politically evaluated. In our current context Costello can be judged as a 'political artist' at two levels, one reflected in the content of his music and the other in his personal

---

[28]   The term 'rhetoric' can refer to: (i) empty special pleading; (ii) the inherently persuasive aspect of language; or (iii) emotive appeals for making a better world for suffering humanity (Simons, 1989). When commercial artists stray into the last of these, their actions will inevitably come under particular scrutiny, especially when they enjoy such visible personal freedom, fame and fortune.

[29]   This term is used in the sociology of deviance to include sub-cultures, which emerge when success is impeded into a typical or traditional career path. Criminality, professional sport and commercial popular music offer alternative life trajectories to unemployment, 'shift work' or a 'nine-to-five existence' (Roberts, 1993; Merton, 1996).

[30]   Many ordinary people will exercise cruel authority over others, given particular circumstances (Milgram, 1963; Zimbardo, 1972; Fromm, 1976).

actions (for example, in his treatment of others, as well as his campaigning and involvement with *Rock Against Racism* and later *Self Aid*).

Costello's amoral imagination and its contemporary moralistic context

Like other artists in the public eye, the *inner source* of Costello's creativity under Thatcherism (NB the *external cultural landscape* for his imagination) was basically amoral. The latter claim about inner life is a truism for all of us[31] and yet its expression, as for anyone with a loose tongue in a post-feminist, racially-sensitive world, put him at risk of quick moral censure.[32] If he used his imagination assertively as his main source of employment, this at times meant that he played with fire.[33]

His words, with the synergy of his melodies, were his stock in trade and sprang from his imagination, with no inbuilt filter, because the imagination, by definition, has no conscience. To be an innovative songwriter he *had* to experiment with transgression and, like many artists grazing contentedly on a diet of fame and the attention of others, he could be capricious and opinionated. His off-the-cuff comments about other writers being like a 'race of pygmies' may well have caused some BBC viewers to wince. That possible reaction highlights this point well, about both the nature of the imagination and the pitfalls of ego inflation in the music industry. Costello's imagination casually and simply voiced the 'pygmies' metaphor. He had no apparent sense of shame or embarrassment about dismissing the writing talents of others or deploying a phrase with racial connotations.

The problem for him was the recently acquired conversational etiquette of the 1980s. This was part of the cultural field in which his position as an artist was being judged; not *just* the content and style of his songs were under scrutiny. In particular, 'identity politics' (see Chapter 8) and the feminist convention that 'the personal is political' meant that everyone, including artists, was learning to mind his or her words. Increasingly during the 1970s, words and power were considered to be inextricably linked, even if, on the right, there was a self-indulgent pride in rejecting 'political correctness'.

---

[31] Within a psychoanalytical framework, creativity resides in the imagination, which begins in the very early life of the infant. This may account for why creative artists so often 'act out' immaturely. Creativity can be thus thought of as 'regression in service of the ego' and it allows artists to remain just 'this side' of madness but always also at risk of 'malignant regression' (Kris, 1952; Greenacre, 1960). This perspective is useful but it risks psychological reductionism. Creativity in practice occurs in a *context* (Wilden, 1980) and it implicates groups of people, not just individual artists.

[32] If we all said what we thought or imagined all of the time, then social life would soon become, to say the least, difficult. Etiquette is one manifestation of the 'civilising process' (Elias, 1969) and guilt, anxiety and shame are the prices we pay for being civilised, when we struggle to keep our impulses in check (Freud, 1989).

[33] Costello learned from this, even if painfully. The incident to be discussed in Chapter 4, in which he was accused of racism, was to haunt him for many years.

It was Costello's claim to legitimacy in the field of a left-wing culture that posed the problem for his reputation. Had he been a conservative or apolitical writer maybe none of this would have mattered. This tension for Costello – between his righteous indignation, which fed and reflected his political value system, and his position as a flawed ordinary human being, at times prone to offending others – is not peculiar to him but could apply to anyone in the public eye. We return to this occasional tension in the chapters that follow.

Chapter 3
Nostalgia Denied

Even when one is no longer attached to things, it's still something to have been attached to them; because it was always for reasons that other people didn't grasp.

– Marcel Proust[1]

The two songs we have presented for discussion up to now ('Tramp the Dirt Down' and 'Alison') have touched upon two major aspects of Costello's songwriting, which he moves between: the micro politics of intimacy and the macro politics of his host society. Although those particular songs are about women (and we address sexual politics more in Chapter 6), the macro and micro aspects of the notion of 'politics' have a much wider connotation for us, in relation to the inner and the outer, the subjective and the objective or 'habitus' and 'field'. For example, in this chapter we consider these both/and, rather than either/or, matters in relation to the dimension of time in Costello's work. Time passes for us all between birth and death and we all adopt a subjective position about this reality. We argue here that, by exploring Costello's particular *subjective* position, articulated in his lyrics and public statements, then aspects of his *objective* social context can be also illuminated, and vice versa.

As a socially progressive writer, his encounter in the 1980s with the right-wing revolution of monetarism, consumerist triumphalism and militarist adventurism in a spent imperialist force was depressing and galling. The aspirations of the left throughout the 20th century were being blown away by the apparently unending adaptability of capitalism and its unstoppable thirst for war economies and new forms of capital accumulation.[2] For another British writer at that time this evoked a direct conclusion of 'Paradise Postponed' (Mortimer, 1985) but Costello, more elliptically, offered us nostalgia denied.[3]

Costello may remain linked, in the minds of some music writers and fans, to a period of Punk and New Wave in the late 1970s, but this was never going to be

---

[1]   From *In Search of Lost Time*, trans. C. Prendergast (1995).

[2]   The legendary moments for the left in the 20th century were largely about heroic disappointment, a cue in itself for collective nostalgia: the Russian revolution betrayed by Stalin; the Spanish civil war and the optimism of Catalonia lost to fascist Franco; and the failure of nerve of the British labour movement in relation to the General Strike of 1926. Thatcher was going to become par for the course with her breaking of the miners' strike and, more widely, her subversion of trade unionism.

[3]   A comparable Miltonian allusion can be found in *American Pastoral* (1997), Roth's dark elegy about American life post-Vietnam. In its first section, 'Paradise Remembered', the author explores the hypnotic futility of nostalgia, when faced with current horrific challenges and legacies.

his resting place or main site of celebration. The reason for this was that some of his emotional attachments were to the very period being rejected by many of his contemporaries: the music of the past. (This rejection of the past may have been a point of peer group solidarity for Punk's fan base but some Punk musicians would later express their respect for bands such as the Rolling Stones, who in their turn had in the past incorporated the appeal of the Blues.)

Although a recurring rhetoric of pop trends is the binary of 'new good, old bad', in truth most of the time we find modish innovations represent some aspect of inheritance, with allusions acknowledged or not. This point is made by Inglis (2000) in relation to the 1960s and their domination in British popular music by The Beatles. The reified image of this allegedly hermetically-sealed 'brand new' period understated the cultural impact of the 1950s on the creative inspiration and work of Lennon and McCartney.

A legacy recycled and elaborated across four decades is exemplified by the bridge formed by another New Wave artist. During Costello's early career, Paul Weller's work connected 1960s US black soul and white UK 'mod' bands under its influence (for example, The Small Faces), with subsequent 'Brit Pop' bands of the 1990s, such as Oasis, Blur and Ocean Colour Scene. Like Weller, Costello never joined any chorus of rejection of the past, despite the label imposed on him as a New Wave artist.[4] And if that message needed to be made clear, his third album was a double endorsement of his respect for history. First, it celebrated an old style of US popular music (at the time decidedly unpopular among the young in Britain). Second, it offered respect to that style by covering songs already written by others. But before returning to the content of his music at the turn of the 1980s, let us establish the case for Costello's nostalgia denied.

Costello and finitude

A condition reality imposes upon us all is finitude. We can recall the past, we have to deal with the present and one day we will die. These three points about our personal timeline are approached differently by us all and addressed by religious and secular ideologies in a variety of ways. For this reason, given the focus in this book, here we examine Costello's own particular approach to life and death. A point arising from songs examined in the first two chapters is that Costello's view of heaven or hell is not in the afterlife but in the here and now.[5]

---

[4]   We argue in Chapter 7 that New Wave contained a dominant conservative wing of the New Romantics, whereas Costello, on its critical edge, represented an older version of radical Romanticism.

[5]   This is a common position in 20th century existentialism. For example, we have from Albert Camus: 'What does eternity matter to me? To lose the touch of flowers and women's hands is the supreme separation' (*The Outsider*, 1961).

Another indication of his existential musings, about time attachment and the meaning of our finite existence, appears in his discussion of the inanimate world not just intimate attachments. For example, we have his reflections on the 'Hoover Factory' (1980, from *10 Bloody Marys and 10 How's Your Fathers*, an album largely comprised of 'B-sides'). Costello used to pass this beguiling art deco building, on the Western Avenue near to London, when he was younger and it clearly made an impression. In a sort of nostalgic reverie, he talks of its 'splendour' and speculates about its wonder when it was 'brand new'. And then he muses: 'It doesn't matter if I take another breath. Who cares? Who cares?'

In this short, simple and sweet song, Costello's existential position is there: his projection into the past, the contingent arbitrariness of meaning and the absurdity of our individual presence on earth. In the documentary of the making of *Almost Blue* we have this statement from him:

> I don't believe in the dying young thing but at the same time I'm inexorably drawn towards that ... I can't work out whether I'm flirting with it or whether it's starting to take me over (*South Bank Show*, November 1981)

Costello left London for Nashville, at a substantial commercial and personal risk. He abandoned his own material. He went to foreign soil and was met by a lukewarm record producer. He chose to record a form of music that was probably stereotyped as redneck sentimentality by his typical fan at home.

However, this brave or reckless expedition also stirred up some intrigue in Britain. His visit to Tennessee to record *Almost Blue* became the focus of a full-length television arts programme documentary. It was presented favourably by the writer Melvyn Bragg on London Weekend Television's *South Bank Show* in which he made his existential statement quoted above. Costello later reflected:

> Going to Nashville to make *Almost Blue* was about *affection and curiosity*. I didn't think for a moment what it meant for my career. I didn't think what it meant to engage [former Beatles' engineer] Geoff Emerick to make *Imperial Bedroom*, with those big orchestrations. It was a money-is-no-object exercise. (*Rolling Stone*, 22 September 2004, emphasis added)

Note how he had acquired 'affection and curiosity' for this style of music in his musical development. He particularly admired the best of musical Americana, in the work of artists like Gram Parsons and Roy Orbison. This skilfully performed and emotionally tender style of music is discussed more in Chapter 6 in relation to women. This chapter connects with that discussion in relation to a broad emotional agenda about tenderness for heterosexual male writers, when they explore sentimentality, vulnerability, regret, self-pity, hurt pride and loss. These together culminate in a type of writing which we could summarise as nostalgic longing.

Costello's imagination also extended to vicarious reminiscences at various points, when he reconstructed parts of the lives of his family members. By 1989, in two songs from *Spike*, there are explicit allusions in his writing to the life of his grandfather, who was an Irishman anomalously in the British army during the First World War (on the 'potato parade'), in 'Any King's Shilling' and to his frail elderly grandmother in 'Veronica' (written with Paul McCartney).

Nostalgia and the taboo on tenderness

Later in his career, this existential theme about sad longing for the security of place, real or imagined, in relation to the Irish diaspora is expressed in 'The Long Journey Home' (1998), the title track of a US television series on the Irish in America. This song (produced by The Chieftains' leader Paddy Moloney) refers to the anguished predicament of swathes of Irish people obliged to depart for Great Britain or the USA (see Chapter 5). But, from the time period of interest to us, we have Costello dreamily 'thinking about the old days of Liverpool and Rotherhithe' (in 'New Amsterdam' from *Get Happy!!*)[6]. Both of these places are firmly located in his younger past.

However, by 2004 Costello was emphatically denying that he was nostalgic by nature, when discussing singing his earlier material:

> I wouldn't sing anything for nostalgic reasons. *I am the least nostalgic person you will ever meet.* And I have no concern for posterity. I believe when you're gone, you're gone. (*Rolling Stone*, September 2004, emphasis added)

There are three ways to explain this disavowal, which are not mutually exclusive. The first is simple *self-deceit* as part of his self-interested public rhetoric about the importance of his most current project. As we noted in Chapter 2, for all commercial artists interviews are mainly marketing opportunities. The second possibility is that Costello genuinely may not look back longingly, when actually *performing* his songs. As he indicates, he truly may not be motivated by nostalgia to sing older, rather than newer, numbers. He may just sing them. The third possibility is that he *imagines* nostalgia as an experience of others *but it is an experience that does not touch him* at all as a person in his life. This prospect is important to bear in mind more generally about lyricists (or poets or novelists). They do explore the experiences and actions of others in their writings and their characters are not *necessarily* expressing their own thoughts and feelings.[7]

Notwithstanding these possibilities, at times the content of his lyrics seem to betray sentiments of longing for people, time and place. Empirically, it is

---

[6]   This song may have been set in New York ('New Amsterdam' was its old name) when he was feeling homesick and is also the scenario for some of the work on *King of America*. Costello's nostalgia about London life is at its most fullsome in a later song, 'London's Brilliant Parade' from *Brutal Youth* (1994).

[7]   We discuss this point in Chapter 6, when examining Norman Mailer and his feminist critics.

simply not tenable to claim that Costello and nostalgia are strangers, even if it is he who makes the claim. Basically he is simply too good at exploring nostalgia, in his own lyrics and especially those of others, for us to dismiss it as nothing but an act of his imagination (the third caution above). And if he is not a nostalgic person, why does he invest so much 'affection and curiosity' about this form of experience in the offerings of other musicians on *Almost Blue* (discussed below)? Surely that investment in and of itself reflects nostalgia. The reminiscences he appears to lovingly record and perform render his disavowal above, to say the least, enigmatic. Going further, the statement may suggest that Costello is protesting too much and that he is still, as in younger days, struggling with tenderness.

In those early days of his career Costello permitted himself tenderness in words that pined for past time and place but he often struggled to do this in his lyrics about current personal intimacy. However, this is not about Costello's idiosyncratic psychopathology but reflects a wider cultural 'taboo on tenderness', especially for heterosexual men (Suttie, 1935). It may be a recurring symptom of the tension between patriarchal authority and the threat of its displacement by matriarchy with social and political progress (Gerson, 2009). We return to this point in Chapter 6, when discussing Costello's ambivalence about women and intimacy.

As for looking back after death, this is an interesting but different point. Does Costello care, in an imagined future, what people will think of him? That reflection *ipso facto* is a present one and so it might actually indicate that he is unconcerned how others *currently* evaluate his work. We await the future and the past has gone, so now is the only place to consider them; an existentialist (and Buddhist) truism that returns us to Costello's untenable disavowed concern with nostalgia.

Nostalgia is a profoundly existential matter (Sedikides et al., 2004). It relates to lost times, people and places (or some combination of these) and is a constant reminder of that loss, in our conditions of lonely finitude and the eventual scenario of the hour of our death. It creates particular conditions of poignancy, like small occasional funerals we are permitted to attend about our own passing. It gives meaning to our lives as we journey to death.[8] Costello is no different from the rest of us in this regard and so his denial about nostalgia should not deflect us from trying to unpack the significance of his actual tendency to look back over his shoulder at both his family's past and the celebration of a musical heritage that was part of his habitus.

---

[8]   As one of Saul Bellow's characters announces in *Mr Sammler's Planet*, 'Everybody needs his memories. They keep the wolf of insignificance from the door.'

Nostalgia and *Almost Blue*

The content of *Almost Blue*,[9] an album of Country and Western covers from Costello, is overwhelmingly, almost unbearably, nostalgic. If there is any doubt about this conclusion, look at it song by song: eleven of the dozen original tracks[10] have a surfeit of maudlin regret and self-pity about lost loves or lost opportunities from past times. On the first, Hank William's singer asks: 'Why don't you love me like you used to do?'

This version is cranked up by Sherrill to a furious tempo, disrespectfully subverting the intended mood of the song. In the *South Bank Show* documentary he seems to impose it on the band as a joke, provoking their understandable perplexity and suspicion. However, it was Costello that started the game of hide-and-seek about the tempo of the number, confessing that on the first take he was already playing it more like a Jerry Lee Lewis piece of rock and roll. In response to this affront, Sherrill can be seen whispering and giggling with the record engineer and then suggests to Costello that the track needed to be even faster. Once the take was finished, Sherrill spoke to Costello from behind the glass of the recording booth and told him that Hank Williams had left his grave and was on his way over. (The song was covered subsequently by, amongst others, Van Morrison and the Red Hot Chilli Peppers, and so has now become a 'standard'.)

Next on the album we have Don Gibson offering us a man who has sweet dreams every night about a lover he simply cannot forget.[11] On the third track ('Success' by John Mullins) the singer has been put in second place by a successful partner and he now spends all of his evenings alone. Continuing the theme, Costello then sings the lyrics of Etheridge and Parson's 'I'm Your Toy', asking his ex-partner to remembering the way she cried in the past. This is followed by Merle Haggard's lament about booze (the one genuine friend he thought he had established in life) betraying him about obliterating the pain from the past ('Tonight the Bottle Let Me Down'). By the sixth track, we are in a divorce court with a judge who was insensitive to the pain of a man who had loved a woman for so long and whose world had now stopped ('Brown to Blue'). Then we have 'Good Year for the Roses', which we examine in more detail below.

On track 8 Charlie Rich's character is in a drunken stupor concerned about the traditional loyalty of his lover ('Sittin' and Thinkin''). Then in the next song, the bluebird in the tree is not singing like he used to and there is a blue note in each song since his lover has gone ('Color of the Blues', from George Jones and

---

[9]   Note that there is no title track on this album but 'Almost Blue' subsequently reappears as a track title on *Imperial Bedroom* (1982).

[10]   When re-released in 1994, eleven more tracks were added, including some duplicated live versions.

[11]   'Sweet Dreams' was a hit when first sung by Faron Young in 1956 but subsequently was largely popularised by a version from Patsy Cline in 1963, the year she perished in a plane crash.

Lawton Williams). On track 10 Billy Sherrill's 'Too Far Gone' has a singer that knows that he has 'loved you too much for too long'. The penultimate track is more in the accusing menacing style typified by Costello's own lyrics from other albums of the period. It is the exception that proves the rule for this one. A woman and her 'yakety yak' are making the singer 'nervous about holding a baseball bat' ('Honey Hush' from Big Joe Turner). But, just to remind us of the central message of the album, we finally return to the main theme, with Gram Parsons and Pam Rifkin and their singer whose 'love still pines for you' ('How Much I've Lied').

By this final track we have an amalgam scenario, across these covered songs, of a man pining for lost love in past times and heading irrevocably for cirrhosis of the liver or suicide (whichever comes first). When we consider the twelve tracks in the round, the album is so obviously *doubly* nostalgic. Not only are the lyrics dominated by the sentiments demonstrated above, but on *Almost Blue* Costello is exploring (with 'affection and curiosity' to use his own words) an objectively recognised musical tradition incorporated subjectively and with great respect into his habitus from the past and in the present.[12] He is personally searching back for something, without regard for the cost to his career or his bank balance (see quote above from *Rolling Stone*, September 2004). With hindsight, any of us may accept this claim with our own particular degree of confidence. However, taking the emotive voicing in his recorded performances and his considered track selection together, it must be difficult for any of us to believe that Costello really is 'the least nostalgic person you will ever meet (*sic*)'.

Let us now look specifically at the track released by Costello as a single from the album.

Tribute, pastiche and appropriation: the workings of 'Good Year for the Roses'

This song was recorded originally by George Jones, an early collaborator of Costello's in the USA. It reached number 2 in the US Country charts in 1970 for Jones, and for Costello in 1981 it made number 6 in the British charts. It has been covered by others since, including Counting Crows. One of the twelve covers that make up *Almost Blue*, Costello recorded 'A Good Year For the Roses' in Nashville in May 1981.

The music and lyrics, written by Country composer Jerry Chesnut, had been recorded in Nashville ten years earlier by George Jones and released on the Musicor album *George Jones with Love* (1971). Costello's cover version was produced by influential and distinctive Country-Pop producer Billy Sherrill. Sherrill was among those producers responsible for the more mainstream Country sound coming out of Nashville in the 1960s and 1970s. This 'Countrypolitan' sound was a response

---

[12]   This is a reminder for the reader that habitus is not only about our inherited habits, values, possessions and competencies from the past. It is like a 'live document' open to ongoing modification, albeit strongly determined by childhood experiences in our family of origin, social class and schooling.

Example 3.1   The 'slip-note' piano style

to the more traditional Country sound produced by studios in nearby Bakersfield. George Jones's original was produced for Musicor by bassist and bandleader Bob Moore. Ironically, this was to be Jones's last Musicor release as he moved to Epic specifically to record more with his then-wife Tammy Wynnette and utilise the producing, composing and arranging talents of – Billy Sherrill.

Whilst the Attractions track stands close analysis in isolation, the context of is one of Costello's admitted fondness for Country music (and specifically the work of George Jones, with whom, to Costello's bemused delight, he had been invited to duet two years previously). Given this context, the historical perspective of Costello's appropriation of genres and the thread of this chapter 'nostalgia' invites us to compare these two recordings on at least some levels. In particular we look at what elements Costello took, amplified or discarded of Country to make his own work, and the significance of production and producers in the recording process of the period.

The song, in either version, is marked by a medium ballad beat comprised of even quavers: where they differ is primarily in instrumentation. Bob Moore's 1971 production features characteristic Nashville 'slip-note' piano (Example 3.1). This was possibly even recorded by pianist Floyd Kramer, who innovated the style and balanced featured appearances and recordings with steady and frequently anonymous session work. Aside from Jones's voice, the piano is the main melodic feature, heard over a wash of strings and shepherded by acoustic guitar, double bass and rim-click back beat.[13]

The Attractions' 1981 arrangement replaces Jones's standard acoustic Country line-up of piano and acoustic guitar (by 1971, 'hackneyed' would be a fair appraisal of the orchestration) with electric organ and pedal steel. Though the album was frequently assumed to be a tribute to Costello's childhood hearing of 1950s Country music, Costello claims his 'in' to Country came with Gram Parsons and the Byrds (*Almost Blue* CD liner notes, Rhino reissue, 2004). The instrumental choices on this recording possibly reflect this attraction to the younger generation of Country players and Costello's closer identification with the 1960s sound, as opposed to the 'classic' Country sound of acoustic guitars and upright bass.

---

[13]   The slip-note style is so called because of the preponderance of appogiaturas played within chords. This feature can be noted in every bar of the bass clef in Example 3.1, and at the opening of bar 4 in the treble clef.

Example 3.2 Guitar strum and bass on 'Good Year for the Roses'

Example 3.3 Drum and bass patterns for 'Good Year for the Roses'

Costello's acoustic guitar is almost subliminal throughout, picking up slightly towards the end of the song, and the pulse that the guitar provides on the original is translated to Pete Thomas's snare, played with brushes. The Costello version is 8bpm faster than the Jones version, a small but crucial difference. George Jones's band sounds relaxed in the pulse and the underpinning lilts along. The apparently light strum on the guitar nevertheless contains strong accents that match the bass pattern, and the desultory feeling of the strum is accentuated by a delayed up-stroke in the first beat and a relaxed 'spread' to each down stroke (Example 3.2).

The increase in tempo of Costello's version is made more apparent by the differences in drumming and bass pattern (Example 3.3). The bass now anticipates both major beats in the bar and is just more present – warmer, richer and electric in tone. The drums are high in the mix, and there is a loud and insistent hi-hat sound, replacing the warm cross-stick heard on the Jones version. The more regular, insistent nature of this pulse and the volume and sonic detail of this regular 'chick' sound is intrusive, considering that most of this arrangement is marked by a variety of soft textures, a lack of attack on notes and a warm overall tone.

The other crucial elements of the Costello version are the organ and lead guitar, heard throughout the track and contributing heavily towards the more progressive Country sound. The guitar is played by pedal steel player John McFee, who was also the lead guitarist on 'Alison' and 'Stranger in the House'. This last track (an out-take from *My Aim is True*) was the song sent to George Jones. It inspired him to invite Costello to do a duet (on his 1979 album *My Very Special Guests*), and the organ is, of course, by Costello stalwart Steve Nieve.

After the first verse, the string section and vocal backing (female 'aahs') enter, and there is a general swell into the chorus, a textural density maintained throughout most of the rest of the track, due to regular insertions of string backings and vocal 'oohs'. Whilst the swirling interplay between pedal steel and organ really creates the ambience on this song, they (and the string/vocal soup) also fill up every sonic space.

Moving from detail back out to the overall sound, George Jones sings the song easily, his voice way out in front of the band and his masculine vocal tone cushioned with a broad reverb. This is classic Country: whilst we require elements of guitar, bass, drum rhythms and strings to fully establish the genre, Country music is, more than anything else, *narrative vocal music*. George Jones would subsequently move away from this style towards the more popular 'Countrypolitan' sound spearheaded by Billy Sherrill.

In Costello's version, his vocal is spatially flatter; more closely recorded and more immediately present, and occasionally tonally obscured by other elements impinging on his frequency range, and reflects the influence of Sherrill and the 'Countrypolitan' sound.

At this point we have to take care not to create false relations between the two recordings. The original production was something that Costello certainly would have heard, it being one of Jones's biggest hits and Costello's own choice for a cover (and frank tribute). However, Costello also chose Sherrill: by the early 1980s Sherrill had produced George Jones for a decade, both with and without Tammy Wynnette. (George Jones would *only* record with Billy Sherrill from 1971 until he moved to MCA in 1991). Jones had a tough time throughout the 1970s, struggling with alcohol and cocaine addiction. He had far fewer hits and was so frequently absent on concerts that by 1980 his nickname was 'No-Show Jones'.

Nevertheless, with Sherrill, Jones had three hits in the early 1980s, one of them preceding Costello's 1981 Nashville date. Listening to one track, 'He Stopped Loving Her Today', and the hit album it comes from *I Am What I Am* (1980), we can hear the same combinations of elements as are heard on Costello's recording: a closer, less distant vocal, electric bass, denser string and vocal backings, and more instances of melodic ornamentation (pedal steel, piano and harmonica).

With this in mind, Costello's choice of Sherrill (Jones's producer throughout his weakest years) argues against a strictly nostalgic reading of 'Good Year For The Roses'. Costello could have favoured a more traditional approach, possibly recording in the more 'purist' Bakersfield studios. However, his speculative desire to emulate Jones lies less in wanting to be as-Jones-was and as he had heard Jones, than in an (equally speculative) desire to be in the same shoes as the 1981 George Jones. In the latter regard this would mean recording with Billy Sherrill and (further speculation) being on the road to recovery from a broken heart and extensive substance abuse. As we noted earlier, the songs selected for the album *Almost Blue* are in the main a maudlin tribute to the latter scenario of male distress and degradation. Costello could personally identify both with George Jones and all the imagined characters of the songs throughout the album he compiled.

Sherrill's contribution to 'Good Year For The Roses' is typical of his output at this time – a dense, multi-layered arrangement. The main non-Sherrill elements are, naturally, The Attractions. The British band can produce all the sounds and rhythms required to emulate Country music, but the exact parameters that define genres performed at their apogee are frequently ineffable and comprised more of nuances than gross events. Whilst the arrangement is certainly effective, the differences in style between the British and American musicians, and the reported early conflict or confusion between Costello and Sherrill, point maybe towards a form of hubris on Costello's part, when trying to write a part for himself in Country music, by recording an album of covers in the home of the Nashville Sound.

Discussion

This short chapter warrants its own space for three main reasons. First, Costello's emphatic denial of nostalgia is bemusing to the honest observer of his music. We try to account here for this disavowal from him but ultimately we are speculating about a topic which remains difficult to fathom. When Costello makes assertions about his position or intentions, during his public displays in interviews, it is difficult to know what to believe and when he is crying wolf. In Chapter 7 we return to this point and question whether Costello ever *really* wants to be understood by his critics, fans or journalists. As a result of this manifest ambivalence, by Chapter 9 we can do little but record the contradictory nature of Costello's self-presentation.

Second, his recording of Country music, which proceeded self-consciously – and with some anxiety, as the above song analysis notes – was part of some sort of existential project for Costello. It was bound up with a particular period in his life characterised by emotional rawness. His love life, and his bruising over the race incident that we consider in the next chapter, meant that he was entering a period of emotional turmoil that was to last for a few years in the mid-1980s. He toyed with his life coming to an early end. He was not sure what the point of it all was at times, according to some of his interview material available. Whatever was going on in his mind at the time, he was discovering how to be an existentialist in practice because he was becoming preoccupied with finitude and choice.

Third, the inner disturbance that was clearly present about his life during the early 1980s opens up for us a number of considerations, which we explore further in subsequent chapters. This disturbance was both a reflection of, and inspiration for, his musical creativity during the 1980s. We return to this particular point when considering the song 'Battered Old Bird' in Chapter 8.

The depictions that were to emerge of him being angry not tender were understandable, but so was his irritation about those depictions. In particular, Costello was faced with the dilemma of how to claim personal integrity about his writing: he was preoccupied with the resolute 'honesty' of his music in his public accounts. On the one hand, he projected this image of dogged authenticity and was even venerated for it.

In Chapter 6, we look at this matter in relation to his early critics respecting his candour about difficult material in his lyrics. On the other hand, his guilt and distress about the break-up of his first marriage meant that he wanted to retain a policy of strict privacy. The poignancy of the song 'Good Year For The Roses' (whether intended or arrived at by coincidence) is that it is about a break-up of a relationship and the presence of a baby. In part at least, that was the actual distressed and distressing scenario in which Costello found himself in relation to his wife and child in 1980.

Thomson (2004) notes, that in the early days of his success, Costello soon developed a very strict position about eschewing personal disclosure and he even invoked the threat of his manager Jake Riviera 'breaking legs' if the policy was violated. This gives us a partial clue about the topic of this chapter. If nostalgia is endorsed positively then it is about celebrating, or dreamily *and openly* wallowing in, the past. Costello could not afford to embark on such a path because it was at odds with his strict privacy policy to protect himself and those near to him.

If this hypothesis is correct, then a dilemma ensues for artists *both* claiming their authority from their experience *and* risking the disclosure of their 'warts and all' personal history. The outcome is that messages to the world, in both interviews and lyric writing, by necessity then have to be coded and their personal sources not disclosed. But once they are coded, what happens to authenticity? Does it mean that the *sentiment* is honest but the words used disguise true events? If the answer is in the affirmative, then it means that the motive is honest but the message, to some extent or other, is dishonest: we are left with a variable mixture of candour and deceit.

In Chapter 6, which considers his attitude towards women, we return to the way that Costello processed this general artistic dilemma. That chapter also examines further a topic introduced in this one: the modern crisis of masculinity. Whatever we make of his inner twists and turns about tenderness, we know that Costello struggled with the experience. Not only was it confounded by anger and bitterness in his exploration of heterosexual intimacy, he struggled to write many songs that were *purely* tender. Even rare examples of these attempts, like 'Stranger in the House', when looked at in detail, are more about 'poor me' self-pity than the gentle adoration of another. Our guess is that his real enough desire to be tender had to be handed over, in whole or part, to other writers. This is one aspect, then, of his choice to record *Almost Blue*. That reliance on others for the purpose of exploring tenderness returned later in his career, when writing with Burt Bacharach or when recording another covers album, *Kojak Variety* (1995).

Conclusion

This chapter has focused on a disavowed aspect of the work of Elvis Costello: his nostalgic impulses and interests. The emotive topic of looking back in longing resonates for most of us in our lives and so it is an experience that does not necessarily require apology or denial. However, commercial artists are not any of us. Their private lives are *both* the source of their creativity (at least in part) *and* a potential threat to their reputation, if turned against them by the mass media and critics. Costello dealt with this dilemma in his own particular way, shaped in part by the particular web of intimacy he inhabited in the early 1980s. If the lid was kept on disclosures about private events to do with his family and erotic life at that time, this was not to be the case in relation to his volubly expressed private rancour about some music from the USA. This is the cue for our next chapter.

Chapter 4
Race and Nation

There are no humane methods of warfare, there is no such thing as civilized warfare; all warfare is inhuman …

– James Connolly[1]

The 1980s marked an important period for British capitalism. Britain's imperial power was all but over and its industry-based economy, centred upon manufacturing, was being abandoned in favour of finance capital and its attendant consumerism, to ensure capital accumulation for an elite few. What would become known as 'Reaganomics' in the 1980s was to be the platform for the catastrophic recent legacy of 'casino capitalism' and the 2008 crisis of international capital. In 'the City', bankers and traders were to become ultra-rich but for much of the population, especially the young of working age, it was about low pay in non-unionised insecure settings[2] or unemployment.

The switch to consumerism created the illusion of an enlarged middle class but in fact the new working class was emerging in low-paid service industries of shops, call centres and goods delivery systems. In the British context, these changes overlaid colonial processes. The latter had generated cultural legacies from 19th-century imperialism, when cheap raw materials imported from the colonies, such as cotton and sugar, had enabled their conversion to goods in British manufacturing. These needed to be transported. Labour shortages and downward pressures on labour costs in Britain ensured that cheap labour from the colonies or ex-colonies-to-be were also imported.

By the mid-20th century Britain's post-colonial character defined the nature of its precarious industrial base and shifting workforce patterns. In the 1950s, African-Caribbean workers were brought in to staff public transport systems in large cities, like London, Birmingham and Sheffield. In the 1960s, labour costs were kept down in the textile industry of the Midlands and North of England by flows of immigrants from the Indian sub-continent. This began a trend still evident (but now in relation to EU migrants) of foreign labour being prepared to tolerate poor conditions of work considered unacceptable by indigenous workers under welfare capitalism.[3]

---

[1]   From 'Can Warfare Be Civilised?' (1915), accessed from The James Connolly Society website.

[2]   Until the 1980s our image of personal oppression about work was in relation to the grave toll of unemployment, but thereafter *insecure employment* was to have a greater adverse effect on mental health for working-class people (Rogers and Pilgrim, 2003).

[3]   This created one of many contradictory post-Second World War racist narratives in Britain of this sort: migrants are coming to take 'our' jobs and women and they are going to

Culturally this alteration of the balance of British neighbourhoods and workforces was to have mass psychological effects, the most important of which was the stimulation, and often justification, of racism. Whereas some parts of Britain had a multi-cultural presence since the 19th century (for example, African and Chinese seamen settled in ports like Bristol and Liverpool), the Caribbean and Indian sub-continent migrants were more visible and more widespread, at the very time when British imperialism was on its deathbed. The country's economic strength and geo-political role were now in severe jeopardy, evoking understandable reactionary impulses in white indigenous Britons harking back to prouder times.

The pre-war rise of Oswald Mosley's British Union of Fascists, with its emphasis on anti-Semitism,[4] gave way in the 1950s and 1960s to a more diffuse form of race hate about immigrants, from far right parties like the National Front and the British Movement (Thurlow, 1987). Their recent legacy can be found in the British National Party. Some of their legitimacy was facilitated by populist statements from right-wing Conservative politicians like Enoch Powell and, later, Norman Tebbitt (see below).

And both the older and ongoing trends of immigration were not just about the markers of skin colour. There were also the cross-flows of population between Great Britain ('the mainland') and its nearest colony across the water, Ireland. This ensured that British racism was going to be more complicated than prejudices about the look of a person's skin alone. Another complication was that the Irish, like 'South Asian' and the African-Caribbean people were disproportionately poor. This has meant (its impact is still being witnessed) that alterations in the health and well-being of these groups were affected by a mixture of *both* racism in its various forms *and* poverty, making it difficult at times to disaggregate the impact of each (Abbots et al., 2001; Leavey et al., 2007; Nazroo and Iley, 2010). These interconnecting processes ensured that what are now called the BME (Black Minority Ethnic) communities of Britain have been socially excluded and their well-being jeopardized on a number of fronts.[5] Racism affected access to jobs and housing. Poverty ensured direct and negative physical and mental health

---

scrounge benefits 'we' pay for. They are also bringing their wives and children to use 'our' schools and health services.

[4]   The orthodox ideology of German fascism emphasised an international conspiracy of Jews, within both communist and capitalist elites. Costello's track 'Less Than Zero' from *My Aim Is True* (1977) was an early note from him about his anti-fascist sentiments. Because of its allusion to 'Oswald', Costello was prompted to rewrite the lyrics for a US audience ('the Dallas Version') to prevent any confusion with Lee Harvey Oswald, the accused assassinated assassin of President Kennedy.

[5]   As well as the main groups noted earlier, other minorities were put into the ethnic mix during the Second World War. For example, there were combatants from North America and Poland, as well as prisoners or internees from Germany and Italy, some of whom remained in Britain.

impacts, as well as indirect cultural impacts around educational and employment aspirations.

Moreover, for those from BME backgrounds raised in Britain (second- and third- generation) additional stressors were encountered about their identity and values. The emergence of the 'post-colonial identity' became relevant to any socio-historical understanding of the politics of race in Britain. Those born and raised in Britain were in a contradictory position affecting the sureties of their self-identity (or 'ontological security') but also allowing them particular freedoms and opportunities to speak more than one language or experiment with political and cultural loyalties. Since the 1950s Irish and African-Caribbean people have been over-represented in psychiatric populations (suggesting that, apart from a proneness to poverty, this existential ambiguity might disproportionately drive these groups crazy). British-Asian teenagers have been unsure whether to embrace or reject Western values and dress codes – let alone where their political allegiances lie or which cricket team they should support.[6]

Costello and British post-colonialism

In the light of the above picture, we can reflect on the extent to which Costello could assert himself as an auteur. At the outset, so much of his persona and rhetoric of self-justification rested upon a form of anarchistic individualism: the sort of obstreperous posturing and pushy irritability that attracts admiration and exasperation in equal measure from onlookers. He had much to be arrogant about (we return to his arrogance in Chapter 7 and his egotism in Chapter 8). He was very bright and extremely well versed in the Western popular musical traditions of the 20th century. These personal resources provided him with a particular wealth of insight and competence denied to many of his equally ambitious peers, in the music industry of the late 1970s. He and his fans were faced with the inspiring image of a self-possessed young man who, by a mixture of creative exuberance and a love of individual freedom, was developing into an ideal-type auteur. His future seemed to be in his own very capable and creative hands.

Whilst Costello seemed to be living in an autonomous artistic space, the sources of that individual edge in the field of commercial music were not of his making. The generations above him, especially his father and grandfather, had already sketched dominant aspects of his life script as a talented and stroppy musician. And that context of musical production was one of post-colonialism. His experience and that of his wider family system, through three generations during his upbringing, was Anglo-Irish, a point we pick up again Chapter 5 when

---

[6]   'A large proportion of Britain's Asian population fail to pass the cricket test. Which side do they cheer for? It's an interesting test. Are you still harking back to where you came from or where you are?' This view was offered in the *Los Angeles Times* in 1990 by Norman (now Lord) Tebbitt, an aggressively Thatcherite Conservative minister.

discussing his ambivalence about the USA. His apparent contempt for England ('the whore of the world'), as an Anglo-Irish writer, has already been noted in Chapter 1.

So, not only did post-colonialism provide him with a family script about becoming a critical and thoughtful musician, the 1980s also provided him, within that role, with a particular external social, cultural and economic focus for his musical imagination. This was a time that invited creative opposition and Costello thus had found his time. That relationship between his subjective inner world (of knowledge and imagination) and his objective outer world of a post-colonial British context, one with particular and discernible cultural and economic features, is how we can understand some of what he wrote and why.

Colonial power from Europe relied on a mixture of military, religious and cultural domination, imposed largely upon the continents of the southern hemisphere. In the case of Britain, this meant swathes of Africa, Asia and Australasia, as well as the important exception near to home (as noted above) of Ireland. Physical domination took two forms, both of which were to have resonances in critical popular music writing, from those like Costello and for the ethnic background of those attracted to musical performance (post-colonial BME groups being over-represented).

The first form was direct enslavement: Britain was at the centre of the slave trade. The latter is the reason that Africans were in the Caribbean and North America, as part of an economic arrangement about the production of, respectively, sugar and cotton. British capitalism worked these raw materials into retail products at home. The second was military adventurism, which was met with a range of degrees of physical resistance from those invaded.[7] Thus the history of British imperialism, like that of other European colonial powers, is a history of violence against enslaved and exploited people. In turn this produced a culture of anti-colonial performance within the colonised, both as a form of subversive protest and as a way of preserving their (frequently suppressed) perspective and history. Some of the descendants of these peoples were to furnish popular music with successful performers and lyrical themes.

In the case of Costello and his Irish ancestry, this provided him with a sensibility about race and nation and the role of military violence within British colonial conquests. A superficial biographical reading of Costello's relationship with race is linked, in the main, to his infamous drunken 'nigger' statement. We deal with this later but have deliberately not foregrounded it in this chapter in order to put his complex relationship with colonialism into a larger context.

Turning to a relevant example of his music: the song 'Pills and Soap' is important in that it was banned by the BBC, on the grounds that it was party political in intent, during the run-up to the 1983 General Election. Denying this, Costello claimed, possibly to outmanoeuvre the ban, the song was about animal

---

[7]   For example, the current aboriginal confidence in Australia is different to that of New Zealand. The former did not resist violent invasion by the British but the latter did.

welfare.[8] The animal theme in the song is present but minor; the rest is undoubtedly about human oppression in Thatcher's Britain. If it was about animal cruelty at all, this seems to have been also an important metaphor for ordinary people being treated like animals. For example, his Noah's Ark metaphor placed vulnerable people alongside those of other species: 'children and animals two by two'. On the other hand, it contains the important lines: 'You think your country needs you, but you know it never will. So pack up yer troubles in a stolen handbag. Don't dilly dally boys, rally round the flag.'[9]

This seeming pedantry about the ambiguities of the song is worth mentioning because the political message of 'Pills and Soap' was possibly scrambled in the wake of Costello's tactical denial. His disclaimer could as easily have been taken at face value by Thatcher's opponents, as by the BBC. We do not have this analytical dilemma about the song 'Shipbuilding', which is a straightforward commentary on the Falklands conflict.

A recent programme on BBC Radio 2 (25 June 2012) was devoted to this song, as a lens into the Falklands expedition and legacy. Costello provided an interview for the programme and his calm reflective mood makes an interesting contrast with our summary of his demeanour in the 'Tramp the Dirt Down' views offered on BBC television in 1989, when promoting *Spike*. In 2012, he makes it clear that the media coverage of the Falklands conflict, which he was monitoring, while on tour in Australia, stimulated him to produce 'the best lyrics I've ever written':

> Rupert Murdoch honed his black arts in the Australian media before he became an American. In that country, the level of lurid, inappropriate and downright false reporting in his papers and on his television stations in Australia added to the horror of watching it … It was already horrifying to see the glee that *The Sun* and such papers marked things off in the conflict, almost as if we were watching a football tournament … There was no debate and anybody that said otherwise was characterised as some kind of a wet or traitor … I've never been a great one for the 'which side are you on?' type song – they suit other people. I've never tried to write the straightforward, unquestioning, love song I feel other people do better that than me. And similarly with this, I didn't want to write a straightforward 'this war is wrong', even though that's what I kinda believed … We were in a time of conflict between portions of something, which Margaret Thatcher went on record to say didn't exist – society … It was not that hard to imagine there being a need to provide both the means to get to people to the conflict the need for the people to take part in the conflict. And in my

---

[8] His reported conversion to vegetarianism at this time is recycled in journalistic pieces about him.

[9] The musical reference 'packing up yer troubles' is to the First World War song 'Pack up your troubles in your old kit-bag and smile, smile, smile' written in 1915 by George and Felix Powell.

understanding of history, especially British history particularly,[10] they nearly always get a working class boy to do the killing ...

This long, but still abridged, quotation is offered to show just how far Costello has come during his career, in relation to rendering his lyrics and his motivation for writing them transparent. In the interview about 'Tramp the Dirt Down' he was much, much, more evasive than in this account. Let us now examine 'Shipbuilding' in some detail.

The workings of 'Shipbuilding'

The making of this song and its various recordings involve a little more complexity than some of the others we offer in the book for analysis. It was written by Clive Langer (co-producer of *Punch the Clock* with Alan Winstanley). However, he was unhappy with his own lyrics and so asked Costello to take the arrangement away and independently write new words. The final version used Langer's melody and Costello's lyric. The words take us through the contradiction for unemployed working-class families, at the time of the Falklands conflict. The shipyards were being offered work to provide vessels for the military, at a time when orders had dried up and they were facing the threat of closure. However, the new ships were in demand to transport the shipyard workers' sons to their death in the South Atlantic.

In all, the British forces lost 255 personnel during the Falklands War and as in all wars the majority of these were NCOs and enlisted men.[11] These doomed combatants of Thatcher's task Force[12] in the song were going to 'be back by Christmas', with resonances of the First World War mantra (oft repeated again at the start of the Second World War) of 'it will all be over by Christmas'.[13] This is another example, as in 'Pills and Soap', of Costello creating a critical sense of

---

[10]   This is another point of emphasis from Costello that *British* colonialism uniquely utilises working-class cannon fodder. However, this trend was also present in other nations and Britain was not uniquely exploitative of young male aggression, pride, nationalism and temporary self-deluded invincibility. Also, the ruling class in Britain and elsewhere sacrificed *their* young, sometimes leading from the front, though often not.

[11]   The Argentinean forces lost more than 600 personnel in the Falklands and there was significant outrage in Britain at tabloid headlines (from Murdoch's *The Sun*: 'Gotcha') that presented war as a game between two governments, and jingoism was blinding the population to the fate of those on both sides.

[12]   After the 1983 General Election, a cartoon postcard appeared of Thatcher laying a wreath on Remembrance Day, with the simple caption 'Thanks boys!' However, while the Falklands War probably boosted her electoral success to some extent, a more important factor was the split off from the Labour Party of the SDP, which divided the left-of-centre vote and let the Conservatives retain power.

[13]   This device to invoke the birth of Christ was also used by John Lennon and Yoko Ono in 1971 in their recording of 'Happy Xmas (War is Over)'. The pacifist message

continuity about British militarism in the 20th century. 'Shipbuilding' was not an isolated political attack on Thatcher about the Falklands but it is probably the best known commercially in Britain. For example, from Argentina appeared 'Reinna Madre' (Raul Porchetto), 'Tudo a Pulmon' (Alejandro Lerner) and 'Yendo de la cama al living' (Charly Garcia). From Britain we had a range of critical contribution: the Anarcho-punk band, Crass, produced 'Sheep Farming in the Falklands', while other offerings included Pink Floyd's 'The Final Cut', Billy Bragg's 'Island of No Return, 'Another Man's Cause' from The Levellers, and 'Spirit of the Falklands' from New Model Army.

A salient aspect of the development of 'Shipbuilding' was that both Clive Langer's melody, and Costello's ambitious, concise and affecting lyrics were both written with a particular voice in mind. Robert Wyatt's version was recorded for Rough Trade a year before Costello's album version on F-Beat. Unlike 'A Good Year for the Roses', which was a frank and honest tribute to George Jones, Costello's motive in recording and releasing a song written for another singer, concurrent with its original release, is less obvious. Rough Trade released Wyatt's version of 'Shipbuilding' in 1982 and it charted at number 36 in May 1983. This was neither low enough to be entirely off the radar (and thus available to be convincingly re-released without the taint of being a 'cover'), nor high enough to garner Costello the plaudits he probably deserved as songwriter.

Punch the Clock was recorded in the first quarter of 1983 and released in August, and at the time of recording, Costello (and Langer) would have no idea that the original version was going to reach a wider audience. Possibly the newer version was included on the album solely to document and reclaim what Clive Langer called 'the best tune I've ever written or probably ever will'. Langer quoted Costello as saying, 'I've written the best lyrics I've ever written'. The disparity between 'Shipbuilding' and the rest of *Punch the Clock* poses a question for us. If Wyatt's version had failed to chart, would Costello still have positioned 'Shipbuilding' in the middle of this album of energetically produced yet fairly lightweight material?

To our listening, 'Shipbuilding' is an achingly beautiful ballad presented in an understated arrangement, hidden between the glossy pop productions on *Punch the Clock*. It is strikingly different in tone, arrangement and sensitivity to the rest of that album, which is dominated by romantic songs featuring synthesisers, horns and filter effects. Viewed with hindsight, we know that this period of Costello's songwriting career was critically regarded as a lull in creativity. Even contemporary reactions to *Punch the Clock* dwelt on a lack of the rich lyrical offerings and attention to sonic detail compared to the sophistication of *Imperial Bedroom*. Maybe the inclusion of 'Shipbuilding' was simply down to a desire to raise the album's compositional 'batting average'. A path not taken might have seen 'Shipbuilding' set aside to grow into a separate album of similar high-quality

---

focuses on the hypocrisy of Christian countries at war, in defiance of their sixth biblical commandment, 'Thou shall not kill'.

material, but at the time Costello may have felt he needed to release these 'best lyrics' immediately, to prove that he could still produce inspirational poetry.

It would be invidious to compare the respective *merits* of the Wyatt and Costello performances here. However, a musical comparison reveals some interesting *technical* resonances and differences in the two versions. For example, we find the impact of Steve Nieve's piano performance on both. On the Wyatt version, he plays a little more gently and possibly with more rhythmic variety, especially in the piano solo (replaced by Chet Baker's trumpet on the newer take by Costello). On the latter version, Nieve's playing is darker, sparser and occasionally stentorian. The piano dominates both tracks and so arguably Nieve had as much a hand in the final product as the writers. Also, we find Costello delivering a vocal line and lyric that had been expressly composed for the rather different vocal style of Robert Wyatt.

With these background contextual nuances in mind, comparing the two productions is fascinating for the listener. With Costello-provided backing vocals on Wyatt's version, Langer produced both (and played organ on the earlier track). There is certainly no hope of fooling the listener in a blindfold test. By 1983, both vocalists had inimitable and mature personal styles, with unique voicing features of tone, articulation, attack and decay. Other differences can be noted. Nieve's piano (already mentioned), the choice of acoustic bass and brushed drums to accommodate the more jazz-oriented Wyatt, and the hypnotic backing vocals and minimal organ are all noteworthy. The latter are transmuted into richer strings and organ on Costello's version, backed by a filtered electric bass and a drummer using a stick on the cymbals, for added clarity in the pulse.

From our reading of it, as a composition, 'Shipbuilding' is a potted masterpiece. For all the harmonic ingenuity involved, the organ padding, strings and occasionally rhapsodic piano, the version recorded by Costello sounds lean and honed. This neatly reflects the bleakness of the subject: he is effectively posing the central question, 'will we be re-employed to build tombs for our children?' We can see how this effect is achieved by studying the structure of the song, the melodies and underlying chords.

There are elements of melody and harmony in 'Shipbuilding' that recall such illustrious antecedents as Brian Wilson's 'God Only Knows' or David Bowie's 'Life On Mars?'. Comparing the first lines of 'Shipbuilding' and the latter is almost like drawing a distinction between subject and object. 'It's a God-awful small affair' resonates with melancholy over major harmonies and a chromatically descending bass. 'Is it worth it?' takes a phrase with a near-identical deep structure – the move from major 3rd to major 2nd to major 3rd on accented beats – but places all this in the context of descending harmonies in the related minor scale. Compare one with the other and the emotional effect is a plunge from sadness viewed at a distance in another, to a deep and personal existential despair of one's own.

Melodically, the song develops by two-bar phrases becoming progressively denser, moving from crotchet rhythms to quavers and then retarding lines at their close with the same rhythmic motif represented by 'boy's-birth-day', 'got-filled-in', 'get-killed-in', and so on. This rhythm always lands on beats 2, 3 and 4 of the

Example 4.1   Verse melody for 'Shipbuilding'

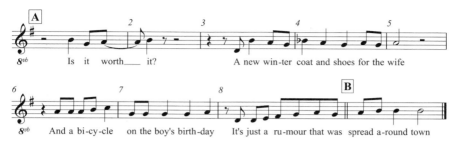

Example 4.2   The role of A in the melody of 'Shipbuilding'

bar, and is analogous in speech to finishing every sentence with the word 'and'. This device implies continuation or persistence and it drives the song implacably yet is barely noticeable. Compare this with the greater sense of resolution we get when a phrase ends on the strong third beat, 'Spread a-round-*town*' or, more clearly, 'diving for *pearls*'.

As in many arts, it is axiomatic in songwriting to develop one aspect of the piece (say, harmony) whilst reining in excesses in other areas (melody, rhythm) to highlight this positive effect. Example 4.1 shows the melody for the first eight bars of Costello's vocal (henceforth the 'verse', in whichever form this material is presented), and it can be seen that the range is small, predominantly a third (G^2–B^2).

Ingeniously, not only do these three notes G, A and B comprise the bulk of the melody (occasionally the B is flattened), but the whole piece revolves around the different harmonic relations built up on the melody notes A and B. This is particularly the case in relation to the note A, which is heard in at least seven different harmonic contexts throughout the song. The B is variously supported by G major or E minor chords (Example 4.2: mm. 1–2), or plaintively against an F major triad (m.3, 'With all the will in the *world*').

After Costello begins the verse, we immediately hear A in the context of E minor. There it is played over the dominant (Example 4.2: m. 3, 'Is it *worth* it?' in Example 4.1). It reappears in the context of imperfect cadences in both G major (Example 4.2: mm. 5–6, '*for the wife*' in Example 4.1) and G minor

(Examples 4.1 and 4.2: mm. 7–8), as the 5th of Dm (Example 4.2: m. 9, '*and a bi*cycle' in Example 4.1). Finally we find A on 'With all the *will* in the world'. There it is presented as the third degree of an F major chord, and 'Fighting for *dear* life', a sequential development of the phrase before, when it occupies that same bittersweet #4th step that the B takes in the F chord (Example 4.2: mm. 10–11).

Note that all these different A's frequently are sung to emotionally significant words. Once Langer had created this wonderfully euphonic set of chord changes (and, one assumes, melody), Costello uses the lyric and specifically the individual placement of words to condense emotions and extract the maximum impact and significance from each statement. This device combines both verbal and musical elements.

Costello *could* have written 'Why should I live?', 'Has life value?' or any number of other first lines that carry the same approximate meaning and number of syllables as 'Is it worth it?', but neither these nor many others concentrate the impact of the significant syllable 'worth' on the questioning imperfect cadence represented by B7 – and to be even more specific, the questioning (that is. rising) inference of the interval A–B. To clarify: here we have an imperfect cadence (Em–B7) that implies a movement away or out from the tonic, the question that would be answered musically by a perfect cadence (B7–Em: the answer). The pitches heard over the B7 chord are A and B, rising an interval of a tone. In speech, a rising pitch often confers a question, and similarly in music – most songs begin with rising pitches, a movement that confers an expanding expository nature to the phrase.

So we have solid musical corroboration and emotional reinforcement in the music of Costello's query in the lyric. Costello takes some musical material that has intrinsic and unique values (which are qualitative but not necessarily ascribable) and uses the words to ascribe an emotion to the musical phrase. Costello has used his lyrical skills to imbue the combination of the word 'worth', the first-inversion B chord and the note A with an existential, almost desperate quality.

Taking a similar look at some of the other, differently harmonised A's in the song and the way Costello has yoked their basic musical effect to his lyric: the A in 'With all the *will* in the world' is a solid third degree of an F major triad (a determined A?), whilst the A 'Fighting for *dear* life'– could that be a plangent, yearning A? The phrase is almost identical to the preceding one. However, replacing the F major with an Eb major puts the A pitch in a tenuous and fragile position.

Now try and imagine the song with all these significant syllables (worth, will, dear, wife, bicycle, boy, diving, pearls, and so on and so forth) falling flatly on first beats of bars and root notes in tonic chords and dominants, each uncoloured and effectively undernourished by the harmonic environment. Then consider that although the song has only three short verses, plus a handful of other lines, it conveys a deep and complex message about the interrelationships between war and capital, between employment, production, existence and soldiering. The

Example 4.3   Key changes in 'Shipbuilding'

Note: the upper line of Roman numerals shows the scale degrees of G major, the parent scale. The lower line gives alternate readings based on perceived modulations into E minor and D major (and minor).

graceful balance of lyric, melody and harmony is nowhere more evident than in 'Shipbuilding'.

Turning to the harmonic craft of the song, just look at the chords themselves. 'Shipbuilding' is an elegant example of functional harmony. This is harmony that serves to focus the narrative drive of the melody. The song also contains well-crafted modulations, based upon often deceptively simple voice leading; the changes between individual pitches (voices) that signify concomitant changes in the overall harmony. It is a mark of Clive Langer's harmonic control that the melody moves back and forth effortlessly between the keys of G major and E minor (and arguably through A minor, D major, D minor and G minor, too – in the first twelve bars of the song alone).

Example 4.3 shows the movement through these keys in the introduction and first verse, beginning on an Am chord over a bass line that steps down through G and F# to settle on a D7 over two bars, firmly establishing the parent key of G (mm. 1–4). However, the verse begins in E minor, signified by a brief chromatic passing chord (B7, mm. 4–5). Between mm.7 and 9 we move into a D major tonality that is immediately undermined by further movement of the F# to F (mm. 9–10), leaving us briefly in D minor, before Cm–D7 in mm. 11–12 creates the expectation of a perfect cadence in G minor, and finally resolving beatifically into G major on the phrase 'just a rumour that was *spread* around town'. Once we arrive in the key of G major – the B section – we remain there, using typical I, IV and V chords until the modulation, via a connecting B7/F# chord, back to E minor for the second verse, 'Well, I ask you …'.

The structure of the song then is also worthy of comment. The B section appears in different guises, allowing a song comprised of very short sections to develop into a more interesting structure – Table 4.1 gives a possible structural analysis of the song with some brief descriptive elements to aid the listener.

Table 4.1   The structure of 'Shipbuilding'

Intro	–	4 bars	piano and organ.
A	–	8 bars	'Is it worth it?' Organ out, bass and drums in.
B^1	–	5 bars	'…spread around town'
A	–	8 bars	'Well, I ask you…'. Strings and organ in.
B^2	–	9 bars	Strings out in 4th bar. Rising bass figure
C^1	–	6 bars	'…will in the world'. Organ swells.
A	–	8 bars	Trumpet solo over piano/organ/bass/drums.
B^2	–	9 bars	Vocal in. Rising bass figure.
C^2	–	6 bars	'…skilled in'. Strings back in.
C^3	–	7 bars	'…will in the world'. Rhythm lull in 4th bar.
A	–	8 bars	'…diving for pearls'. Trumpet in.
B^2	–	9 bars	Echo on trumpet from 3rd bar.
C^2	–	6 bars	'…skilled in'. Strings back in.
C^3	–	7 bars	'…will in the world'. Rhythm lull in 4th bar.
D	–	9 bars	'…diving for pearls'. D7(b9) pedal. End on Em.

The structure of the song is additive, beginning with a verse and adding a little more to each iteration:

$A + B^1$
$A + B^2 + C^1$
$A + B^2 + C^2 + C^3$
$A + B^2 + C^2 + C^3 + D$

Example 4.4 The effective slow and delayed resolution in 'Shipbuilding'

Following the first verse, B appears to be a chorus, but after the second verse it is developed over a bass line rising an octave diatonically in seven bars from a low C to resolve back into G major. By alternating Em and D7 chords and including a recurring piano motif that draws the ear further towards the E minor tonality, the line manages to pass through G without a sense of closure in the home key, prolonging the line and delaying the resolution (Example 4.4). More a bridge than a chorus, the rising bass and twice-deferred resolution creates the impression of something like an evaded cadence (from an inverted dominant to first-inversion tonic, in this case D7/A to G/B) that allows for the continuation into the C section and an eventual perfect cadence.

Moreover, this C section contains the powerful lines and a cadential resolution, which sum up the position of both the soldier and the shipyard worker. But the resolution is twice delayed by additional lyric lines (C[2]), which define the fatalism of the workers in the face of the dilemma. This is followed by a transformed version (C[3]) in which the rhythm section 'retreat' on the D7 dominant, creating the sense of a pause without breaking the pulse. In the first instance, this sets up a second trumpet solo over the A and B[2] harmonies – what one would normally expect to be a fade or play-out. However, as the cycle of structural elements draws back to this point, C[3] is heard yet again, with Costello producing a suspended dominant by singing a G over the D7, and this leads to the *true* coda. Here the dominant pedal is maintained for eight bars, with the occasional addition of the b9 (Eb), drawing our ears towards a resolution in G minor (as in the verse).

But there is one final twist in store for the listener. There is an abrupt resolution to Em, justifiable in harmonic terms as the similarity between G and E minor, and between D7b9 and a heavily altered B7 (the dominant of E minor), is close enough to make this a surprise rather than a shock. We are denied our blissful major resolution in G major and forego the tragedy of a dour G minor resolution; resolving to the E minor is penumbral, wry, not hopeless – but not joyous either.

There are several possible reasons for making this kind of compositional decision. Among the best could be that E minor is a kind of sidestep that neatly breaks the pattern of expectation building up in the repeated sequences of E minor to G minor to G major to E minor to G minor and so on. The mounting D7b9 implies the G minor that we (from experience) would expect to be transmuted to G major. But it resolves from a D7 to an E minor and is something we have not heard in the song since the beginning of the very first verse. It has long since been drowned out in our memory by other cadences.

Costello says of the lyrics, 'I wasn't trying to be alarmist or morbid in any way'. However, he was definitely pointing out the irony of the situation, while respecting the dignity of the workers and personal bravery of the combatants involved. He hints at a number of political points in the lyrics of this song. These include: the barbarity of a war economy; the insatiable demands of capital; and the recent silencing of the shipyards and the destruction of working-class communities. But this sad (and effectively Marxian) formulation from him is pregnant with the possibility of change and the prospects of an alternative regime of peace, solidarity and prosperity for ordinary people.

To get from one to the other requires a shift in consciousness (not to mention society, government and economy), so distant as to be impossible, and so Costello seems to end the song on a dreamy sentiment. It ends with a fermata that could imply something politically unfinished. This question mark over an imagined and better future for mankind in 1982 can be contrasted with a different one about his political credibility a few years earlier. We now turn to that contrast in order to highlight one of the many ambiguities of Elvis Costello as a 'political' songwriter.

Costello and the Holiday Inn bar incident

The sophisticated political sensibility and poignant sentiments, which we now associate with 'Shipbuilding' and some of Costello's other songs of the 1980s, form an important context for the early negative judgment he was subjected to as a result of an unbecoming drunken racist rant. Above, we indicated that we would defer this section for the very reason that Costello's position about race and nation required a proper context of discussion.

The incident, which was to haunt him occasionally for the rest of his career, occurred in March 1979 and was rapidly publicised in the USA. It started with some banter about music with Stephen Stills and his backing singer Bonnie Bramlett, in the Holiday Inn bar in Columbus, Ohio. As the heat rose with time and drink, Costello, in an angry anti-American diatribe, reportedly alluded to James Brown and Ray Charles as 'niggers' (one 'jived-assed' and the other 'blind and ignorant' respectively).

The following day the incident was leaked to the press by Bramlett.[14] Costello was on public trial and the dislocated shoulder he suffered in the brawl with his adversaries was the least of his problems. His explanation for the drunken debacle and his expression of sorrow for the offence and storm in its wake appeared in *Rolling Stone* on 2 September 1982. However, the fallout, especially in the USA, was considerable. Given the commercial importance of the US market, Costello's inebriated folly was serious in its implications. For some, it also placed a question mark over his commitment to progressive politics.

When Ray Charles was later asked about the furore, he commented: 'Anyone can get drunk once in his life … drunken talk isn't meant to be printed in the papers and people should judge Mr. Costello by his songs rather than his stupid bar talk.' As Thomson notes when reflecting on this opinion, Charles 'showed the kind of maturity and restraint that few on either side of the battle-lines had been able or willing to display' (Thomson, 2004: 6). As we demonstrated above and elsewhere in the book, Costello's considered political values were indeed expressed more productively and acceptably in his lyrics than in his 'stupid bar talk'.

The fair caution by Charles about rushing to judgement over Costello's drunken spat is important for a number of reasons for our discussion. The accountability of private views and particularly about offensive terminology was becoming an important cultural trend in the 1980s (we consider this more in relation to women in Chapter 6). Also, the offence taken by Stills and Bramlett was primarily about Costello's attack on US music. Note, then, that this was *not* a political discussion about race. The focus of the row is important because Costello's offensive and not denied use of a single word, 'nigger', became the scandal, not the substantive drunken exchange about popular music across the Atlantic. Costello, more than many, has shown a devotion to a range of musical influences from the USA (see Chapter 5) and so to attack Stills and Bramlett, rather than going with their love of their home-grown music, was, to say the least, perverse but not out of character.

Costello's general contrariness also needs to be considered in explaining the offence given and taken. His *post hoc* account in his contrite press statement was that he made his comments in order to shock his argumentative company into an abrupt end to the dispute. Quite how being aggressive and shocking would end antagonism, rather than fuel it further, may not make sense to many of us, but does to a mindset which believes in 'topping' an opponent with a shocking diversion or killer blow. His drunken state might account for it but, as is clear in our description of his personal style in this book, Costello *generally* enjoyed being contrary in his

---

[14]   Bramlett toured and worked with Eric Clapton in 1970 on his first album and co-wrote the track 'Let It Rain'. This ironical connection can be noted in relation to our comparison below of Costello with Clapton in relation to racism.

encounters with those he viewed as adversaries.[15] Even when sober, he was not renowned for his quiet diplomacy, prosaic precision in his use of words, his non-defensive openness to personal feedback or his empathy for others. This leaves us with a sense of a man who, like many people, simply enjoyed being argumentative and provocative: he has a 'fight or flight' orientation in his encounters with others.[16]

Given these relevant considerations about the appeal for tolerance made by Ray Charles, we also need to look at Costello's cultural and political track record. Nothing that he had done before that incident (or since) would warrant a description of him being a racist, quite the reverse. He played at gigs for *Rock Against Racism* and was the producer of the first album of the Ska band The Specials, which was formed for explicitly anti-racist reasons.[17] In a remake of their hit 'Free Nelson Mandela' in 1988, Costello was a backing vocalist.

At the time of the controversy in 1979, Costello's father, Ross MacManus, publicly came out to emphasise the sensitivity about racism in his family (as Irish in England, see Chapter 5) and his absolute conviction that his son was not a racist.[18] Costello's own guilt about the incident possibly is reflected in this recollection in his September 2004 interview with David Fricke in *Rolling Stone*:

> I had a heartbreaking moment last year[19] [with his wife Diana Krall]…As Ray's coming out, a woman is leading him. He gets to within fifteen feet of us, and they stop. The woman says, 'He wants to meet Diana'. I had to turn away. That wasn't the right moment. It would never be the right moment, really. It would be one of those things: you have a friend who goes into rehab and he says, 'Remember that ten dollars you lost? I stole it from you'. It would have been like that. Why did he need that?

Furthermore, the Ohio incident and Costello's subsequent contrition can be put in the normative context of his political position about race, compared to some of

---

[15]   See Chapter 7 and his encounter, while with Nick Kent, with an employee of Island Records.

[16]   The psychoanalyst Wilfred Bion, investigating small-group dynamics, observed that we all tend to have one of three unconscious personal 'valencies' about 'basic assumptions' operating in relationships: fight or flight; dependence; or pairing. In the first we assume that relationships are about winning or losing, in the second it is about relying on a comforting leader and in the third it is about relying on the productive outcome of two people in communion (Bion, 1961).

[17]   A decade earlier in Britain hits emerged from The Equals (with Eddie Grant) and The Foundations and so Ska was the most recent incarnation of 'two tone bands'.

[18]   Costello's use of the word 'nigger', as a general attribution of an oppressed identity, can be found in his line about the cannon fodder of British militarism ('one more widow one less white nigger') in the song 'Oliver's Army' from *Armed Forces* (1979).

[19]   Ray Charles died in 2004 just before this interview.

his famous peers from the 1970s and 1980s. Whereas Costello actually immersed himself in anti-racist causes and worked well with black artists, other reputations have been less marred, despite their far more dubious political features.

Costello's offence occurred in a drunken private state and was only made public by an aggrieved and spiteful antagonist, but this was not the case, for example, with Eric Clapton or David Bowie. Their very public views from the same era seem to have been forgotten and have not been a recurrent basis for personal criticism, or affected their celebrity status or public standing, in contrast to Costello's weeping scar.[20]

Clapton's prolonged and very public attack on people of colour in Britain[21] was particularly ironical, given the debt he owed black musicians in the blues and reggae traditions he plundered for his work. For example, his first commercial hit was a version of Bob Marley's 'I Shot the Sherriff'. In the recent BBC4 television documentaries, *Reggae Britannica* and *Blues Britannica* (2009–11), the role of Clapton in covering and popularising Jamaican and Blues music is noted. However, no allusion is made to his publicly declared racism, despite the first programme pointedly describing the rise of Rock Against Racism (see below).

The paradox of Clapton (a white racist, who was expropriating the commercial appeal of music rooted historically in the oppression of Black people) raises a question about whether any of us can and should separate the aesthetic and cultural aspects of music from their political origins and intentions. In interviews Clapton claims to be uninterested in the racial background of a source of his music, only its aesthetic appeal to him. The silences in the television programmes noted also caution us against relying on journalistic accounts of popular music which, even when reasonably well researched as in these cases, ultimately 'play it safe' about criticising pop heroes. In these programmes, Clapton's 'God' image was retained, despite the known events involving his boorish xenophobia in 1976.

The critical focus on Costello, and not the likes of Clapton and Bowie, may be linked to a point we raised in Chapter 2, when Griffiths (2007) introduces an exasperated query about 'bitter left wing guys'. Whereas, Bowie was politically confused or ambivalent and Clapton incorrigibly ethnocentric, Costello wore his socially progressive credentials on his sleeve. Thus, little better could or should have been expected from Bowie and Clapton, but Costello's political accountability was possibly more relevant for his fans and critics alike. It also

---

[20]   For example, in 1976 David Bowie, in his 'Thin White Duke' persona told us: 'I believe very strongly in fascism ... People have always responded with greater efficiency under a regimental leadership.' By 1980 Bowie had given up collecting Nazi paraphernalia and disavowed such views.

[21]   Clapton's extensive onstage racist rant at a concert in August 1976 in Birmingham included: 'I think we should vote for Enoch Powell. Enoch's our man. I think Enoch's right. I think we should send them all back. Stop Britain from becoming a black colony. Get the foreigners out. Get the wogs out. Get the coons out. Keep Britain white. I used to be into dope, now I'm into racism." (cited in Street, 1986).

explains why Costello himself has felt the need to be accountable in his interviews at times. Bowie could remain whimsical, or account for his passing fascist views by a temporary cocaine-induced imbalance of the mind, and Clapton could be cavalier and unrepentant. Costello, by contrast, probably fully understood the political gravity of the private Columbia incident, for the very reason that in good conscience, when sober, he was implacably opposed to racism and used to reflecting on its nature. His allegiances as a social activist support this conclusion.

In the late 1970s there was a shared political context connecting Costello and Clapton, which was the emergence of the Anti-Nazi League in response to a resurgence of activity of the far right National Front. A musical outcrop of this, in 1976, was Rock Against Racism, the stimulus for which came after two of its founding members, Roger Huddle and Red Saunders, wrote a letter of complaint to the popular music newspaper *NME* about Clapton's publicly avowed racism.

Thus, whereas Clapton was instrumental in provoking Rock Against Racism into existence, Costello joined its cause, working with anti-racist musicians like The Specials. Whereas Costello, in his public reflections, remained anguished about his drunken private expletives with a provocative audience of two, Clapton's indignation from the right was never going to give way to subsequent contrition about his live rant to thousands of fans. As recently as 2 December 2007, in an interview with Melvyn Bragg on *The South Bank Show*, Clapton restated his admiration for Enoch Powell, the 'Little Englander' Conservative politician who sternly incited race hate against migrants in the 1960s.

On 20 April 1968, at a Conservative Association meeting in Birmingham with a strategically invited press presence, Clapton's hero made his famous 'rivers of blood speech'. Powell warned of the consequences of New Commonwealth immigration to Britain: 'As I look ahead, I am filled with foreboding; like the Roman, I seem to see "the River Tiber foaming with much blood".' He was a classics scholar who wanted to give his ethnocentric rhetoric gravitas by such bombastic historical allusions. Despite his 1976 onstage racist rant at Birmingham, Clapton went, in 2004, to Buckingham Palace, where he became a Commander of the Order of the British Empire (CBE), a title offered to, but declined by, Bowie in 2000. Powell was a particular hero of both Eric Clapton and Margaret Thatcher, a point which places Costello unequivocally in a discernibly different political stable.

Conclusion

In this chapter we have prioritised for consideration Costello's exploration of race and nation, especially his view about Britain as a post-colonial power at the time of his early commercial success. He was involved in two controversies in this regard. The first was a theme about his hostility to British military adventurism, culminating in one of his songs, 'Pills and Soap', being banned by the BBC and another emerging as probably the best known, and now oft recorded, song about the

Falklands War, 'Shipbuilding'. This has been an extension of our discussion of his contempt for England (explored in Chapter 1, when we looked at 'Tramp the Dirt Down') that will be picked up again in Chapter 5 with regard to his attack during the 1980s on the Anglo-American political compact of Thatcher and Reagan.

The second controversy discussed in this chapter was his drunken spat in Ohio, which was to make him the focus of criticism about his disparaging use of the word 'nigger'. We have considered this in the context of private and public discourses and the increasing tendency during our period of consideration for the former to be held accountable within the latter. We pursue this point further in Chapter 6. This incident also allowed us to weigh up the psychological factors about the group setting he was in, his inebriated state and his personality, and to place those in the context of his use of a single expletive being open to attack or exculpation from others.

That wider social context was illuminated further by alluding to two other commercially successful artists from the period, David Bowie and Eric Clapton, whose transgressions were far more serious. Although their extreme right-wing statements were very public and sustained, politically their reputation has been questioned much less than Costello's. Moreover, their services to the British State have been formally recognised, with them both being offered CBEs (an outcome unlikely for Costello for the foreseeable future).[22] We have argued that his accepted status as a critical and progressive political song writer explains this discrepancy, as it increased demands on him for personal accountability. This continues a point we developed at the end of Chapter 2. We now turn from his position in and about Britain in the 1980s to his views on the trans-Atlantic relationship of the time.

---

[22]   His service to popular music has, however, been recognised by British academia. In 2005, he was awarded an Honorary Doctorate from the Department of Music at the University of Liverpool.

Chapter 5

The Special Relationship with the USA

A nation that continues year after year to spend more money on military defense
than on programs of social uplift is approaching spiritual doom.

– Martin Luther King Jr[1]

Introduction

In Chapter 1 we noted that, despite being unlikely bedfellows, Thatcher and
Costello had a few shared interests. One was an appeal to Christian themes for
sources of inspiration and the other was their preoccupation with the USA, even if
these common concerns took them in different ideological directions. As a haughty
British nationalist, Thatcher could look on fondly to her seeming equivalent in the
USA, President Ronald Reagan.

Thatcher, like Blair subsequently, bristled with pride about an international
presidential-style role. Consequently, her narcissism stylised a relationship, which
is functionally important for any modern day UK premier. She could view the
USA as an ex-colony, which had been gifted the beauty of the English language,
British Protestantism and its work ethic, representative democracy and the seeds of
capitalism – which, together, had brought global progress. All of these elements of
a traditional conservative narrative were close to her heart. However, a convenient
silence in this self-regarding Anglo-centric view was that, by the middle of the
20th century, Britain was in fact a burnt-out imperialist power, whilst a long-gone
colony across the Atlantic now blatantly dominated the 'free world'.

The extent of the global domination enjoyed in recent times by the USA
was summarised in the State of the Union address, made by George W. Bush on
20 January 2004, entitled 'America Will Never Seek a Permission Slip'. Bush
made it clear that the USA's mandate to act at will was superior to that of the United
Nations, the organisation with alleged international political legitimacy. After the
downturn of 2008 the global domination from the USA now looks less persuasive,
especially with its debts to China. But, in the 1980s, the residual economic health
and geopolitical influence of Britain was heavily reliant upon the USA.

All recent British prime ministers have known this historical position and a
priority call on being elected is to the President of the USA, to sustain the notion
of an equal and mutually faithful 'special relationship'.[2] With the latter comes a

---

[1]   From 'Beyond Vietnam', an address delivered at the Riverside Church, New York
City, 4 April 1967.

[2]   This rule applies to British leaders of all political hues. All of them have to affect
a warm obsequious stance in relation to the US President, independent of personal or

barely veiled undertone of contempt for the brash ex-colony, which has not been limited to the political right.[3] Indeed 'American' or 'Yankee' imperialism has been a proud pretext for hostile slogans from the left; to be 'anti-American' has at times been a badge of honour, rather than an admitted form of ethnocentricity or Old World snobbery. And yet, so much of US culture has, quite understandably and properly, been endorsed and enjoyed by the very same left-of-centre critics.

Thus ambivalence was not limited to any one social group or individual in Britain and Europe generally,[4] a point to bear in mind when we explore Costello's *particular* mixed expressions about the USA. So this is definitely not about his individual psychopathology, though he has struggled with the more general cultural phenomenon of equivocation in his own particular way. This bears examination because it is an important aspect of his music.

We noted that, in his childhood, his father's occupation as a singer and his mother's involvement in record retailing furnished their shared household with a rich collection of music. Much of this was from the USA. It is no coincidence that many years later music reviewers were to muse on the prospects of Elvis Costello becoming his generation's 'Sinatra'. In Chapter 3 we explored that connection across time in relation to nostalgia; in this one we will focus on his relationship with the USA.

Costello expressed his ambivalence recurrently, in a variety of ways, from the styles of music he loved to extend, cover and rework, or the accent he applied at times as a singer, to the content of some of his lyrics and his attitude towards the record companies. The outcome of that approach-avoidance position was variable and not always within his individual control. For example, we noted in Chapter 2 when discussing the song 'Alison' that its soul roots were in 'Ghetto Child' by the Detroit Spinners and that it culminated commercially in the syrupy version made famous by Linda Ronstadt. Thus, both its start and finish was the USA and Costello brokered the round trip, but he was not always in the driving seat.

Also, as we noted in relation to the drunken rant incident in Chapter 4, the public focus understandably came to be about race; but it is also noteworthy that Costello's deeper meant jibes were part of a perverse belligerence on his part

---

ideological sympathies and differences. This culminated in the disastrous collusion of Blair and Bush in relation to Iraq.

[3]　　In US–European relationships, some of the most hostile prejudice has come from conservative elites on both sides. For example, the French have resisted US cultural influences in various ways and ethnocentric Republicans in the US have openly expressed contempt for the French. George Bush is said to have noted contemptuously to Tony Blair that 'the French do not even have a word for entrepreneur'.

[4]　　There is a recurring European ambivalence about the USA in the lack of agreement from social scientists about a country that variously is venerated as the epoch of human liberty and criticised for its bullying imperialism or even its seeds of fascism. Claus Offe's *Reflections On America* (2005) summarises this ambivalence in the work of Tocqueville, Weber and Adorno. The last of these rejected American cultural products, including popular music, for their alienated and commodified role, whilst later, on returning to Europe, praising the welcoming humanity of the American people.

about the alleged *inferiority of US music*. When sober, Costello clearly venerated it though other sentiments were obviously released when he was drunk. Given the good living he has come to make in the USA since then and the prestigious collaborations he went on to develop (for example, with Burt Bacharach), those sentiments may now be buried much deeper than in the period we are considering.

The aphorism that England and the USA are two countries 'divided by a common language' has a contested origin. It was certainly quoted with confidence by Winston Churchill (who had an 'American'[5] mother) but was probably invented originally by George Bernard Shaw. The Irish playwright spent most of his life living in England. Like Costello, Shaw was embedded in a complicated and dynamic trans-Atlantic and Anglophone cultural triangle.[6] Both succeeded in making a public impression with their command of English while being aware that, in times past, the Irish tongue, like others across the whole Celtic fringe, had been suppressed brutally and nearly extinguished under colonial rule. Great Britain was a resented coloniser of Ireland, as well as of the USA. But unlike the latter, which had kicked out the British in the late 18th century, the Irish remained subjugated well into the 20th century (and in part still are, according to Irish nationalists and republicans).

Moreover, the Irish diaspora emerged as a direct political influence in the USA. By the end of the 19th century, over a quarter of the Irish population had sailed there, largely propelled by starvation under British rule. This migration was to prompt a later, dramatically orchestrated and emotive Costello song, 'Long Journey Home', written with Paddy Moloney of The Chieftains. It contains the succinct punning line, 'I'm bound to find a better life than I left behind'.[7] The song is an example of the recurring nostalgic outlook from Costello we explored further in Chapter 3.

Irish-Americans soon became evident in the US governmental apparatus (often as police officers, politicians and officials) and even eventually produced their very own President.[8] The popular support for this impact came from the sheer scale of the Irish-American voting presence. Today around 35 million Americans consider themselves to be of Irish heritage. Their political pedigree is evident in city, State and Federal politics, exemplified by the O'Neills and the Kennedys. Even the bête

---

[5]   One indication of US cultural domination is that 'America' has wrongly become loosely synonymous with two vast continents. For example, it is difficult without being pedantic and clumsy to indicate that 'North American' (let alone 'American') might refer equally, to Canadians.

[6]   One of Shaw's provocations about the USA was: 'Americans adore me and will carry on adoring me until I say something nice about them.'

[7]   See the title track of *Long Journey Home*, the 1998 multi-artist album produced by Paddy Moloney.

[8]   J.F. Kennedy, the 35th President of the USA, was the great-grandson of eight Irish migrants who all arrived there in the mid-19th century. More recently Barack Obama has enjoyed the voting benefits of confirming some Irish ancestry.

noire of modern US politics, Joseph McCarthy, was of Irish stock. Despite his humble birth in rural Wisconsin and his pugnacious lack of grace, he commanded extraordinary influence for a while within the East Coast urban elites of the 1950s, when he was also a family friend of the Kennedys. This has created a tension in the co-existing Irish-American narratives of *both* dispossessed historical victimhood *and* more recent political opulence within the elite establishment.

English by birth and tongue but from Irish roots and immersed in the products of US culture, Costello was embedded in this cultural and economic triangle and complexity. Thus it is possible that his creativity can be framed within a post-colonial context of both confusion and opportunity. Like other post-colonial artists he might generate some variant of trans-national transcendence. At any moment, England, Ireland or the USA could become points of attraction for Costello's imagination; and they did. As with other post-colonial writers, this creativity would be expressed boldly and imaginatively in the language of the coloniser. Moreover, as a musician, he could adapt aspects of influence, with much confidence, from all three countries; and he did. But this confidence and opportunity have also been linked to a confusion of identity and strong mixed feelings. The latter creates the prospects of both artistry and madness. For example, the tiny sparsely populated country of Ireland has had a strong and disproportionate international presence in the creative arts but it has also produced disproportionate levels of mental disorder, including psychosis and substance misuse (especially alcohol abuse).[9]

King of America?

Evidence about Costello's ambivalent stance towards the USA can be gleaned from four main sources. The first, already alluded to in Chapter 2, was the documented extensive presence of American music in his household and his love of singing US ballads as a child, both from the 'middle of the road' crooning tradition of his father's big band background. Later, Progressive Rock, Country and Western, Soul and Jazz were put into the mix by Costello, who has relentlessly honoured and extended all of these US-derived stylistic traditions, separately and in combination, in his own songs and 'covers', for over thirty years. The word 'eclectic' (applied at times understandably to Costello's music) might miss the point about this range of influences, as it might imply a sort of random pick-and-mix inferiority, rather than layers of a rich US heritage.

The second was his commercial reliance on the US-dominated music industry, in terms of record company involvement and the important and very large and so lucrative concert circuit in North America. This reliance promised fame and

---

[9]   For a review of this point see Rogers and Pilgrim (2010). The apparent predisposition of the Irish to both madness and creativity opens up a wider and general question about the boundary and link between the two outcomes across all cultures: a topic for another book.

fortune, but it also risked commercial bondage for Costello. As we will note later in Chapter 7 he reacted visibly to that constraint.

The third was the ambiguous context of the USA for his generation, as part of the cultural landscape his imagination inhabited.[10] Any child in the British Isles growing up in the decades, not just the immediate period, after the Second World War was surrounded by US popular music, the products of Hollywood and then, increasingly, 'American' television. Thus, this was not only Costello's world but also the world of all of his peers. This ensured that his US allusions and sources would resonate, to some degree, with the bulk of his British audiences and fan base, even if the latter had explored them less knowingly and in less detail than Costello.

The fourth source of evidence about his ambivalence was the emotional resonance of his family history, which has appeared occasionally in his songs. For example, the song 'Veronica' (written with Paul McCartney) referred to his frail grandmother. But, in relation to the Irish-American musical connection, his grandfather Paddy was an important point of reference, both as an interesting life story and as part of the family script of performing music. Paddy was born of Irish migrant parents in Birkenhead (over the Mersey from the city of Liverpool). Following the death of his father (it was rumored in the family that he was murdered), Paddy ended up in an orphanage and from there went on to the British military school of music.

Paddy's story personifies the colonial confusions created at the time and not uncommon in the Anglo-Irish community. An Irishman born in England, he was wounded fighting for the British in France in the First World War and was then moved to Dublin in 1916, not returned to the front.[11] Costello recounts in an interview in *Folkroots* in 1989:

> So he ended up in the British Army in Dublin in 1916 on the wrong side, as you might say. I'm not saying that James Connolly came to him and said '… keep your head down' but some Scallies that he knew there said 'You'd better watch out'. It's a good starting point for a story that could happen anywhere.

The 'good starting point' led to two clear references in Costello's songs. The 1916 period is alluded to in 'King's Shilling' on *Spike*. In the 1920s Paddy went on to work

---

[10]   With the exception of the 'British invasion' led by the Beatles and the Rolling Stones in the 1960s, during the mid-20th century most of the commercial Anglophone popular music industry had been shaped from the USA, both in terms of its artistic roots (like Jazz, the Blues and Rock and Roll) and its technological apparatus of production and distribution (the large record companies).

[11]   At Easter in 1916, an insurrection by Irish Republicans in Dublin was suppressed by the British Army after a week. Although its leaders were executed, it was an important milestone on the path to Irish independence in the 20th century. The scenario is portrayed at the start of the film *Michael Collins*.

as a musician in New York and it was that period that Costello refers to amongst others in 'American Without Tears'[12] from *King of America* (1986). The starting scenario is a man in a New Orleans hotel who goes out to seek company in a bar. He encounters two English women, an ex-beauty queen and her friend. Over the course of the song, we find a story about them being courted and then transported to the USA as GI brides, who no longer speak English but now 'American without tears'.

This song was part of an album with several tracks that make lyrical allusions to the USA but also create an ambience of the latter through the musicians and the instruments deployed. For example, the song foregrounds the accordion and its lilting quality resonates very strongly with a Cajun style (with the first line positioning the scene in the Southern States). Also, with a telling irony used by Costello, he appears on the front of the album in a crown typical of the British monarchy but he is also wearing what looks like a very ornate and gaudy cowboy shirt. This might be a joke but it is also a serious sign, intended or otherwise, of an historical contradiction. The USA does not now have a monarchy but it did before 1776, when independence was declared and the British were expelled.

From the past to the present: the workings of 'Peace In Our Time'

If *King of America* was for Costello an ambivalent historical celebration of Americana, during the 1980s he also encountered much in contemporary US society that offended him and incited his creative impulses. We noted in Chapter 1 that the brutal social consequences of monetarism had been a context of provocation for Costello. The shared adoration Thatcher and Reagan had for this particular ideology created a particular bond between them, but there was also the matter of a shared advocacy of militarism to impose their power.

We can explore this connection and Costello's response to it by looking at a song from *Goodbye Cruel World*. This album was recorded in 1984, with critics generally being unimpressed by its quality. This was Costello's ninth album and the second to be produced for F-Beat by the team of Clive Langer and Alan Winstanley. 'Peace In Our Time' was the final track on the original album. The liner notes to the 1995 Rykodisc reissue express clearly what a conflicted period this was for Costello. He was struggling to maintain a clear artistic vision in the face of personal upheaval and widening rifts both in the band[13] and between Costello, Langer and F-Beat. Here is a typical summary from the liner notes of Costello's own reflections on the quality of the album:

---

[12]   Costello released a second version of this song ('American Without Tears, No 2, Twilight Version') with a very different lyric and musical arrangement, on the 2002 reissue of *Blood & Chocolate*.

[13]   We explore the personal conflict with his bass player Bruce Thomas in Chapter 7.

Congratulations! You've just purchased our worst album ... many would agree
... I can explain everything ... My gravest mistake for all concerned was in
asking Clive Langer and Alan Winstanley to produce this record ... 'Pop Music'
was among the things about which I was dempressed [*sic*] and demoralised ...
I fought every attempt to apply the Clanger/Winstanley method to these songs
... two tense and fairly unproductive weeks of playing 'live' [in the studio] ...
I'm almost certain that Clive wished he could get out of the project but stuck
it out more as a friend than a professional ... I agreed to let them [Langer and
Winstanley] work their magic on a few cuts and give the record company some
commercial focus ... It was a happy, if fatal, compromise.

This is not a condemnation of Langer and Winstanley. Costello, though often
known for attacking others and tetchily defending himself, on this occasion is more
than ready to take responsibility for the quality of the work. As he put it: 'this is
far from a criticism of Clive and Alan's abilities. In truth I didn't need a producer,
I probably needed a nurse (or maybe a priest).' Thus, Langer and Winstanley did
not let him down; it was the other way round.

When referring to the meaning of our focus here, 'Peace In Our Time', Costello
makes just one brief allusion: 'If it now seems like a relic of those days of anti-
nuclear dread then I hope it stays that way.' As is often the case, Costello is being
cryptic. Does he hope that the song itself is consigned to history or the anti-nuclear
threat it recorded? Even the word 'relic' is ambiguous, with, yet again, religious
connotations it could imply a laudable bit of heritage, as with the relics of saints
in the Catholic tradition that are venerated. Alternatively (and probably) it might
refer to a dead and unattractive residue, especially in an ageist culture, where the
present is celebrated and the past automatically held in contempt.[14] Costello, in a
1989 interview for *The Musician* about *Goodbye Cruel World*, seemed to confirm
his ambivalence about it:

I'm not really bothered with being a nostalgia act. I've never been afraid of
saying 'fuck everything else that I've done before.' The good thing is that I don't
feel there's anything to be embarrassed about. I've made some bad tracks, a
couple of albums that didn't quite come out the way I expected, and one of them,
Goodbye Cruel World, is just a bad record. But nothing I'm absolutely ashamed
of yet, which isn't bad for 12 years. If I want to pull a song out from 10 years
ago, there's always one I can honestly put my hand on my heart and say, 'I don't
feel foolish singing this.'

---

[14]   The dilemma of shame about the past was put to Costello by his father. In an
interview with BBC's Radio Merseyside, Ross recalls advising Elvis at the start of his
career not to disclose his family background to the music press, as it might be held against
him, because of the passé status of big band music. The dilemma was solved by Costello's
manager, Jake Riviera, insisting on him being a closed book to outsiders to encourage
intrigue and curiosity. The strategy seems to have worked to date.

Both the cryptic self-deprecation in 1995 and the above slightly more ambiguous evaluation in 1989 (*which* song, we might still ask, was he happy to sing subsequently?) may divert our attention from Costello's value-judgement at the actual time of the album's release. Adulterous, depressed, drink-sodden and without a nurse or priest, Costello was still a good judge of his own material. Moreover, despite, or maybe because of, his low mood, his troubled inner world was resonating productively with his outer political context. In that personal context of *both* inner *and* outer disturbance and distress, Costello had a knack of writing emotive songs, with plaintive lyrics. An earlier example we could cite is 'Riot Act', which retains much ambiguity about regret. It could be a sung confession about his drunken rant in Ohio, his adultery, the end of his career or even the end of his life. It was positioned on *Get Happy!!* (1980), immediately after the track 'I Stand Accused'.

With the exception of its middle verse, 'Peace in Our Time' is far less ambiguous than 'Riot Act', with its teeming wordplay,[15] even if they were both born from contexts of personal and political distress. In 1984, Costello picked out the former as the best of a bad bunch, from what he calls 'a bad record'. For an album agreed by all voices, including that of the artist, to be very weak, the song does stand out as somewhat different from the rest. By intention or not, 'Peace in Our Time' was part of a constellation of political commentary from Costello, which we can now see with hindsight included 'Pills and Soap', 'Shipbuilding' and 'Tramp the Dirt Down' from the Thatcher period in Britain.

This song is not an isolate, if we think about Costello and his already established contempt for militarism. Many of songs from the 1979 album *Armed Forces* had a similar theme and his pacifism and belief in the sanctity of life underpin many of his lyrics (for example, when he attacks the barbarity of capital punishment). However, in this particular song we see an emerging trend in the 1980s, which by the end of the decade was fairly clear. Costello began to make more pointed and transparent allusions to actual political (in this case military) events and so his lyrical references were becoming now less diffuse or obscure, though the mists of uncertainty never cleared completely.

This shift from idiosyncratic personal allusions and fragmented expressions of his imagination, in the great bulk of his songs during his career, to a more transparent narrative style brought him for a while closer to a folk-song tradition, especially in relation to the rhetoric of 'protest singers' in the 1960s (see later). With that shift came both the opportunity of political catharsis for himself and arousal for his listeners and the risk of the loss of flexibility of his more habitual poetic imagination. Songs that preach or protest create these gains and losses.

'Peace in Our Time' is structured very traditionally: a four-bar intro, two verses followed by attendant choruses, an instrumental solo followed by one more verse-chorus, and a coda. The first verse is situated in 1938, the second sometime later

---

[15]   The lyric of 'Riot Act' is an example of Costello's extraordinary cleverness with words.

and the final verse refers to US politics in the 1980s. The chorus reference is simple: 'And the bells take their toll once again in a victory chime'. Its second line praises God sarcastically for the alleged attainment of peace in our time.

The title of the song is a common, albeit slight, misquotation from an event alluded to in the very first line. On 30 September 1938, the British Prime Minister Neville Chamberlain returned to England with the 'Munich Agreement'. This was a piece of paper, just signed by him and Adolf Hitler, in which the latter agreed to ward off prospective military hostilities with Britain and cease current ones in Europe. Later that day, from 10 Downing Street, Chamberlain issued an explanatory statement with this quickly regretted flourish:

> My good friends, this is the second time in our history that there has come back from Germany to Downing Street peace with honour. I believe it is peace for our time. We thank you from the bottom of our hearts. And now I recommend you to go home and sleep quietly in your beds.

The next day Hitler's armed forces occupied Sudetenland. Within a year Britain and Germany were at war. The sting in the tail of the first verse of the song refers to the post-war settlement by which Germany's reconstruction was paid for by its erstwhile enemies. Normal trade between the old European colonial powers was soon resumed.

The chorus is a sarcastic lament with a play on the word 'toll' (to indicate both a bell ring and a body count).[16] The second verse is the least clear in meaning in the song and has two separate referents, we can reasonably speculate about, though we emphasise that this is conjecture. The first half may simply refer to paranoid surveillance in a police State – one peacetime eventuality of authoritarian militarism, to be found at the time both in Eastern Europe and in the dictatorships of South America, like Pinochet's Chile, so favoured by Margaret Thatcher. The reference to babies reappears in 'Tramp the Dirt Down' (see Chapter 1) and is an image that Costello seems to like, to connote a mixture of vulnerability and innocence in ordinary suffering humanity.

The second half of the verse probably refers to the dread and remorse of Robert Oppenheimer. He was a socialist and professor of physics at Berkeley, credited with developing the nuclear capability of the USA during the Second World War. In his memoirs he cites a passage from the ancient Hindu text the *Bhagavad Gita*: 'If the radiance of a thousand suns were to burst at once into the sky, that would be like the splendor of the mighty one … Now I am become Death, the destroyer of worlds.' After Hiroshima and Nagasaki nothing would be the same again.

The third verse is an explicit attack upon Ronald Reagan and his military machine. It cleverly condenses and scores no less than three political points in a very few lines. The first couplet refers to the invasion of Grenada by the USA

---

[16] In a Wikipedia entry, Paul Inglis (the 'Pope of Pop') reports that Costello has hinted that he had 'lifted' this chorus from another song.

in 1983. Grenada is an ex-British colony and the military incursion by Reagan initially and embarrassingly provoked Thatcher's ire (in a context of widespread international condemnation). The Caribbean island had a left-wing government allied to Castro's Cuba and was seen as a threat to US interests in the area. The presence of US students on the island was used by Reagan as a rationalisation to justify his invasion of a sovereign state, in a blatant contravention of international law. The 'might is right' justification for US military interventions, usually at odds with UN conventions and consensus, has been a motif of their foreign policy throughout Costello's lifetime.

The middle lines of the third verse refer to the 'Star Wars' technology developed by Reagan's regime. The real title, of 'Strategic Defense Initiative', referred to investment in a complex technological apparatus, including space-based sensors, to anticipate attack from the Soviet Union. This initiative, if successful, would have dramatically altered the nuclear power balance between the West and East. In turn, this would have dangerously de-stabilised a political stalemate of peace created by the precarious logic of mutually assured destruction.

The final lines of the verse refer to two political competitors. The first was the White House incumbent, Ronald Reagan who was already showing the early signs of dementia. He was renowned, at the time, for being the manipulated dupe of his intelligent and more coherent advisors and lobbyists. The second was John Glenn, who was the first US astronaut to orbit the earth in 1962. Glenn made an unsuccessful bid to become the Democratic presidential candidate in 1984, at a cost to himself of $3 million. Thus Costello asks: 'There's already one spaceman in the White House. What do you want another one for?' The word 'spaceman' is a cruel pun about Reagan, which only worked as a device by Costello being equally dismissive of Glenn in the final line of the verse. It also works by continuing the space-age theme from the middle of the verse.

The number of words required for our prosaic interpretation of this final verse confirms the capable poetic efficiency of Costello as a lyricist. However, we need to qualify this compliment. The trick of successful evocative condensation is shared by poets and lyricists but it is indiscriminate to evaluate their work as a single art form.[17] Although Costello adopts many poetic strategies (he connotes rather than denotes, he decides the length of the lines and punctuation, he uses symbolism, imagery and condensation at will) it is not fair to judge him, or any other lyricist, purely as a poet. His job is to fit words to music to create a synergy of meaning and feeling. Generally he is very good at this task, as this song, 'relic' or not, demonstrates.

Taken as a whole piece, the lyric of the song condenses a depressing and anxious story, from the late 1930s to the mid-1980s, in which State-inspired nuclear terror, with the USA at the forefront, flooded the public imagination. More

---

[17] Poetry cannot always be put well to a melody. If the phrasing or word length is too complex then the song does not work – poetry *may* 'sing' but lyrics *have to*. A line of poetry that scans well when spoken may jar when put to a tune. Conversely, a clever or stirring lyrical line in a song may fall flat when and if it is simply spoken.

importantly, the real and ready presence of those abundant arms threatened the very existence of life on earth. Turning to the melody and musical production on the record, we can see how the poetic competence of Costello and his use of structure and harmony to accentuate the significance of his lyrics is manifest in 'Peace In Our Time'.

Assuming the album credits to be accurate, neither Bruce Thomas nor Pete Thomas is represented on this track – there are no drums or bass. It is likely that the arrangement was worked up between Costello on guitar and Steve Nieve and/ or Langer on organ and piano. There is an occasional brass phrase and some sort of processed 'clang'. The latter eccentric sound is short with many conflicting overtones, and it sounds like a piece of metal scaffolding pipe being hit with a hammer. The sound does not resonate in the same 'space' as the other instruments. It is a sample complete with reverb, processed and gated to provide us with a discrete sound event within the arrangement.[18] It should be regarded less as a pitched 'note' added to the harmony than as an element of *musique concrète*, a noise chosen for what it adds to the ambience of the track. In the context of tolling bells and thanking God this dull, metallic clank helps to undermine the sincerity of Costello's faith, aiding our comprehension of the lyric and its satirical implications.

The lack of bass and drums gives the track a fresh and natural 'unproduced' sound, despite it being carefully built up from four or more layers of guitar and keyboards. Listening to the song without delving too deeply into the lyrics, the overall feel is almost that of a Christmas hit, with sleigh-bell rhythms, churchy organ harmonies and some warm brass. There is also something about the forthright rhythms and trombone melody that, to our minds, evokes Northern collieries and mill-towns. Costello outlines the changes on an acoustic guitar with a waltz strum typical of country music: one-two-and-three-and, one-two-and-three-and ... Concurrently, Nieve prods away at an organ with an insistent crotchet pulse. The guitar has been mixed down underneath the warmer, less-cutting keyboard to lose some of the crunchy high-end attack.

During the introduction, the changes of chord from F to C to A7 are accentuated with additional tracks of piano and guitar, the guitar playing rippling broken chords and the piano providing some bass in sonorous open voicings. These additional piano and guitar parts drop out in the verse to be replaced by organ padding – at first pianissimo in the left hand, then chiming in strongly at the close of the verse with a second-inversion A chord, the organ key attack and the natural harmonic richness of the chord voicing creating an almost bell-like timbre that melts into a more familiar Hammond-and-Leslie tone with delayed (but deep) vibrato.

---

[18]   A gate is a filter which only processes signals between certain pre-set dynamic parameters. In their most basic application, gates can be used to eliminate unintentional and unwanted sounds that occur within the studio, such as the buzz of drum snares, or intakes of breath on vocal tracks. Conversely, they can also be used to isolate specific sounds within a recording. The 'clang' on 'Peace in Our Time' is effectively a sample of not only the sound, but also the space it was recorded in.

Example 5.1 'Peace In Our Time' motif

Melodically, the whole arrangement is built upon two motifs: the trombone figure that bookends the piece and provides an instrumental solo in the middle, and the arch-shaped figure that comprises the germ of the entire melody (Example 5.1). Heard beginning on the 3rd rising to the 5th and back (Example 5.1.a), we later hear it extended up to the flatted 7th to create a cadence (Example 5.1.b), transposed to the 2nd with some ornamentation (Example 5.1.c), and eventually the same motif forms the climax of the vocal using augmentation – employing the same pitch progression with augmented note values – and repetition (Example 5.1.d).

In fact, this motif is reiterated in each line of the song. Later on, when we are in the dominant region with the melodic focus on the 2nd and 4th degrees, and quite prepared to hear this phrase resolving to the tonic '… as the evening de-*scends*', Costello maintains our attention by hanging doggedly onto the 4th degree – G – playing it insistently throughout the second half of the verse: of the twenty measures between the move away from the tonic chord and the resolution to D '… and the *bells*', twelve are dominated by G naturals. Upon reaching the chorus, having stretched our capacity for Gs, it makes melodic sense to do the same with an A over the tonic, employing a descending (occasionally ascending) bass note against an otherwise static chord. The preponderance of this device throughout the song – even entering into the trombone melody in the coda – recollects European waltzes and chansons that Costello is probably referencing

Example 5.2 Trombone intro for 'Peace In Our Time'

Example 5.3 Trombone between verses in 'Peace In Our Time'

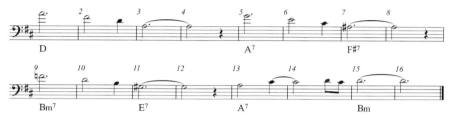

through his abiding love of Country music, a repository of influences from Irish, French, German and Spanish-Mexican music in addition to Afro-American Blues.

Costello says in his 1995 liner notes: 'In the instrumental refrain trombonist Jim Paterson plays the melody from another unfinished song of mine: "World Without End".' The use of this trombone melody is another excellent example of musical economy, providing continuity throughout the arrangement. At first hearing, the introduction is in the middle range of the instrument. The melody is simply an arpeggiation of the corresponding harmonies that, having established an opening tonality of F major, modulates immediately to an (expected) D minor tonality (Example 5.2).

However (and compare this to the modulatory cadences in 'Shipbuilding'), the verse turns out to be in D major. This creates a brighter, more positive ambience, even more than if the verse had been in the same F major key as the intro. When the trombone melody is heard for the second time (the solo), between verses 2 and 3, its context – and function – has changed. We have had fifty measures of D major and an abrupt modulation back to F major (in order to repeat the intro) would sound clumsy and artificial, so the trombone melody is transposed up a 6th into the home key of D major, allowing it to enter with the resolution of the chorus '... Peace in our *time*'. This brings it into the upper, 'tenor' range of the trombone, giving it a brighter sound and keeping the overall tone light and upbeat – accentuating the bite of the satirical intent.

Beginning this line in the key of D major immediately creates an harmonic problem to be resolved. Where the intro modulated from F through C7 to A7 and thus to D at the top of the verse, the solo swiftly finds itself on an F#7 chord, leading us into the key of B. To follow the lead of the intro/verse and head off into B major at this point would have been very interesting but out of character with the rest of

Example 5.4   Trombone coda of 'Peace In Our Time'

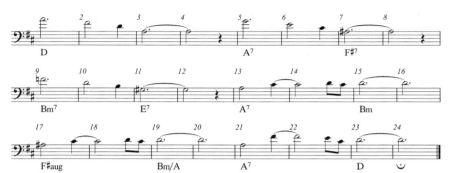

the piece, so the line progresses by sequence (Example 5.3) through Bm7–E7 to arrive at an A7 chord. A7 being the dominant of D major, this is an ideal place for the verse to pick up from. Costello could have begun verse 3 two bars earlier if he'd wished to, but instead he chooses to insert an interrupted cadence, resolving to the 6th. (The interrupted cadence is typically used to delay the climactic resolution of the perfect cadence: V– vi being followed by V–I. In this case, vi is immediately followed with I (the beginning of verse 3); yet another instance of Costello constantly turning 'to the light' harmonically within this piece.)

This melody appears once more after the last chorus, as a coda to the whole song. Now the composers have free rein to create something melodically and harmonically satisfying with which to end the piece; it needs to create a true sense of finality after the previous harmonic wrong-footing and sidesteps we have been presented with. Using the additive form whereby the solo is an extension of the intro, the coda is thus an extension of the solo. With a nod to the descending, chanson-like device used in the verse, the modulation inherent in the interrupted cadence is embraced. For a brief moment we seem to be wholly in the key of B minor with the inclusion of the A# (Example 5.4). However, the melody note remains a D and the next chromatic note in the descent is A, the 5th of D major. This is enough to re-establish our home tonality and Costello resolves decisively to D major in the next four measures.

Costello delivers the lyric in, what is for him, a relatively natural and unforced manner and transparent delivery which he later – coinciding with the more clichéd lines – underlines with emotional swell and a throbbing vibrato ('…a piece of paper in his hand', '…the whole world in his hands', '…peace in our time'). The elision required to fit some of the wordier lines to 4- and 8-bar phrasing creates some interesting effects – the way that 'And I slip on my Italian dancing shoes' falls in a rhythmic unit of four beats over the underlying triple metre – is very satisfying. (Tuplets are rhythmic figures that subvert the prevailing time signature; in duple metres (2/4, 4/4) these are usually triplets or, occasionally, groups of five or seven.

Less common, but very elegant, is the quadruplet in triple metre. Commonly known as 'waltz time', 3/4 already possesses a rhythmic lilt not found in duple metres; it is the only time signature to be directly allied to a dance. Inserting bars of four even beats in triple metre produces the sensation of an illusory retardation in the time, by literally fitting more into the bar without being constrained by the metrical sub-divisions, and of almost skating over the pulse.)

As can be seen in other songs, Costello likes to save modulations and chord changes until they tie in with the emotional punch of the lyric, and vice versa – here, after the four rising 3rds that emphasise the pealing (and punning) lines 'And the bells / take their toll / once again / in a victory chime', the phrase 'And we can thank God' lands on the subdominant. In a hymn, this would be effective cooperation of liturgy and harmony in the interest of promoting and sustaining faith in God. Throughout this song the apocalyptic fatalism of the subject matter, combined with effusive thanks to a God that provides peace at the expense of thousands of deaths, invite us to question Costello's sincerity. Later, Costello deliberately retards the melody at the climax of every chorus, using a more emotional delivery and augmentation (extension of note-values) to over-dignify the lyric, creating satirical effect. The eponymous phrase is so drawn-out it is delayed by a whole bar; one would say that it is dragged out through gritted teeth, but for Costello's hushed and reverent delivery.

Thus, when we overview the confessional mode of Costello's reflections on the album embedding 'Peace in Our Time' (with his allusion to needing a priest), and the hymn-like feel to the song, it seems to contain more than its fair share of religious resonances. The words are a lament about the collective sins of the political class and its recurring penchant for the seeming glories of war and the geo-political advantages of military force. Like 'Shipbuilding', the theme of anti-militarism and its role in impeding the development of a peaceful and socially just world appear in this song. What both songs do, albeit in different ways, is also problematise the USA–UK political alliance. We pick up on this point below, when discussing the tensions created by the lack of US support for the Falklands War and the awkward fact that the US invaded Grenada. The latter was a British colony until 1950 and it continued to be a member of the British Commonwealth after 1974.

Discussion

This chapter has used two songs as vehicles to explore Costello's particular ambivalence about the USA. As we noted in the introduction, this is by no means a quirk of his, given the wider mixed feelings that Europeans, especially those in the UK, often express about Britain's ex-colony and now dominant geopolitical partner. In the case of Costello, the picture is further complicated by his Anglo-Irish identity. 'American Without Tears' and 'Peace in Our Time' both reveal the capacity of Costello as a lyricist to mix personal and political themes, with the first biased to the personal and the second to the political. Both songs also move dramatically through time, evoking for the listener a large span in the middle of the 20th century.

In the first song, Costello is working with material imagined rather than experienced, as he was born in 1954 and the time explored largely focuses on the 1940s. However, he grew up in the context of a powerful narrative, fuelled by emotive stories of love and death, of memories from the Second World War. That narrative flowed through everyday conversations in families, in the mass media and in cultural products like film and music. Fascism had been defeated but this had been touch and go at times. Loved ones had been lost to death or migration, and democracy had been mortally threatened. The role of the USA, from the British perspective, was ambiguous – a needed ally arriving late on the scene.

Britain came near to being invaded eighteen months before the USA entered the war at the end of 1941. The successful retreat at Dunkirk in 1940 just about held off the prospect of Britain under Nazi rule, without direct US involvement (though the USA had been providing important background resources). However, active US military support was required for eventual triumph and this had consequences that were personal as well as political, especially in relation to love and death in British families.[19] For this reason, songs like 'American Without Tears', which highlight differentials of wealth and influence between the UK and the USA, are powerfully evocative of the Second World War and its legacy in the post-war period. But the final verse and its allusion to Costello's grandfather remind us not just of an unbalanced bi-partisan linkage. For him, as noted in the introduction of this chapter, Ireland made up the third point of a cultural and political triangle.

For the Irish, the USA was not a patronised and gratefully embraced ex-colony but a land of hope, one which provided migrants with the prospect of health, wealth and liberty, not starvation and colonial subjugation. Also, at the time of the Second World War, Ireland was neutral (making it suspect for many years in the eyes of Britain and its allies). During the 1930s, militant Irish Republicanism was divided between pro-fascist elements and those volunteering to fight alongside anti-fascists against Franco in Spain.

Irish neutrality, during the 1940s, raised the possibility – and provoked rumours – that German spies could be nearby in Eire and that the Irish might be tempted by a form of 'my enemy's enemy is my friend' political logic. However, there were Irish in the British armed forces and Irish people on mainland Britain were loyal to the war effort. To complicate matters, both Britain and Germany had serious plans to invade Ireland, as strategic options during the war.[20]

---

[19]   The USA entered the Second World War on 8 December 1941, the day after the Japanese attack on the US navy in Pearl Harbor, Hawaii. The atomic bombs dropped on Hiroshima and Nagasaki were a brutal reminder of the ruthless approach the USA has adopted towards its enemies, when required, to protect its interests.

[20]   In 1940, the British designed its invasion *Plan W* and Germany's equivalent was *Unternehmen Grün*.

Thus, Costello's allusion to his grandfather points up a recurring cultural and political ambiguity: during the 20th century, Irish troops were co-opted by powers outside of Ireland. They fought and died in the First World War as British combatants. They might have (as in Paddy's case) ended up fighting 'on the wrong side' when quelling Republican insurrections. In the case of the USA, Irish American troops fought alongside the British in both World Wars.

This reminds us that the 'post-colonial' identity and its many contradictions are, like many other socio-political phenomena, shaped by warfare.[21] It is little surprising then that Costello's imagination wrestles with, and within, the cultural triangle we note about Britain, Ireland and the USA. It is also not surprising that militarism and warfare are a central topic, for him, within that exploration of the trans-Atlantic triangle. This point is a cue for the second song we examined.

Costello's personal context for 'Peace in Our Time' was one of turmoil, of inner and outer disturbance. The distress of that time in his life could account for his tendency, in later years, to create an emotional distance from the album *Goodbye Cruel World*, a defence made easier by its condemnation by critics. However, given Costello's capacity to be bloody-minded, he could have defended his work. After all, he usually plays to his own agenda, not one set by others. Also, we drew attention to the ambiguity of the song 'Peace in Our Time, being designated by him as a 'relic'; probably, but not necessarily, being a code for regret and a need to forget a painful past.

With regard to outer terror, his emotional state may have sensitised him to the ongoing US-led military aggression in the world of the early 1980s, which existed for all on earth at the time.[22] He was not unique in reacting to this ongoing threat of nuclear annihilation. The 'Star Wars' ambition of Ronald Reagan was simply the most recent of several points of provocation to the producers and consumers of popular music. Anglo-American popular music expanded in scale after the Second World War and so reflected and reinforced the fear and nihilism of its young consumers. Costello was born into that historical period and it is scarcely surprising that he, like many of his contemporaries, would react creatively at times to a context of outer terror, alongside those who were pushed into denial and short-term pleasure-seeking (Nuttall, 1968). The presence or absence of a future became a matter of constant reflection and prediction for young people, and remains so today.

The Cuban missile crisis of 1962 stands out, because of the frightening brinkmanship between the Soviet and US leaderships. Whereas in the 1980s

---

[21]   The episodic *civil* war in Ireland during the 20th century did not attract Costello's creative attention (compare this with Bono or The Cranberries about 'the Troubles'). Also, one of Costello's collaborators, Paul McCartney, produced one of the most radical lyrics about the conflict ('Give Ireland Back to the Irish') in the immediate wake of Bloody Sunday in 1972. Banned by the BBC, the song went to number one in the Irish Republic.

[22]   When people, for whatever reason, experience periods of distress in their lives, it is common for them to be highly sensitive to external threats, which can create further distress for them.

Reagan's plans were a mixture of boastful sabre-rattling and science fiction, in 1962 the world was a whisker away from real and immediate destruction. Reagan, who never fought but had acted in several patriotic war films,[23] let slip, in 1981, that he believed that a limited nuclear battle was feasible in Europe, without necessitating a full-scale global exchange. Not surprisingly, protests about this cavalier proposal were not limited to his Soviet adversaries but were also heard from his NATO allies.

This one-off comment from a President, who largely lacked credibility outside his immediate obsequious political circle (which included Thatcher) and US voter base, was not a full repetition of the conditions of the 1960s, when bellicose rhetoric was common on both sides of the Cold War. For this reason, we tend now to associate the 1960s, not the 1980s, with a peak in musical reaction to political posturing about the use of nuclear weapons, but both periods are relevant to compare. Reagan was a dangerous President. In 1981, he announced the stockpiling of neutron bombs and the following year (five months before the 'Star Wars' boast) he initiated the MX missile system. This was in breach of the international anti-ballistic missile treaty, signed between the Soviet Union and the USA in 1972.[24]

Prior to that treaty, the prospect of nuclear annihilation was verbalized – with fear, loathing and sometimes graveyard humour – from the early 1960s by 'protest singers'. The best examples are 'Talkin' World War III Blues' and 'A Hard Rain's A-Gonna Fall' from the album *The Freewheelin' Bob Dylan* (1962) and the angry and foreboding 'Eve of Destruction' (written by P.F. Sloan and recorded by Barry McGuire in 1965).[25]

But Costello's response was also shared by some contemporary songwriters, at a time when, as we noted above, the Cold War was far from over and Reagan was playing fast and loose with the future of the human race. For example, other offerings came from Frankie Goes to Hollywood in their 'Two Tribes' (played for a John Peel session for the BBC in 1982, but becoming a longstanding single hit in 1984) and Nena's '99 Red Balloons', recorded in both German and English in 1983. Also Sting offered 'Russians', his critique of the Cold War and its nuclear threat, from the album *The Dream of the Blue Turtles* (1985). Even earlier, in 1980, Paul Weller's 'Going Underground', penned for his band The Jam, alludes to his exasperation with Thatcherism as it was getting into gear. The song alludes

---

[23]   Reagan was in the US armed forces during the Second World War but for medical reasons was never posted abroad to see action. He spent those years making propaganda movies for the war effort.

[24]   The USA ended this treaty formally in 2002 after the dissolution of the USSR.

[25]   A longer period of musical engagement with the nuclear threat is presented in *Atomic Platters* (Bear Family, 2010). This multi-media presentation (5 CDs containing more than 100 songs, a DVD and a lengthy explanatory booklet) covers that first phase of concern from the Second World War to the end of the 1960s. This is well-trodden territory that Costello is exploring in the 1980s.

to 'nuclear textbooks for atomic crimes' and laments public spending on the arms race rather than healthcare.

A final point to note in relation to the content of 'Peace in Our Time' is that it refers to a time in the early 1980s, when, despite the emerging strength of mutual commitment between Thatcher and Reagan, they had to express some personal disappointment with one another over two strategic military interventions. This song refers to one of them; the 1983 invasion of Grenada which angered Thatcher because she was not warned or consulted. Another relevant song for this point, which we looked at in Chapter 4, is 'Shipbuilding'. Reagan's government remained neutral about the Falklands conflict and tried at the outset of hostilities to act as a broker between the UK and Argentina. The fact that Thatcher and Reagan buried their differences about both conflicts privately, and so quickly, in order to ensure a solid publicly-declared alliance, is telling.

After taking advice, Reagan rang Thatcher on 26 October 1983, the day after the Grenada invasion. He apologised for the lack of consultation and begged Thatcher's indulgence, mainly arguing that operational necessity had meant the invasion happened in the way it did. Thatcher sympathised immediately, drawing parallels with her own constraints about the Falklands expedition (rhetorically rendering them partners of equal importance). They went on to discuss how to install a government on the island more in tune with the interests of the USA and the UK. The call was ended by Thatcher referring to her need to attend to a 'tricky' debate that day in the House of Commons. Reagan supportively signed off with 'Go get 'em. Eat 'em alive', reminding us that he viewed adversarial exchanges, in party politics, as a sort of cannibalistic playground game.[26]

Finally, that transatlantic personal alliance of the right embodied by Thatcher and Reagan has, over the years, witnessed a parallel in the life of Costello. After Thatcher left power he continued to work with US artists in social activism projects. These included work with Emmylou Harris and others in the Campaign for a Landmine Free World, and benefit concerts and recording for victims of the Hurricane Katrina devastation of 2005. His main US collaborator in the latter was Allen Toussaint, who he has worked with since 1983, including on the album *Spike*. Thus, although Reagan died in 2004 and, Thatcher in 2013, their regime of power was in part responsible for continuing creative political opposition, up to, and including, the present day. Costello has been an evident, though not singular, player in that opposition in the field of popular music.

---

[26] The full transcript of this call is available now as it has been declassified. See the Margaret Thatcher Foundation website, where this and other exchanges with Reagan can be read in full.

Chapter 6
The Post-Feminist Context

I do earnestly wish to see the distinction of sex confounded in society, unless where love animates the behaviour.

– Mary Wollstonecraft[1]

Introduction

Costello emerged as a successful commercial artist in the late 1970s, at the very time when second-wave feminism peaked in its influence. 'Second-wave' feminism, typified in the writings in the 1960s of Betty Friedman and Simone de Beauvoir, went beyond broad objective concerns of earlier feminists in relation to matters, such as voting rights and the economic disadvantage in marriage created by patriarchal property rights.

By the 1970s, these traditional protests about objective gender disadvantage were extended to powerful subjective concerns about respect and freedom and so enlarged the feminist strategic agenda to include social rights. This was no longer (just) about the macro politics of equality of *opportunity* but also about the micro-politics of personal recognition and its role in equality of *outcome*. This was summed up in the Women's Liberation Movement slogan 'the personal is political' (Hanisch, 1970), which indicated that iniquitous socio-economic arrangements were mirrored in recurring daily processes of women's oppression.[2]

This fresh wave of consciousness amongst women created a new etiquette. Prior to this, women were treated well by the rules of patriarchy (cherished or protected as vulnerable like children – 'women and children first' in an emergency) or badly (they were patronised and personally discounted at best; objectified, raped and killed at worst). This tradition was challenged dramatically with second-wave feminism, which created a new discourse about etiquette and women's rights, which we touched upon in Chapter 2 when examining the challenge this created for Costello.

---

[1]   From *A Vindication of the Rights of Woman with Strictures on Political and Moral Subjects* (1792).

[2]   Occasionally the inverted form is heard ('the political is personal'), making all individual men potential or actual enemies of all of the women they encounter. That version has been linked more with radical, rather than socialist, feminism.

'The worst thing that's happened to feminism since Jack the Ripper'?

Quite quickly Costello's song output had generated a reputation of misogyny. For example, as early as 1978 Fred Schruers, writing in *Circus* magazine about the tour after *This Year's Model*, offers this:

> It's 1:30 am in the Bootlegger Lounge in Syracuse, NY. Elvis Costello, the one with the owlish stare and the spitting mad vocals, the man whose songs may be the worst thing that's happened to feminism since Jack the Ripper, is leaning solicitously towards an elegant brunette in a low cut black dress.

There we have it in a nutshell. Costello is being compared to a mass murderer of women and is caught in an act of lascivious behaviour, grooming a victim. And, after this introduction, this piece from Schruers was not at all critical. Quite the opposite: it praises the artist and his songs. It ends with a statement about the tension or contradiction we examine in this chapter.

> Elvis Costello, then, is definitely this year's model for a rock star. Tougher than punk, more touching than MOR, a better beat than disco – and all with integrity. The kind of integrity that approaches rage, and makes for crashing, cathartic rock & roll concerts. Sitting in the dark bar in Syracuse, Elvis is apparently talked out. He launches out of his chair like a banty rooster trying to fly, gives one of his electric, swivelling gazes around the bar, and heads out – hand in hand with his future. (Schruers, 1978, emphasis added)

Schruers is impressed by a credible auteur with clear and honest intentions. The notion of 'integrity' brings us back to a central dilemma (addressed above in Chapter 2 and to be pursued a little further in Chapters 7 and 8) about authenticity in a commercial field requiring opportunistic self-advancement, impression management and performance. In Costello's case here and in later examples, like the interview with Tracey MacLeod we examined in Chapter 1, these endorsements from critics or fans about Costello's authenticity or integrity seem to rest on two aspects of his work.

The first is his apparent willingness to be emotional (especially in relation to angry indignation): he 'did' anger, not tears, in public at least at that time, but occasionally there was much tenderness in his lyrics, which critics tended to selectively overlook, to his irritation. However, this oversight was encouraged by Costello's own preferred persona and rhetoric, although later complained about by him (see later and Chapter 7).

With regard to emotional expression, we share a dubious cultural assumption that to be emotional *ipso facto* is to be authentic ('express your true feelings', 'speak from the heart', and so on).[3] This axiom about the emotions is of course

---

[3]   Note how 'integrity' in the way connoted by Schruers refers to something 'approaching rage', suggesting that integrity is about emotional expressiveness. This returns

highly challengeable. Whilst privately we have true feelings (and even then we can deceive ourselves with our inner voice), once we publicly express them then they become a form of communication and have rhetorical value, like any other statement. We *can* express them truly but we are all also capable of expressing them disingenuously and for instrumental or manipulative ends.

Politicians and entertainers necessarily become expert at this and in the case of histrionic individuals this becomes a rewarding lifestyle to gain power over others. In the case of talented actors and confidence tricksters, their emotions are on tap, for contrived but convincing performances. Instantly they can become someone else, in another time and place; that is, emphatically *not* one's true self in the here and now. Thus, emotionality and authenticity cannot and should not be conflated. This caution even precedes one already rehearsed in Chapter 2 about the pressures that shape 'impression management' in commercial artists.

The dilemma, about understanding the link between emotional experience, emotional expression (not the same as the first), and whether or not emotions are *inherently* authentic or open to abuse in the manipulative fakery of artists, has tested antiquarian philosophers and modern psychologists alike. Moreover, there is even ambiguity in whether or not emotions should be deemed to be negative or 'base' constraints on the higher virtues of rationality and duty to others, or whether they are virtuous *because* they reflect authenticity (Zaborowski, 2012). An example of such uncertainty is in the work of Descartes, who viewed the emotions as broadly good in nature but cautioned that it was the way and context in which they were *expressed* that determined whether they were vices or virtues. With this jury of experts still out, then all of us have to come to our conclusions about making sense of those we may praise or condemn in their social performances, whether they are ordinary people or commercial artists.

The second important aspect to discuss in this chapter is the matter of candour, which follows up the first point about the distinction between inner experience and its outer expression. Should feelings and the views linked to them be constrained in the interests of others, or is the 'truth' better out than in? We dealt with this at the end of Chapter 2, when discussing the matter of transgression within art and the amoral character of the imagination.

If an artist just says things in an interview or in their lyrics in an uncensored way, what does it mean and how might it be judged? Does it reflect an ideological stance about speaking the truth unto power or is it merely the unreflected-upon outpourings of their chaotic amoral inner lives? Do artists just say or sing or paint or dance what other people just think or imagine, but keep to themselves? And is that OK-should artists have a privileged dispensation within our moral order to do this without censure or control? Does it make them special, like wayward children set free to entertain and impress us by their freely expressed artless impulses in

---

us again to a problematic in the discourse of popular music about authenticity, which we address episodically in this book.

the service of artistic achievement? But before moving on to these matters we can take stock about a simple empirical matter – was Costello being fairly accused?

Judged or pre-judged?

Those knowing Costello's career will be aware that much of his songwriting (even to the present day) explores the dynamics of heterosexual relationships. They will also recognise (see above in this chapter) that claims about his misogyny were made very early. Whether they were premature is a subjective judgement we can all make with hindsight. But whether they were early is objectively not in doubt.

Look again at when Schruers made his comment. It was 1978. At this stage Costello had only released two albums and the latest (his first with The Attractions) was still being road-tested. Also look again at what Schruers said: 'the man whose songs may be the worst thing that's happened to feminism since Jack the Ripper'. If commercial artists can be accused of playing to their audiences for dramatic effect, this is certainly also true of the easy cheap shots that can emerge from music journalists trying to grab the reader's attention in the first paragraph.

This comparison with Jack the Ripper is logically, empirically and ethically misguided in several ways. The Ripper was anonymous and his identity never discovered, whereas Costello was the transparent named author of his acts. The Ripper brutally eviscerated women, whereas Costello wrote emotive songs about heterosexual intimacy. The Ripper existed prior to feminism, whereas Costello was operating in its very midst. In the latter regard, the comment from Schruers is inherently anachronistic. The Ripper logically could not be one of the 'worst thing(s) that happened to feminism' because he pre-dated it as a political ideology. He violated *women*, not a political strategy for female emancipation.[4]

Whether Costello, or any other named man in the cultural field of the day, should be accused of undermining rather than supporting feminist goals is the begged question, in the light of him being labelled by some as misogynistic. Silly comparisons with mass murderers do not help us in this legitimate inquiry. With hindsight, one of Costello's biographers makes the following comment about the contents of the album *My Aim is True*:

> Songs ranged from the complex and surreal ('Waiting for the End of the World') to the unsympathetic ('Less than Zero') and misogynistic ('I'm Not Angry'), and while critics lathered praise on the record, they also wondered what real pain could be involved that enabled Costello to write to such songs, ones that crossed the borders of human emotions so strikingly. (Clayton-Lea, 1998: 27)

---

[4]   Apparently more has been written about Jack the Ripper than all of the US Presidents put together. Contestation about a single perpetrator and an undetected identity has sustained an unending legend about the horrors of London in 1888 (Curra, 2011).

Thus the melodramatic rush to judgement from Schruers about misogyny was not isolated. For example, Mitch Cohen in *Creem* magazine (February 1978) considered that 'the only questionable thing about Elvis Costello is how far he'll take his misogyny, how long he'll keep blaming women because he was raised on romance and has had it pulled from under him'. Moreover, if these were examples of an early pre-judgement maybe they were also prescient about how others were to label Costello. For example, we have this retrospective view from Colin Beckett online in *Stylus* (1 September 2003): 'Costello's first two albums created the image of an outraged misogynist, but *Armed Forces* broadened his misogyny to full blown misanthropy.'

We can also note here that feminism, as a moral framework, was being mediated and voiced by *male* critics. (When writing this chapter, we have not found women critics attacking Costello, though they may have been out there but missed by us.) At the same time, it is unlikely that most female listeners would exactly be charmed by creepy lines like 'When you feel strange hands in your sweater' (from the song 'Everyday I Write the Book'). Costello himself flatly denies accusations of critics for example, when maintaining that his lyrics were not anti-women but anti-fashion. (In some of his later songs on *All This Useless Beauty* (1996) Costello produced some clearly pro-feminist lyrics.)

With regard to Schruers, his Ripper analogy also needs to be placed in the context of the rest of his review – which was glowing. There is a stance he is taking to Costello's work by the end with his complimentary emphasis on 'integrity'. And this apparent contradiction might point up why Costello's work was and remains controversial about women (this we explore later), but a psychological and semantic caution needs to be noted about the narrow conflation of candour and personal 'integrity'. Honesty cannot be selective because selectivity is inherently a form of dishonesty. However, and this is where the tension creeps in and Costello and other artists can stand accused: honesty is not the *only* moral impulse governing being human.

For example, etiquette, courtesy or diplomacy can also be read as attempts to ensure compassion, respect and recognition for our fellow human beings. They could be understood as the human conscience (or 'super-ego') collectively writ large. These blueprints, from various political and religious ideologies about how we *ought* to treat one another moment-to-moment, are important constraints on selfish and hurtful acts. They also have a downside though. They can be a constraint on freedom of expression. Also, their attentive advocates can readily fall from grace: righteousness and purity risk immediate dangers to anyone preaching them. With diplomacy comes duplicity, and with primness, hypocrisy soon follows. Moreover, sometimes these moral strictures are incommensurable. Compare feminist arguments with those of radical Islam. Both have very clear views about the nature of propriety in gender relations but they are fairly different.

In the context of these moralistic considerations, at issue here is simply how much 'artistic licence' should be granted in a civilised society. If artists should be at liberty to offend, then ethically maybe there should be some demonstrable gift evident from them in exchange.[5] That gift might be the struggle to authentically explore our inner and intimate lives, as well as any aspect of being-in-the-world. This type of offer and creative struggle is what we encounter in the work of poets, lyricists and novelists who we come to enjoy and respect.

What the variegated traditions of psychoanalysis have demonstrated is this. We are all complex bundles of desire, who are struggling to tame our passions and selfish intentions in order to co-exist with others. As a consequence, we are all liars and cheats. We deceive ourselves and others in order to avoid the pain and threat created by authentic expression. As social animals we cannot simply and always express ourselves at will in a free way; there are consequences for others and in turn that means consequences for our own survival, because we are interdependent beings.

Serious artists test the limits of exploration of this complicated world of being human. When they do, they may at times find themselves playing with fire. As early *homo sapiens* soon found out, flames certainly illuminate but they can also be painful and even lethal. Costello played with fire *when writing* about the politics of intimacy at the very time when feminism was asserting, for mass adoption, its own version of the super-ego writ large. Feminists were saying 'this is how it should be for the whole of human society', whereas Costello, and other frank artists, was saying 'from the way I see it this is how it is'. One position is normative and prescriptive ('the personal is political'), whereas the other is imaginative and descriptive ('the personal is messy and complicated and this is my experience of that complexity'). It is easy, though, to see why the latter position might clash with the former.

The validity of the claim about the range of song topics listed by Clayton-Lea and his note on the critics' speculation about Costello's pain motivating his emotional explorations is certainly underscored if we examine albums nearby in time. For example, the comments could reasonably apply to the contents of *My Aim is True*, *This Year's Model* or *Armed Forces*. In the context of feminism, his insistent exploration of the micro-politics of intimacy on many of the tracks of these albums was going to be tricky.

Was Costello simply a typical young patriarch of the post-Second World War period, who treated women with casual contempt? Was he being brazen and aggressive in the face of imminent feminist censure? He was certainly full of rage, which could be read as machismo. But feminists at the time were also full of rage. Rage and even violence are not solely male preserves,[6] even if most violence,

---

[5] The term 'gift' here is used to indicate that, at root, this is not a commercial point but one about creative outcomes prior to their financial worth being established,

[6] This point is graphically illustrated by the assassination attempt on Andy Warhol, who was shot by a member of SCUM (the Society for Cutting Up Men) on 3 June 1968. Empirical studies of intimate violence demonstrate that it occurs in heterosexual, gay and lesbian relationships at similar levels of prevalence and in the first of these male and female victims equalise in frequency the more that gender inequalities reduce in society (Rogers and Pilgrim, 2010). This position is empirically strongly defensible though in relation to *sexual* violence, where men are overwhelmingly perpetrators in relation to women, girls, boys and other men.

official and illicit, is dominated by male perpetrators and victims. So if rage is not inherently male and patriarchal, what is it about Costello's early songs that might attract the attribution of misogyny? A related question is whether Costello's own behaviour, rather than his songs, might have attracted the attention of critics, who labelled him as misogynistic.

Both of these questions, one about his music and the other about his personal conduct, need to be placed in the time period in question. Nowadays the field of popular music has normalised a more general cultural trend towards 'pornification', whereby commercial artists (both men and women) are typically packaged as sexual objects or are surrounded by the latter as a supporting cast, for example in raunchy music videos (Attwood, 2009; Paasonen et al., 2007). In the 1970s and 1980s, this was not the norm in the field and so any critical attention about sexual politics tended to focus on these two questions about lyrical content and the sexual morality of the artist. The female vocalist Madonna probably did most to move us into the third area of current pornification, with her lead being taken subsequently by artists like Britney Spears, Beyoncé, Christina Aguilera and Lady Gaga. Whether this is sign of feminist progress is a moot point (Levy, 2005).[7]

Costello cannot be accused of having anything to do with that politically ambiguous pornification of popular music. If anything, some of his lyrics are quite puritanical and he has never deployed eroticised packaging in his performances or video material. However, Griffiths (2007) is correct to note that the women in Costello's songs are *limited* in their roles (to lovers, present and past) and do not seem to appear as people in non-sexualised roles in society. The one exception here is Margaret Thatcher (see end of this chapter). During the 1980s, he tended to use women mainly as backing singers in his collaborations (Claudia Fontaine, Caron Wheeler, Chrissie Hynde and Cait O'Riordan). However, he did write with the last of these: for example, they co-wrote 'Tokyo Storm Warning' from *Blood & Chocolate*.

When considering this pattern, and the limited agenda about gender in Costello's lyrics, Griffiths does not dismiss Costello as being merely misogynistic but nor does he endorse him as a sensitive post-feminist product. Thus we are left with the other question about Costello's private conduct. On this point, there is no evidence, from his biographers at least, that he was, in any sense, peculiar for his time, place or occupational field. Life on the road with the band would have brought with it habitual opportunities for casual sex, some taken. More relevantly, his main relationships are not a matter of secrecy. Neither are they a cause for particular celebration or opprobrium.

---

[7]   By the 1980s, our period of interest, contrasting ideological positions began to emerge *within* feminism about pornography, with the anti-porn orthodoxy being challenged by some liberal or 'sex-positive' feminists. Andrea Dworkin's work typified the former and Camille Paglia's work the latter. Madonna and her recent raunchy pop tradition favour the 'sex-positive' form of cultural expression.

He has been married three times, first to his teenage lover and then to two partners he met in the field of commercial music. He married Mary Burgoyne in 1974 and they had a son, Mathew, together. He subsequently had an intense sexual relationship with a fashion model, Bebe Buell. Costello later denied the assumption that the song 'Party Girl' was about Buell but conceded that it referred to a brief fling with an art student. In an interview with Nick Kent in 1991 (in Kent, 1994), Costello admitted that 'the trouble with being an adulterer and a songwriter is that you always write songs in code'. He went on to say: 'I'm not glorying in it. And I'm still not happy about all the pain it caused by ex-wife.' This seems like a variant of ordinary guilt-tinged account of adultery admitted by anyone, not consistent with hatred for the opposite sex. An early working through of this angst is found in the song 'Accidents Will Happen'.

In 1986, he married the bass player from *The Pogues*, Cait O'Riordan, but they parted in 2002. In 2003, he married the jazz singer Diana Krall, who bore him twins, Dexter and Frank, in 2006. At the time of writing they remain married.

That is the basic story, with no evidence that these intimate relationships warranted accusations of Costello being anything even approximating to Jack the Ripper (Schruers' taken-for-granted narrative in 1977). Costello was, and has been, unremarkable as a heterosexual, working in the music industry.[8] Given the prurience of the tabloid press, if he had not been unremarkable they would have found and publicised the grounds for any such suspicion.

It is true that, in public settings, Costello has been extremely guarded about his private life. In Chapter 3, we discussed the role of this policy and its possible link to him denying that he looked back on his life for creative ends. However, the mass media has a tendency to seek and find scandal for commercial reasons. With the exception of the 'race incident', provided on a plate for them by Bonnie Bramlett (see Chapter 4), journalists have had little to toy with in the life of Costello, compared to many others in the music industry. His public life has been met with plaudits about his musical erudition and some jibes about being curmudgeonly (there are many parallels in this regard to his friend Van Morrison). But this is normal 'rock and roll'.

The common chaos of intimacy

So if the attribution of misogyny was to have any empirical basis, we are left looking at Costello's lyrics and his preferred way of performing them, not his private life, according to the evidence that exists about it. Then the discussion does become interesting. It invites us to separate out Costello's demonstrable personal preoccupations about sex and women in his songs on the one hand (see below) and the caution that these are products of his imagination on the other,

---

[8] Compare him, for example, to Bob Marley who had eleven children by seven different women by the time he died at the age of only 36 years.

even if that imagination will melt erratically into cues from his personally-lived experience. The blurring of the two creates much confusion and contention in any post-feminist discussion of cultural products, a point that is general and certainly not limited to a consideration of Costello.

For example, in an infamous debacle of a debate in 1971 between Norman Mailer and his feminist critics, including Germaine Greer and Diana Trilling – with, amongst others, Betty Friedman and Susan Sontag in the audience, joining in the attack – the novelist defends his work and its contents. At one point, in a state of irritable exasperation, he insists that his critics wrong-headedly are attacking his characters *as if they are him*. From Mailer's perspective, his critics could not view his characters as products of his imagination, only as mouthpieces for his misogyny.

This type of conflation is also at the heart of the argument about Costello and his attributed misogyny. He does say some really spiteful and creepy things about women in his songs. He is obsessed by voyeurism, exhibitionism and sado-masochism, sharing some of these themes of sexual 'perversion' or 'variation' with Madonna,[9] so is in good or bad company depending on which post-feminist reading we prefer. He silences lovers, and domestic violence comes and goes in his songs.

So does all of this content mean that Costello hates women? It might do. Alternatively, it could simply involve him imaginatively exploring tensions around sex and the hate which habitually emerges at times alongside the love in intimate relationships, whatever their sexuality.[10] This is not *just* about exploring power between men and women but it does include power play between intimates, whatever their gender. The data about gay and lesbian intimate violence footnoted earlier highlights this point. So the tensions Costello explores could stand for intimacy in general and are not *only* about the male–female dynamic. For example, when heterosexual or homosexual relationships finish, one or both partners commonly feel and express rage and despair in their loss. Also, when couples are together, control, not just power, is also a recurrent point of dispute or accommodation. Sexual activity, or its lack, and money, or its lack, are recurrent topics of tension on both counts.

A moral – or, more precisely, moralistic – discourse about sexual relationships, whether it is from feminism, fundamentalist religion or any other ideology, cannot speak to or explore the complicated experiential churn of actual relationships. The latter include, over time, variable mixtures of lust, trust, distrust, dependency, emotional and practical support, care during sickness, respect, power, control, possessiveness, fears and compensatory expectations from past attachments, adoration, hatred, sentimentality, blind faith, jealousy, fear of abandonment (the list goes on). People repeat mistakes in intimate relationships and may also struggle not to repeat them. It is all very complicated, as we know from honest accounts from people who live together.

---

[9]   Costello does not have a high opinion of Madonna – see Chapter 7.

[10]   Costello only deals with heterosexuality and so makes his particular contribution to a 'hetero-normative' discourse.

With this fluid complexity, any honest and intelligent examination of the common chaos of intimacy, which contains calculative or deliberative forms of thought *and* intuitive or emotional aspects of our experience, has to be left to psychoanalysis, existentialism and serious artists. Ideologies, like feminism, are inherently prescriptive or normative, whereas these experientially-based explorations require the restraint of the impulse to direct and judge too much. This is less about righteous judgement and more about candid curiosity. As with journalists in war zones, who may well have a particular partisan view about the conflict, the primary duty of the serious artist is to explore and represent what is going on, not to take sides or tend to the casualties.

In a review of a Mailer novel at the time of the chaotic debate noted above, Joyce Carol Oates gives her view about 'what is going on' about the common chaos of intimacy and its associated emotions in the context of second wave feminism; especially hatred. She comments:

> Women have always been forbidden hatred. Certainly they have been forbidden the articulation of all base, aggressive desires, in a way that men have not. Aggression has been glorified in men, abhorred in women. Now, the hatred is emerging. And such hatred! Such crude, vicious jokes at the expense of men! Most women, reading the accusations of certain feminists, will be as shocked and demoralized as Norman Mailer himself. Somehow, in spite of all the exploitation, the oppression, somehow … *there are things about the private lives of men and women that should not be uttered, or at least we think they should not be uttered, they are so awful.* Women have been the subjects of crude jokes for centuries, the objects of healthy male scorn, and now, as the revolution is upon us, men will become the objects of this scorn, this exaggerated disgust and comic sadism. Nothing will stop the hatred, not the passage of legislation, not the friendliest of men eager to come out in support of Women's Liberation. It has just begun. It is going to get worse. And yet, it will probably be short-lived. Hatred goes nowhere, has no goal, no energy. It has a certain use, but it has no beauty. (Oates, 1971: 43, emphasis added)

Costello, like all serious (not necessarily worthy or good, just serious) artists gets his hands dirty with 'things … that should not be uttered'. This is where Oates introduces the highlighted provocation 'or at least we think they should not be uttered, they are so awful'. 'Exaggerated disgust and comic sadism' are there in oodles in Costello's lyrics and, unrestrained, he certainly goes to places which are 'so awful'.

This type of lyrical exploration by him is then either appreciated for its honesty, hence Schruer's need to venerate Costello's 'integrity', or it is dismissed as mere misogyny, hence Clayton-Lea's label of 'I'm Not Angry'. Both are understandable readings of Costello's early songs. Both in their own way could be defended as being 'true' and the second one may be particularly tempting, given that the first-/second-person form is typically used by Costello in his lyrics (see the next section).

Moreover, his emotive often angry and sneering tone of voice is there to underline his spiteful take-home messages and so here we will note a point of relevance to his songs about women, but applicable to all the topics in his repertoire. The punch in Costello's work often is not what he sings but *the way that he sings it*; this truism about the manner of speech also applies to song.[11] This means that we need to consider what Barthes (1977) called the 'grain of voice'.[12]

Costello's voice is technically limited. Indeed, by those with no interest in, or affection for, his work, he might even be thought of as a bad singer. For example, he tends to shout and strain when he struggles to reach notes. But what the listener is never in any doubt about is that when he is despairing, melancholic, sneering or angry, it is very evident in the way that he characteristically *performs* his songs. This is not just about having a 'distinctive' voice (a feature of many singers), it is also about that distinction in some way or other breaking the mould and changing the way that we hear music. Costello might be thought of now legitimately in these terms.

Thus we can reflect on three aspects of his singing performance relevant to the emotional message taken away by the listener (in this case about women and sex). First, the lyrics he writes, and thus sings, are recurrently *emotive* (see below). Second, the grain of his voice always provides a peculiar *emotional overlay* to those emotive lyrics. Third, despite the technical limitations of his voice, Costello demonstrates notable *dramatic versatility* – he can play with his own words and thus encourage different ways of listening and hearing his songs. Together, these three features make Costello's singing performances extraordinary.

Having considered the grain of Costello's voice and its emotional punch in his song performances, we finish this section with a central conclusion. What makes the interpretive difference in approaching his songs is the listener's choice to either identify, with certainty, their content with the *actual viewpoint* of the songwriter on the one hand or, much more ambiguously, to listen to the lyricist's *imaginative explorations* about intimate relationships on the other. The tension noted above between Mailer and his critics is replayed in these competing understandings of Costello's songs.

Women and sex in Costello's early songs

In the light of the above cautions about judging Costello as a misogynist, and the defence offered about his serious artistic aspirations, let us now look at some examples of his early songs and what they contain about women and sex. Whereas in other chapters we have analysed particular songs, here instead we look more

---

[11]   See our note 5 in Chapter 2 above about his lesson about this from Van Morrison.

[12]   Some singers stand out in pop history, for example, Frank Sinatra, Elvis Presley, Buddy Holly and Kurt Cobain, in relation to their extra-ordinary voicing, which can be appraised beyond the technical expectations of concerned singing teachers (Frith, 1981).

widely across several examples of his work, when allusions are identifiable about heterosexual intimacy. Some themes are identifiable, which we summarise here in several points with brief illustrative examples:

Sadomasochism

This theme recurs in Costello's lyrics and can be identified on his first album where we have:

> She's got a ten-inch bamboo cigarette holder and her black leather gloves. And I'm doing everything just tryin' to please her, even crawling around on all fours. ('Miracle Man' – *My Aim is True*)

> He's got a mind like a sewer and a heart like a fridge. He stands to be insulted and he pays for the privilege. ('Man Out of Time' – *Imperial Bedroom*)

> Time to experiment. Make love like a punishment ('Flirting Kind' – *Punch the Clock*)

Physical and emotional abuse

This shades into the previous point arguably but is not necessarily connected to sexual arousal. Here are some examples:

> Wooden bones and pretty lashes. Iodine for your baby's gashes ('Tiny Steps' – *Armed Forces*)

> Oh I know that she's disgusted (oh why's that). Cause she's feeling so abused (oh that's too bad) ('(The Angels Wanna Wear My) Red Shoes' – *My Aim is True*)

> But I can't excuse the cruel words that I use whenever we fight. ('Tears Before Bedtime' – *Imperial Bedroom*)

> It all ends up in a slanging match with body talk and bruises. ('Pidgeon English' – *Imperial Bedroom*)

> And I even slapped your face and made you cry. ('Boy with a Problem' – *Imperial Bedroom*)

Cuckolding, betrayal and revenge

This theme reminds us of Costello's most quoted public confession from 1977 in an interview with Nick Kent. Notwithstanding our recurring cautions about the intentional fallacy and the problem of establishing authenticity in the public statements of commercial artists, it still bears repetition for the reader's consideration. It is cited in all of his biographies and has become emblematic of him as a young artist. Clayton-Lea (1998) ensures that it is placed as the very first epigraph in his book about the artist:

> The only two things that matter to me, the only motivation points for me writing all these songs, are *revenge* and *guilt*. Those are the *only* emotions I know about, that I know I can feel. Love? I dunno what it means really and it doesn't exist in my songs. (Interview with Nick Kent in *NME*, 27 August 1977, emphasis in the original)

Costello may have meant what he said, or thought he did (maybe not). Motives other than revenge and guilt were actually discernable in his songs, as was some notion of romantic love (see below). So this is really a reductive and misleading self-analysis from Costello and one contradicted by his own statements at the time, which we note later. He was a motivated performer as a pre-pubescent boy, before betrayal in intimate sexual relationships logically could even occur. It is not impossible that his cryptic allusion to 'revenge' might refer to people other than sexual partners. We will never know for certain. However, the content of his *early* songs overwhelmingly put women in the cross-hairs of his vengefulness. He complained about other matters (for example, militarism, aspects of the music industry, elites and a burgeoning crass consumerism) but rarely in quite the same *personalised* way. To complicate our interpretive challenge further, the nature of accusation and counter-accusation between parties is not always clear in his lyrics. An example, of this is in the hauntingly ambiguous song 'Riot Act' from *Get Happy!!* (1980). It could be about a woman or his accusers over the 'race incident' (see Chapter 4), both or neither. It is placed deliberately on the album directly after 'I Stand Accused', further engaging our curiosity, especially as the latter song was not written by Costello.

Thus his drive to perform and be successful was more complex than the combined impact of these two emotions. It still makes for a good quote though, even if with hindsight it seemed to be mainly for dramatic effect. But if he was not singularly preoccupied by betrayal and revenge, he did dwell on them quite a bit. For example:

> I may be crazy but I can't contemplate being trapped between the doctor and the magistrate. One of these days I'm gonna pay it back ... ('Pay It Back' – *My Aim is True*)

> You're upstairs with the boyfriend while I'm here to listen. I hear you calling his name. (I'm Not Angry' – *My Aim is True*)

> It's knowing that he knows you now after only guessing. It's the thought of him undressing you or you undressing. ('I Want You' – *Blood & Chocolate*)

Voyeurism

At times this can shade into the above point in relation to cuckolding. Costello often alludes to desire for the female form and the masturbatory fantasies of men. In the first example given, the whole song 'Satellite' could be read as a critique of pornography (there is a direct allusion to a being in 'pornographer's trousers') and is a note from him about globalization and its technological changes (see Chapter 7).

> As he undressed her with his eyes her weakness was his talent. How could she know as she stepped through the lights, that her dress would become transparent ('Satellite' – *Spike*)

> You check her outline. Break her regulations. You watch her legs through several service stations. ('Busy Bodies' – *Armed Forces*)

> So in this almost empty gin palace through a two-way looking glass you see your Alice ('Beyond Belief' – *Imperial Bedroom*)

> I've got this camera click, click, clickin' in my head. I've got you talking with your hands, got you smiling with your legs. ('I'm Not Angry' – *My Aim Is True*)

> All the soldiers taking turns with their attentions. And as they speculate what she'd look like beneath that thin nightgown ... ('Sleep of the Just' – *King of America*)

All of the above material, a sample not the whole case, suggests that Costello is pre-occupied with women, both as erotic objects and as important figures of personal attachment. The unrestrained negativism in the lyrics and the despair and anger in his voice when singing, are hardly indicative of a gentle respectful attitude towards 'the opposite sex'. His preoccupation with 'sexual perversion'[13] does not help his case in this regard.

Whereas Bob Dylan could write one type of song, typified by the sweet romanticism of 'Spanish Boots of Spanish Leather' *and* another of irritable disappointment, typified by 'It Ain't Me Babe', the sense was that Costello was only able and willing to create bleak versions of the latter. An early exception was his 'Stranger in the House', which he wrote alone but went on to perform with George Jones. He struggled to construct many of this type of song but, as we will see, was keen to sing the works of others reflecting its usual softer sentiments (see below). Now we turn to some moderating evidence for those who strongly suspect misogyny in Costello's work.

---

[13]   This is a contested term depending on whether variations in sexual life are judged puritanically or celebrated liberally by any of us. However, the triad of sadomasochism, exhibitionism and voyeurism noted do place a particular emphasis upon the objectification of women in Costello's hetero-normative lyrics.

Not only, but also: Costello and his love of women

Costello's rhetoric as someone who did not know what love meant in 1977, claiming, as he did, its total absence from his songs, was maybe never plausible from the outset. Over ten years later, he was complaining 'The French call me Mr. Hate. I'm not Mr Hate, I'm Mr. Love' (interview with David Wild, *Rolling Stone*, June 1989).

But earlier, indeed in 1978 in a follow-up interview with Nick Kent in *NME*, Costello wanted to make *both* a virtue of his stubborn adolescent aggression *and* complain about the lack of appreciation from his critics about the sensibilities of his lyrics, as well as unfair accusations about his immaturity. Summarising the lack of empathy and imagination of music critics about his work he noted that:

> You can say 'Oh you're just immature, you'll soften up' but I fuckin' won't ... Tenderness, I can feel tenderness and I'm not afraid of it, and *it isn't entirely absent* from either of my albums. (Emphasis added, for contrast with the 'revenge and guilt' claim)

Given that he was only in his early twenties when he made this comment, he probably *was* immature, so can be forgiven for denying that fact at the time he did and for his truculence. As for not softening with age, how could he (or anyone) predict the future? He was a sharp young songwriter not a clairvoyant. Moreover, he seems to be already back-pedalling from his more quoted absolute claim, only a few months previously, about his songs having no love in them. We now have tenderness not being 'entirely absent'. And, indeed, looking back now at his work, if all of the above unsavoury and dark samples of his lyrics warrant representation, they are not the whole picture. There was another side of the coin, even though it tended to hide face-down much of the time in his words.

It is also worth noting that his anger and negativism, as well as the grain of his voice, were probably quite a shock to many listeners (including presumably music critics) and so maybe nihilism, misogyny and even misanthropy stood out in Costello's overall musical message, drowning out the nuances he pleads to be heard. Songs about the opposite sex, according to the dominant pop narrative of the time, were supposed to be about sweet adoration. They were about 'lurv' not sordid impulses or contempt and loathing. Accordingly, this break from the old from Costello would have grabbed the attention of listeners and disguised the more ambiguous qualities of his lyrics, which are certainly there to be found.

To complicate matters further, maybe Costello protested too much. All of that distrust and fury about women may have been what is called 'reaction formation' in psychoanalysis. Earlier than Freud, Spinoza pointed out that:

> no one is disturbed or anxious concerning anything unless he loves it, nor do wrongs, suspicions arise, and enmities arise except for love for a thing which no one can really fully possess ... (Spinoza, *Ethics* 5, proposition 20, 1996)

Maybe he really, really, loved women and so Spinoza's proposition would apply.[14] This hypothesis is supported by Costello's recorded material, when it is looked at in the round. Indeed, all of the above angst, equivocation and turmoil reflect something very obvious: Costello is obsessed by women and understanding heterosexual intimacy. In his early work it preoccupies his imagination, not to the exclusion of all else, but it is highly prominent.

Whether we can call any obsession 'love' is a moot point (are people who are obsessed by anything in love with it?). But he is certainly and unequivocally emotionally preoccupied by women, an existential position inhabited by most young heterosexual men. It is just that, as a compulsive songwriter, this *particular* young heterosexual man had to put it down obsessively in his lyrics. This obsession did lessen with age, though by no means disappeared. In his twenties, Costello was as much a slave to his testosterone as any other young man. In his thirties, he could at last turn some of his imaginative attention to more worldly matters. And he did, although he still complained of being dismissed for his immaturity.[15]

If he really, really loved women then, as all people know who seek meaning in their lives through a strong passion for others, this is a sort of enslavement and thus a potential source of resentment. That resentment can keep fuelling anger with oneself, for the constraint it imposes on one's autonomy, or with the object of one's desire. The ensuing fury can then ricochet inwards and outwards. This pattern might have provided the addictive and compulsive impulses required for Costello passionately to write what he did about *both* love *and* hate in heterosexual intimacy. And for the period of his work we are considering, we can note three pieces of evidence that Costello was quite capable of exploring the tender aspects of heterosexuality.

First, even within his angry or spiteful songs, we can find softer emotions or ones which are ambiguous, such as the line 'making love tooth and nail' (from 'Kid About It' on *Imperial Bedroom*). Another example is the song 'Indoor Fireworks' from *King of America*, which is a melodic amble through a relationship, which contains lines about fighting (yet again) but is also obviously about adoration and longing ('you were the spice of life, the gin in my vermouth'). And then it resolves with his leitmotif of anger – but is it now revenge or regret and is he blaming himself or his ex-partner with the line, 'I'll build a bonfire of my dreams and burn a broken effigy of me and you'? These more nuanced songs give some support to Costello's own plea for understanding from his critics about his struggle with the complexities of intimacy.

---

[14]   See Spinoza (1996). The inverse argument, more frequently used in psychodynamic logic, is that sentimentality disguises feelings of hate.

[15]   An example of Costello's abiding perversity is that by 2010 he also objects to the attribution of *maturity*: 'Content is a word that has never sat well with me. Like "maturity". They are two words I've never liked. I think they imply some sort of decay. A settling.' (Interview with Tim Adams in *The Observer*, 17 October 2010.) It would appear that Costello wants to be appreciated but *never fully understood.*

Second, a few whole songs are within the tradition we are accustomed to associate with romantic love, with sentimental or forlorn feelings predominating and an absence of rancour. For example, 'Stranger in the House' (from *My Aim Is True*, his very first album and identified by his critics as the first sign of misogyny) was noted above, and arguably an exception that proved the rule. Even this song, with its gentle maudlin feel, focuses on self-pity and is not particularly tender about the lost love it alludes to. The song is not about the tender adoration of a woman but a man's disappointment in her for *her lack of empathy for him* and his consequent tragic loneliness. This then, is a masculine 'poor me' offering, not a celebration of womanhood, the well-trodden path of Country and Western music and a cue for the next point.

Third, and this would also be a theme in his later work,[16] Costello clearly enjoyed recording covers, which were in a softer cultural tradition. In his early career, this third option about exploring tenderness via the work of others is the album *Almost Blue*, in which he tries to rescue the unfashionable tradition of Country and Western music from its reputation of trite sentimentality. As we noted in Chapter 3, this generated a single success for Costello ('Good Year for the Roses'). Also, there were isolated examples of this on non-cover albums like *King of America*, where he recorded and slipped in the telling and self-pitying 'Don't Let Me Be Misunderstood' (a single hit for The Animals, but recorded originally by Nina Simone and written by Benjamin, Caldwell and Marcus). The song 'I Stand Accused' from *Get Happy!!*, written by Colton and Smith, was also about infatuation. It is another example of Costello, including on his albums the occasional song about undying romantic love, penned by others.

These examples of covering existing tender love-song material in his early career were augmented later in his co-writing with Burt Bacharach. Both these early and later songs tended to have a coherent message or relatively transparent narrative for the listener. This was out of sync with much of Costello's early sole-authored material, which was notoriously obscure, disjointed or even surreal (see Chapter 8).

Conclusion

This chapter began by reporting accusations of misogyny against Costello. Comparing him to Jack the Ripper was grossly unjust and unjustified. And yet his accuser connected this journalistic hyperbole to a strong sense of admiration about the artist's 'integrity'. That contradiction, in one critic's reading, reflected a tension not only in the work of Costello but also of any male writer at work in the midst of an increasingly self-confident feminist movement during the 1980s.

---

[16] An example in his later work was the album *Kojak Variety* (1995), which contained poignant songs ('Please Stay' (Hilliard and Bacharach)) and nostalgic ones ('The Very Thought of You' (Noble)) as well as traditional fare about lost love ('I Threw it all Away' (Dylan) and 'I've Been Wrong Before' (Newman)).

The comparison of Costello with Mailer, and the furor the latter's work caused in the 1960s and 1970s, was made above because of an important point of commonality when interpreting male artistic products in a post-feminist context. If heterosexual men now write about intimacy from the way they *experience and imagine it*, then the outcome will be evaluated by any reader in that context. Costello's dark obsessions, in part at least fuelled by his (overstated) rhetoric about 'guilt and revenge', would expose him to the charge of misogyny.

In this chapter we have both accounted for that collision course with a judgmental reception, and we have examined why moralisation is simply not enough if we are to do justice to any understanding of Costello's work, or any other serious artist. We have also tried to account for his ambivalence about women and how that was reflected in the type of songs he wrote or selected to perform as covers. The relevance of all of this for our period of interest is not just to attempt a fair minded review of him, when accused dismissively of misogyny. Our perspective also illuminates that second-wave feminism was part of the cultural field of the 1980s in the Western Anglophone countries apprehending and assessing Costello's music or any other cultural product.

If feminism from the left was to be a new evaluative context for Costello and other male artists in the 1970s and 1980s, we need also to return to the obvious context for this book: the ascendency of the right in Anglo-American *realpolitik*. We began by reporting in Chapter 1 his total contempt for a woman; a woman whose passing he wanted to live long enough to celebrate by tramping down the dirt on her grave. Whereas there is no clear evidence that he hated women in general, it would appear that he did indeed hate Margaret Thatcher. Maybe she was a ready target for the spiteful pole of his ambivalence. However, he was by no means alone in his feelings for her in the 1980s.

Whatever might have been said that was critical, justifiably or otherwise, of Costello's sentiments about women in the 1980s, there was one clear interpretive steer for us. The shared objective context of the artist and his critics contained a right-wing militaristic female leader in Britain. Dismissing her jokily as being 'really' a man is a facile (and occasionally still heard) platitude from the period. The trend to depict her as masculine, begun by the satirical TV programme *Spitting Image*, can lead us away from a possibly uncomfortable but undeniable truth: Margaret Thatcher was a woman.

Thatcher's own masculine roots were declared repeatedly by her. Her political heroes were all male – Hayek, Friedman and Powell – and she enjoyed telling journalists that her father had taught her all of her fundamental ethical and political principles. To her embarrassment, one of these journalists (in an interview in the *Radio Times* in 1993) had to point out to her that she had omitted any reference to her mother in the most recent details in *Who's Who*. Thatcher became flustered and promised to rectify the error, but the cat was by then out of the bag about her preferred way of defining herself (see our discussion at the end of Chapter 1 for more on this point).

In the previous chapter, we noted the irritation that Thatcher expressed about the invasion of Grenada. However, on the very weekend in 1983 that it was being planned unilaterally by the USA, her existing complicity with the US war machine was also highlighted. The liberal broadsheet *The Guardian* reported a leaked memo about the installation of more US missiles in Britain. At one site of their installation, Greenham Common, women had already created a peace camp in 1981. It remained there for ten years until the missiles were removed. Ideologically, these feminist pacifists had far more in common with Elvis Costello than with Margaret Thatcher. But we are left wondering what they might have made of his music.

Chapter 7
The Music Industry

The simple fact is that anyone with any talent at Columbia was never given a chance. People would become invisible … almost non-human … if they transgressed certain codes.

– Elvis Costello[1]

Introduction

We noted in Chapter 2 that Costello has been criticised for complaining about the music industry but still profiting from it. This is not an uncommon scenario. Commercial artists are constrained by the demands of record companies, though less so now than in the 1980s, as technological changes have subverted their monopoly of production and distribution. Wikstrom (2009) argues that today the technological changes in the wake of the internet have de-centred the role of record companies and created a more complex set of connections involving artists (whose elites are also less central than they were), independent producers and fans. He traces this systemic change to the 1980s after the invention of the compact disc, with digital recording techniques starting even earlier in the 1970s, though adopted unevenly for a while.

At the time of our interest, even when artists were performing, the demands of their recording contracts limited their autonomy, to various degrees. This chapter dwells on these general points about the ambivalent relationships between artists and the industry that both sustained and constrained them, and examines the particular way that Costello reacted to those challenges and opportunities in the context of the 1980s.

In Chapter 1 we introduced the notion of 'field' from Bourdieu. What was the particular character of the field of commercial popular music in the 1980s that might illuminate what Costello did and why he did it? We can answer that question in relation to three main dynamic processes which interacted and interwove during our period of interest.

First, there was a particular *financial* aspect to the industry which Costello had to consider and respond to. Second, there were particular *technological* features of the field that created the conditions of possibility of his musical products. Third, there were contingent *socio-cultural* factors in the 1980s that created temporary expectations of ideological conformity, or objections to it, by songwriters. These three strands will be discussed now as a general commentary and then Costello's work will be considered in that wider context.

---

[1]   From Elvis Costello website.

The state of the music industry in the 1980s

By the end of the 1970s Punk and New Wave had emerged as a strong cultural reaction against both the spirit of the 'hippy' period of the 1960s and the more recent domination of anodyne and over-produced music. From the 1960s, 'Progressive Rock' had emerged (some of which was to seriously impress the pre-successful, and yet to be named, Elvis Costello). It was characterised by elaborate productions in the studio and expensive multi-media concert performances and a fair claim, much of the time, to sophisticated musicianship. Songs had grown progressively longer, sometimes taken up with complex and persistent guitar or keyboard solos, filling or ending each piece. The three-minute pop song had been superseded by tracks that went on for ten or fifteen minutes. Short simple melodies were elaborated or displaced by 'sonic landscapes'.[2] As for 'Disco' and 'Glam Rock', these were confections that demonstrated the triumph of form over content.

The short sharp shock of Punk met this recent mixed legacy head-on. If Progressive Rock had sweeping and even awe-inspiring sonic landscapes, then Punk had shattering and terrifying sonic riots. Moreover, its emotional tone was different (angry and action-orientated not soft hearted and experientially-focused) as was its ideology (ironical, sneering and contemptuous about virtually everything outside of Punk). It was saying something dramatic to distance itself from the rock and disco norms of the previous decade.

These cultural tensions at the end of the 1970s coincided with some important technological shifts. The first was the elaboration of the use of popular music in films. This was not new. For example, both Elvis Presley and The Beatles had been at the centre of a series of song-focused films in the 1960s and, in the 1970s, the rock opera *Tommy* appeared with The Who as its stars and writers. The elaboration was evident though. Some films, such as *Saturday Night Fever* and *Grease*, were now effectively stage shows put on screen, with the extra flexibility of setting that film provided. In other cases, popular songs were used as a central motif for non-musical films. A good example of this was the comedy *Arthur*, which had the song 'Arthur's Theme' written and sung by Christopher Cross at its centre (with other music supplied by Burt Bacharach).

If the popular music–film interface was an elaboration, an innovation was the appearance of the pop video and the strain it was to place immediately on the traditional dominance of radio presentations and listening. The connection between the two points was that the earlier music films, noted above, were effectively extended promotional material for the artists involved. What was new was that a single song and a very short film were now being packaged and marketed as coterminous

---

[2]   When Bob Dylan's successful single 'Like A Rolling Stone' emerged in 1965 it was considered to be extraordinary because its play time exceeded four minutes: a small but telling sign of lengthy tracks to come.

products. The studio-constructed visual aspects of the song's presentation on screen could then augment or confuse meanings for the listener/viewer.[3]

In 1979, this moment of transition, anticipating the appearance of *MTV* in 1981, was celebrated by the New Wave band The Buggles, who released the nostalgic 'Video Killed the Radio Star' (Island Records). The emerging creative opportunities surrounding pop videos came to be dominated by the traditions set by Disco. All artists used the new format, funding permitted, but it was Disco that came to exemplify the format during this period, though some videos notably explored other, more surrealistic, possibilities.[4]

Other emerging technological changes which shaped musical production, included the shift from vinyl to tape and then from tape to compact disc. The much smaller formatting of these successors to vinyl records altered both the production of music (using the new studio digital technology) and the style of listening. The clunky radio or record player could be left at home and music could be listened to virtually anywhere, using tape (later CD) 'Walkmans', and copies of the latter from firms beyond Sony.

Music went from being 'in the room', with all of its attendant and diverting sounds, to being literally 'in the head'. The studio-generated apportioned chunks of sound in two stereo channels whizzed from one ear to the other or produced a synergy, located somewhere in the centre of the listener's skull.[5] For the first time, the ordinary listener could share the experience of the recording engineer wearing their headphones, at least in relation to the final version agreed.

A final point about technology is also about elaboration rather than sharp innovation. Synthesisers increasingly now dominated the recording and performance of music in both rock and disco music. This was an extension of one aspect of Progressive Rock, where keyboard players experimented with this instrument[6]. The change now was that some bands were playing songs that were *synthesiser-dominated* and its presence was common across the field. Whereas,

---

[3]   A good example of this was Costello's video of the song 'New Amsterdam', which might lead the viewer towards and then away from the meaning of the lyrics – which like most of his songs were already ambiguous.

[4]   A good example of this was Peter Gabriel's 'Sledgehammer' video (from the album *So* in 1986), which probably retains its filmic impact even today for those seeing it for the first time.

[5]   When 'stereo-grams' first developed a mass market in the early 1960s, this effect could only be grasped partially by the listener lying down on the floor with their head between the two speakers, which were fixed a couple of feet apart in the piece of furniture. At the time, gimmicky records of trains going in and out of tunnels or people playing ping-pong became fun.

[6]   Two protagonists exemplifying this in the early 1970s were Keith Emerson and Rick Wakeman.

in the 1970s, bands like Kraftwerk[7] and Tangerine Dream were on the esoteric margins of popular music, in the 1980s the synthesiser was 'mainstreamed' as a formula for commercial single success. It became associated in particular with a continuation of New Wave music. This presence of variants of electronic keyboards on stage became increasingly evident in the versatile playing of Steve Nieve in The Attractions.[8]

Maybe not all of these changes would have the dramatic effect of the internet in the subsequent decade, but they were noticeable nonetheless. They were to alter both the discourse of popular music and, physically, its style of consumption. Apart from the apprehension of music moving from room to head and beginning a trend of atomised audiences, there was also the disruption of the sensory and emotional attachments to the buying of records (their smell and look). The size of an LP permitted forms of artwork that could be dramatic in impact on the consumer. The same artwork squashed into the folds of paper in a little plastic box containing a tape or CD limited both the pictorial artists' scope and the visual pleasure of the consumer.[9]

Macro-economic and cultural shifts

Turning to the macro-economic climate of the 1980s, record sales began to decline, creating for the first time a crisis in confidence in the industry. This was also a time when the Thatcher-Reagan consensus on monetarism and marketisation of public bodies created a culture of atomised individualism. The emphasis during this period was a governmental ideology of consumerism and a shift from production. Together these pushed the lived experience of many from collective to individual concerns.

If the symptoms of alienation of the opposition between labour and capital were taking new forms (from production to consumption), then the listener of music was drawn into that dynamic social process, as were the producers of music. This did not homogenise its forms (arguably diversification was used to test new markets) but there was a convergence of its character. For example, Country music became Pop-influenced ('Urban Cowboy'). Also rock and roll persisted undiminished with new popular forms like Thrash Metal, as well as a strengthened continuation of showy Glam Rock ('Hairspray'), started in the 1970s and still unrepressed by Punk. This, then, marked the beginning of a contradictory postmodern period of globalisation, when everything was sort of becoming the same but also in many ways more differentiated and niche-marketed (see Chapter 8).

---

[7]   Kraftwerk re-emerged briefly in the singles charts in 1982, confirming their role-model status for Gary Numan and others.

[8]   Costello recalls in his liner notes for the 2002 version of *Armed Forces* that Polymoog and Jupiter-8 synthesisers were used by Nieve on the song 'Green Shirt'.

[9]   As a small recognition of this, a 1986 limited edition reissue of *Blood & Chocolate* came boxed in a cute mock bar of Bourneville chocolate, boosting in a tiny way the 3-D capabilities of the tape's packaging.

With regards to the content of successful music during this period, the safe and the inoffensive predominated. The political right dominated the popular media outlets, (exemplified by the increasing monopolising powers of Rupert Murdoch[10]), and the comforts of traditional romance soon became themes to explore for success-orientated writers, in tune with the *zeitgeist*. Combining the two images of tradition and romance, we find the fated Princess Diana entranced by Wham! and their sugary love songs.

A string of happy or zany acts appeared in the charts in the 1980s reflecting this upbeat carefree approach to music. Cindy Lauper told us that 'Girls Just Want to Have Fun', the 'Material Girl' Madonna took her listeners on a 'Holiday', Frankie Goes to Hollywood instructed us to 'Relax' (and got banned by the BBC for suggesting sexual release as the recommended method), Joe Fagin reassured us 'That's Living Alright' and the fittingly named Madness welcomed us to their 'House of Fun'. We had other reasons to be jolly from Adam Ant, Bucks Fizz, Shakin' Stevens, Dollar, Human League, Chas and Dave, Bow Wow Wow, Duran Duran, Bananarama, Fun Boy Three, Culture Club, Thompson Twins and Spandau Ballet. The overlap with the previous decade was also obvious though, with the abiding presence of those like Stevie Wonder, Rod Stewart, Paul Weller, Cher, Dolly Parton, Phil Collins, Bryan Ferry, David Bowie, Elton John, Paul McCartney, Michael Jackson and Diana Ross. And the evergreen Rolling Stones just continued as they meant to go on. Some of these older artists shifted towards the norm of facile romanticism, but not all of them.

During the 1980s, 'carefree' self-indulgence was evident in mass culture. Fashion-wise this culminated in the narcissistic 'New Romantics'.[11] The effete and androgynous fashion celebrated by this trend was traceable to David Bowie in the 1970s and it signalled a dandy-inspired rejection of, or dissociation from, aggressive and anarchistic Punk. It was thus the conservative and dominant wing of the New Wave movement in music, bearing in mind that this was a label applied for while to Costello.[12] This continued the theme in the 20th century of generations of young people determined to enjoy themselves, whatever the political or economic

---

[10]   Murdoch was an open supporter of Thatcher. His attack in 1986 on organised labour at his printing works in Britain was as influential in its impact on the British Trade Union movement as her attack on the mineworkers. Murdoch switched his allegiance to Tony Blair thereafter, which is one clear indicator that the capitalist class was confident in the continuation of neo-liberalism, with the project of New Labour (see Chapter 1).

[11]   A case is made below that *Costello*'s version of Romanticism was older and not limited to concerns about self-indulgence, 'lurv' and fashionable appearance.

[12]   As Covach (2003) noted, New Wave signalled a 'return-to-simplicity aesthetic' in protest against rock becoming 'bloated and corporate' and its performers 'too professional'. However, given the sophistication of Costello's musical talents, this general description may not be readily applicable. Technical simplicity has also been linked to claims of musical authenticity (see Chapter 9).

strictures of their time ('Young Guns (Go For It!)').[13] But this individualistic self-indulgence chafed against what was happening for those on the left. Reaganomics and Thatcherism meant a dour culture for them of defeat and despair. This was exemplified in the UK in the collapse of the miners' strike, the jingoistic drama of the Falklands War and dead hunger strikers in Northern Ireland. A quick glance at mainstream New Wave pop success would tell us nothing of such events and the mood they created, except maybe as a sort of 'photographic negative'.[14]

A vestige of serious social commentary at the start of the decade was from John Lennon's 'Happy Christmas, War Is Over' in 1980.[15] We do not know whether more of this might have ensued had it not been for Lennon's murder that year. And even if Costello, with a few others, was to buck the trend of carefree individualism in the 1980s, every one of *his* single successes was based upon traditional romance, albeit of the maudlin hetero-normative variety. His successful cover of 'Good Year for the Roses' was discussed in Chapter 3.

The response of Costello to the industry

We noted in Chapter 1 that Costello held rather a dim view of his fellow popular song writers in the 1980s (he called them a 'race of pygmies'). At its crassest marketing level this was about cutting his competitors down to size to promote his own talents. This was not a one-off remark from him: Costello disparaged other musicians sporadically. For example, he told Neil Spencer in *NME* in October 1982 'Most people in groups are dullards'.[16] In an interview with Nick Kent in 1991, a follow-up to the famous 'guilt and revenge' piece in *NME* from 1977, he provides a strong defence of his recent writing partner Paul McCartney and refers to his era:

> this was back when being famous actually meant something. Nowadays any fuckin' clown can get on international satellite TV and become famous simply by shooting someone or releasing some inane fucking song. Of course, fuckin' Madonna is fuckin' famous – she's on TV every fifteen fuckin' minutes! (Costello interviewed in 1991 and cited in Kent, 2007: 216)

---

[13]   A 1982 chart triumph for Wham! and summarising the ethical impulse of individualistic effort and opportunism under Thatcher.

[14]   Even the oppositional power of lesser played versions of popular music, such as the Roots version of Reggae, gave way in 1980s Britain to the blander de-politicised focus of 'Lovers Rock', which limited its interest to sugary heterosexual romance. Again we find individualism displacing political radicalism.

[15]   After Lennon's death, the single charted higher than when it was first recorded in 1971. Its original allusion was to the Vietnam War.

[16]   This theme continued. In 2003 he told David Hepworth in his interview in the magazine *Word*, 'Being gifted with words in rock and roll is not exactly difficult. It's not overpopulated with geniuses.'

Although we have addressed the question of Costello's alleged misogyny in Chapter 6, it is worth noting that Kent's reporting of this 1991 meeting in a pub alludes to a 'girl' (*sic*) who was an interloper for a while, and identified only as a record company employee from Island Records. Their complicit rejection of her is reported by Kent in a macho manner. Costello is sarcastic to her repeatedly and Kent describes his face as having a 'menacing glow'. We return to this point in Chapter 9.

To reinforce the point that Costello wants to make, about his own competence compared to those around him, he notes later in the Kent interview 'I was shrewder than most people'. At times this sense of superiority comes through in his lyrics: for example, in the line 'have we come this fa-fa-fa, to find a soul cliché', probably a sarcastic allusion to Talking Heads in 'Let Them All Talk' from *Punch The Clock*.

This binary approach to his own work and role (superior) and the work and role of others (inferior) was not merely the outcome of an inflated ego in the wake of success but was present in the early years.[17] For example, an early acquaintance from his brief stint in the folk clubs of the 1970s, Charlie Dore, recollects Costello' egotism thus, though it is not clear whether she is being admiring or critical of him:

> He was very assured, very much a one-man band … He was intense, utterly focused and single-minded. He didn't suffer fools gladly. He would get very frustrated with people who stood in his way or didn't get it … The attitude was already there. (Dore, cited in Thomson, 2004: 62)

But high self-regard is a collective position taken up by many aspiring commercial musicians and so is not Costello's idiosyncratic psychopathology. To want to be successful requires arrogance not just self-confidence.[18] If everybody in a competitive commercial field has a high opinion of themselves, then one option (though not an obligation) is to denigrate one's peers to shore up one's own grandiose claims. Maybe Costello had grounds for his arrogance and claimed musical superiority. His imagination, musical knowledge, practical talent and ruthlessness could combine to create success. Indeed, our culturally accepted view of the construct of 'intelligence' refers to the relative sharpness of sense that we have and the adaptive advantage that this bestows upon us in relation to others. In this sense, Costello was extremely intelligent as an artist and remains so today.

---

[17]   This binary opposition was not evident, though, for Costello when he was talking about his respected collaborators (of which, in his career, there have been many) or about artists he venerated from the past.

[18]   This point applies to managers in the music industry as well. Allen Klein, who managed both The Beatles and The Rolling Stones, had this view: 'The music business is about 99% no-talent losers who can't stand a winner in their midst. I'm a winner, and if they want to sour grape my success by calling me names, let them. I don't give a shit' (cited in Garfield, 1986: 257).

Moreover, part of the persona of the modern auteur *requires* that there is a self-belief about being a genius peeking out from a plenitude of artistic mediocrity (see more on this below). Within this Romantic tradition, Shelley commented that 'poets were the unacknowledged legislators of the world', to which we could add 'unelected and unaccountable'.[19] This led to a paradox for Costello. To claim a special niche, in which his talents and his integrity were respected, was always ambitious, when faced with a record-buying public, which was diverse in its taste and not always comprehending of his lyrical complexity or sympathetic to his political values.

For Costello, to be special as a musician might inherently mean that he could only court a minority audience. That would have been fine had he accepted that process and outcome. However, he was frustrated by his sales figures (tending to blame conservative forces in the record industry) even though he was still making a very decent living from his 'vocation'. He was also faced with a broad picture of a culture celebrating superficial individual enjoyment, during a period of deep political and economic retrenchment by the rich and the powerful.

Maybe the issue here was not the lack of talent in songwriting (where is the empirical evidence that this fluctuates too significantly as time passes?) but the selective focus of that talent. Costello, then, may have been wrong about a lack of surrounding talent but right about the way that it was being co-opted for trite ends. Air-headed hedonism or manic jollity are recurring historical examples of 'fiddling while Rome burns': dress up in camp clothing, sing fatuous songs, fall in love, enjoy sex, act crazy and get drunk, in any order and to whatever extent personally preferred.[20] Costello and a few others were insistent on introducing another political and ethical agenda within popular music, which was resistive and critical. Maybe that was always going to be an uphill struggle in the 1980s.

The mainstream writers of the time were simply providing the sound track for facile self-indulgence, both mirroring and reinforcing its existence. If popular music is for many *not* a vehicle for authentic engagement with their time and place but is instead an escape attempt,[21] then this should not be surprising. If one is young, powerless and has an insecure financial future, then why not just enjoy the

---

[19]   But, as we noted in Chapters 4 and 6, the politics of race and gender now require that even artists must at some point account for their words and products.

[20]   In psychodynamic terms this relates to 'manic defences' against depressing grim reality. Depression just waiting around the corner for the young generation of the 1980s was articulated eventually by The Smiths. Also singer-songwriters aligned with Costello's critical perspective but less obscure in their lyrics, such as Billy Bragg and his social realism, put romance in its down-to-earth context, with lines of resignation like, 'I don't want to change the world. I'm not looking for a New England. I'm just looking for another girl.'

[21]   The term 'escape attempt' is used as part of the sociological exploration of Cohen and Taylor (1976) with the self-evident title: *Escape Attempts: The Theory and Practice of Resistance in Everyday Life.*

moment? Indeed the more dire the situation, the more that such escape attempts may become tempting and popular.

And the point of writing commercial popular songs is to anticipate and appeal to the contingent needs of the buying public. Maybe Costello's songwriting competitors were not lacking in talent but merely tapping into creative seams about sentimental romance and hedonism during bleak times, in empathic anticipation of the particular mass psychology of the era: its prevalent 'community of affect' (Hebdige, 1979). To resist that trend requires some deliberate obdurate act. Costello was not in a minority of one in this regard. For example, more considered and critical songs emerged from Paul Weller and Paul McCartney,[22] and the social realism and mournful laments of both Billy Bragg and The Smiths have just been footnoted.

The Smiths could make a claim to a more principled defiance of commercial musical fashion than Costello. For example, they rejected the politics of Third World relief, and the Live Aid and Band Aid projects, as a diversion from facing poverty at home. They also refused to adopt the synthesiser, the mainstay of most post-New Wave bands, including The Attractions. They were guests on the Red Wedge tour of 1986, led by Billy Bragg and including The Communards and The Style Council, whereas Costello was not involved. Indeed, there is little in his biography to indicate that he has ever been engaged in party politics. Red Wedge was designed to support a Labour victory in the 1987 General Election.

Costello's own political activity during the 1980s involved a series of contributions to shared concerts. These included The Big One (18 December 1983), Live Aid (13 July 1985) and Self Aid (Dublin, 17 May 1986). In the first he sang 'Peace in Our Time' for the first time and in the second he covered 'All You Need Is Love' from The Beatles. It is not clear whether its sentiments were direct or ironical (given the point of Live Aid being that *more* than the sentiment of love was required to prevent starvation!). The first concert was an anti-Cruise missile benefit, a reminder of the consistent position Costello took about militarism and pacifism. In Chapter 4 we also noted his contribution to Rock Against Racism: he played in its second concert at Brockwell Park in 1978.

Thus, although not party political (cf. those temporarily drawn into the Red Wedge project), Costello still adopted an oppositional mode to the jolly writing norms of the 1980s. His habitus, with resonances in his family script going back generations, knew few other options but to shout 'foul' and to be indignant and contrary in the face of corporate interests and the various wars, symbolic and actual, being waged by the powerful on the powerless. And yet, he was in a contradictory position about this: he too was ambitious for recognition and fame, even if the evidence about his concern for fortune is not clear at this distance of time. He

---

[22]   McCartney is sometimes dismissed for his sentimental preoccupation with 'home and hearth' songs but there is far more to him (Dempsey, 2004). His broader range, with some dark undertones, was evident in the songs on *Spike*, written with Costello; and we noted in Chapter 4 that he took a radical political line on Ireland.

was in the predicament that all left-of-centre commercial artists find themselves. This is why it is easy (and fair) for Griffiths to accuse Costello of some political hypocrisy. With success, comes a loss of a credible mandate for righteous rhetoric about the dispossessed. This is compounded by accusations of domineering or oppressive treatment of work colleagues, which we discussed in Chapter 2.

Apart from this subjective predicament for 'politically progressive artists', there is a relevant objective and supra-personal consideration. If the rich and powerful own and control the means of production and distribution and ordinary people are rendered relatively poor and disempowered, beyond their weak power as consumers, is anything occurring in the political economic structure of society between these two poles of opposition or accommodation?[23] That question is complicated enough to consider if we simply try to understand employed professionals (from newly trained and poorly paid nurses to top civil servants at the centre of government influence). But what of that wide range of citizens who generate their own income, and who stand outside of routine socio-political arrangements of being either employers or employees?

Costello, like all commercial artists, is simply one example of a group of people who are neither ordinary workers nor the ruling class; they exist at various points on a continuum in between, along with, among others, the owners of small businesses, criminals, freelance journalists, general medical practitioners and professional footballers. These roles, like patterns of consumption of popular culture discussed earlier, could be seen, in their own right, as 'escape attempts' from the tedium of regulated nine-to-five life, with the bonus for some of high earnings. An inherent contradiction of left-of-centre artists, like Costello, is that they are embodying a form of elitism, which is at odds with their ideological pretensions about egalitarianism (we discussed this point at the end of Chapter 2). Social equality and the treatment of the oppressed and dispossessed may be sincere concerns for them but they also crave fame and fortune.[24]

Thus, when we consider Costello's objective position, and not just his individual response to it, the following points are relevant to understanding the outer and inner aspects of his life in tandem. If an artist sees himself or herself as morally and politically deserving all of the fruits of their own creative labour, he or she will understandably encounter corporate interests (in this case the record companies in the main, but this point could extend to an artist's manager or production company) as 'necessary evils'. They are 'evils' because they are parasitic upon the artist but they are 'necessary', because an artist cannot also

---

[23]   There are a number of other questions begged by this one. For example, how do we account for the professional middle classes, who might legitimately seem to be part of the working class, part of the ruling class, and a range of shades in between, depending on their status and earnings (Saks, 1983)?

[24]   This tension is expressed most clearly and barbarically by Sylvain Marechal, the French revolutionary, who said in 1796, 'Let the arts perish, if need be, as long as real equality remains' ('Manifeste des Egaux).

produce and distribute their wares on a mass basis. When there is a convergence of interests then everyone is happy with the compromise; we move from parasitism to symbiosis. The artist makes money and enjoys status, consumers enjoy the products bought, companies make profits for their shareholders and a whole workforce in the industry is sustained.

The problem comes when an individual artist engages with this industrial complexity in a resentful way, which was the case with Costello. The identity of auteur will bring with it a range of feelings about *entitlement* to recognition, autonomy and earnings. Many worthy artists are tried out and then written off by record companies. As Frith (1981) noted at the start of the period of our interest, the business relied as much, if not more, on the many that it tried out and then discarded, as it did on its high-earning elite repertoire of artists. Most aspiring commercial artists never make a lifelong career of their ambitions, remaining poor or opting eventually for the same possibilities as anyone else in the field of wage slavery, after a memorable brief flirtation with success.

And when *sustained* success does occur, there remain personal pitfalls. An individual artist may be exploited by their manager, if he or she becomes overly absorbed by writing, recording and performing. This scenario occurred famously in relation to Leonard Cohen with his ex-manager Kelley Lynch.[25] Or, in another example, musicians and other staff who are employed by artists may become resentful about their treatment in terms of remuneration or unreasonable contracts (a version of this is noted below in the relationship between Costello and his bass player Bruce Thomas).

Costello and popular culture in the 1980s: an old, not a new, romantic

Turning to Costello's cultural response to the froth of the 1980s and his dour alternative trajectory to its norms, we find an irony. Again this is about his auteur self-image being pitted against the complex machinery and dominating logic of the music industry, as part of capitalist relations of production, exchange and distribution. Stratton (1983) outlines the latter in the following ways, when arguing that Romanticism is commodified under capitalism:

> The music is not only commodified; in the process it is also distanced, alienated from the artist and becomes an object, which is understood to exist in its own right. It moves from the profit domain of the market place. Reciprocally, the artist

---

[25] In 2005, Cohen successfully sued for the $5 million misappropriated by his ex-manager, but Lynch defied the subpoena and the artist did not receive the money he was owed. As a consequence, his loyal fans enjoyed a spate of money-making international tours undertaken to refloat his personal pension fund. In 2012, after years of harassment from Lynch which left Cohen fearing for his life, a US court found against her once more, but the misappropriated money remained unpaid.

experiences a distancing from his or her music and it becomes a product and is experienced as existing in a different societal context. (Stratton, 1983: 148)

For their part, artists faced with these large economic impacts on the products of their imagination find particular ways of resisting the slight to their egos and their sense of dispossession, while also enjoying financial advantages denied to struggling competitors.[26] In Costello's case, he could reissue material later with liner notes to re-establish his authorial authority. Also, live performances themselves always provide opportunities for re-authoring and so the artist temporarily repossesses what, in Stratton's terms, have become distant and alienated products. If 'Alison' was taken away and sentimentalised by Linda Ronstadt (see Chapter 2), Costello could still sing it the way he wanted to – as if for the first time or in a new way of his choosing – in his own concerts.

Another consideration is that, strictly speaking, the product of commodity in the music industry is the music itself, sold as an artifact (for example, as a record, tape, disc or electronic file). These artifacts (along with other 'merchandise') are what generate profit and they are certainly reliant on the artist, as well as legions of intermediaries and support staff involved in its production and distribution. However, because wage labour (in any sphere) cannot be separated from the person involved, he or she can, and at times does, *feel* like an object or commodity. This is signalled in the epigram at the start of this chapter, where Costello describes himself as being rendered as 'non-human' by Columbia Records.[27] Any of us may feel like 'a cog in the machine' or a 'brick in the wall' but we are not cogs or bricks. We can reflect on what is going on and take action about it (or not). We may be *symbolic* objects, and so can feel objectified, but we remain reflective, and potentially resistive, beings.

To offset that sense of alienation, one option is for the artist to return to a culturally inherited identity from centuries back. The drive to keep control of or repossess commercially produced music can be inspired by both a medieval troubadour tradition of the wandering poet or singer, free and autonomous, and Romanticism, as a movement in artistic production, found in 18th- and 19th-century high culture. Troubadours flourished between the 12th and 14th centuries and were peripatetic singers, poets and general entertainers. Their emphasis on being

---

[26]   A particularly ironical example of this point is the lyric written and sung by Melanie (Safka), 'Look What They've Done to My Song Ma', which was covered by Ray Charles and the New Seekers. It was eventually co-opted by the Quaker Oats Company for an advertising campaign with the changed title of 'Look What They've Done to My Oats Ma'. In the original lyrics, Melanie explored how being a songwriter had brought her to the verge of insanity.

[27]   Griffiths (2007: 2) makes the point that 'Before becoming a professional musician, he [Costello] had jobs like *you and me*: computer programmer for example' (emphasis added). This view from Griffiths makes (common) sense but lots of other roles, including being an academic, are not standard forms of work in production and distribution.

among the people but also having a distinct cultural role and going from place to place has obvious resonances today with other peripatetic musicians, from street buskers to touring rock bands. What they all have in common is the contingent sympathetic patronage of their audiences to ensure an income.

These historical traditions coalesced in the 20th century with the development of an ideal type of the sole artist, typically male, using their art to speak the truth to the world. Stratton cites Graña (1964) who comments on this Romanticism in art. Graña's description includes an emphasis within the Romantic Movement on: the ideal of and freedom of self-expression; the idea of genius; the celebration of the non-rational; 'cosmic self-assertion'; the social alienation of the artist; the hostility of modern society to artistic talent and sensitivity; and world weariness and the 'horror of daily life'. Commercial success ensures that today (as was the case in the 1980s) the latter is kept at a safe distance, being viewed from the stage or out of the windows of tour buses. Life becomes a cosy detachment, with successful artists neither enjoying nor suffering many ordinary experiences.

We can see in the Romantic and troubadour traditions an image that will coalesce as a powerful role in the heroic and dazzling 20th-century auteur: endlessly talented but not always appreciated by others; sensitive beyond the experience of most ordinary people in their audiences; on the margins or just outside of mass existence; and speaking the truth through artistic expression beyond the alienated rationality of modern life. Here is one image, at least, of Elvis Costello (among a few others) in the music industry of the 1980s. He was becoming one of Shelley's 'unacknowledged legislators of the world'.[28]

Thus at the individual level, one aspect of successful artists like Costello existing in the ambiguous space between the ruling class and the masses is that he might expect, and at times achieve, some reversal of the alienation experienced by 'the common people'. Lukes (1967), following Marx, distinguishes four co-present nuances of 'alienation'. First, it refers to a worker's alienation from the *product* of their work. Second, it refers to the *process* of work. Third, it refers to people being alienated from *themselves*. Finally, it refers to alienation from *other people.*

Marx observed these effects under capitalism. Costello was relatively lucky because he could retain some sense of affinity with his products (his music), though for reasons already noted this could not be complete. Barring irritations with the industry, he could enjoy the process of making music, while being paid for that process. Costello's alienation from himself is certainly a thread in his life, but its reasons go well beyond simply his location in the economic system

---

[28]   His BBC interview when showcasing *Spike* (discussed in Chapter 1) gives us a strong clue about this aspiration. He was demanding to be taken seriously about the regime of Thatcherism. This reflects a wider cultural division in the field of popular music between those who are content to be entertainers and others who have political aspirations to change the world through their work.

as a musician; these include other factors related to his habitus. So too with his alienation from others: habitus and field are both relevant.[29] This complex picture leads to a number of contradictions in his actions; more of this below.

Maybe *both* his marketing rhetoric *and* his sincerely held view in private was that he was determined to eschew any complicity with the oppressive political context of the 1980s. He saw himself as part of the cultural resistance to what was happening in the world at the time, especially in Britain (hence his views reported in Chapter 1). We return to his asserted authenticity and his claim to personal integrity in the next chapter.

This stance was at it most credible in relation to his stubborn commitment to the release of 'Peace in Or Time' as a single. He probably knew that its miserable anti-war stance was out of sync with most songs achieving chart success at the time but he still insisted on 'putting it out there', to use a more recent phrase. The practical challenge remained for Costello though, as it does for his competitors in the field, of expressing a plausible form of authenticity in a commercial context which demanded: a) the recurring inauthentic task of marketing of the self; and b) a style of life that disconnected the successful artist from the daily existence shared by most ordinary citizens.

But the longer historical context pointed up by Stratton does not just provide us with a way of thinking about particular artists, like Costello. It also allows us to understand the commodification of Romanticism *itself* within late capitalism. This view can be augmented by that offered by Marcuse (1964) in his notion of 'repressive tolerance': artistic and other forms of deviation from routine rational life are celebrated. These might defuse the prospect of more organised forms of protest against current oppressive power relations and insights about them.

If we read this Marxist-functionalist view, alongside earlier comments about 'escape attempts', then we open up an argument about the essentially conservative character of popular music. This would even include the positioning of what we might call its 'disgruntled protest wing', which was personified by Costello, and by many others before and since. Rather than popular art offering the celebration or rehearsal of alternative realities, as a form of pre-figurative politics, it might, if taken as a whole system, simply be a pathway to de-politicisation and mystification. It could just feed a superficial gullible world of 'bread and circuses'.

This phrase is a metaphor for superficial need satisfaction of the general population becoming a diversion from a serious and shared common duty towards civic life and political responsibility. It came to characterise the frivolous habits common when the Roman Empire went into decline and has become an extended metaphor for other forms of decaying polity since then. The notion was developed as 'prolefeed' by George Orwell in his novel *Nineteen Eighty Four* (1949) but

---

[29]   Offe (1984) divides modern capitalism into three main sub-systems: economic relations of production, exchange and distribution; structures of socialisation like the family and peers; and the welfare state. Costello's actions and experiences can be located in the contradictions within and between the first two sub-systems.

Aldous Huxley's alternative dystopia in *Brave New World* (1932) is maybe nearer to our current state of a 'bread and circuses' culture, with its excessive individualistic consumerism and consequent political passivity. According to Barber (2007), this has already turned adults into children: the dystopia is here and now.

However, other voices suggested that the top-down corporate power of large record companies[30] was only part of the story. Those who bought records might be pacified dupes of the industry (the 'bread and circuses' view) but they might also use popular songs as sources of authentic emotional resonance and even political resistance. All of these are possible, according to Grossberg (1983). He argues that popular music can be co-opted by large and powerful conservative interests but it can also give voice to oppositional, alternative and critical positions in society. Similar explorations about the variable points of passivity or resistance that consumers could adopt can be found in writing about popular culture in the period of our interest (Hall and Jefferson, 1976; Frith, 1981). For example, here Fiske (1987) queries the stereotype of the record companies as a monolithic and irresistible conservative force on behalf of the capitalist system pacifying a docile population. He adopts, but also doubts, the metaphor of cynicism, which, by chance, was shared by Costello in 'Pills and Soap':

> Their skill in sugar coating the pill is so great that the people are not aware of the ideological practice in which they are engaging, as they consume and enjoy the cultural commodity. I do not believe that 'the people' are 'cultural dupes'; they are not a passive, helpless mass incapable of discrimination and thus at the economic, cultural and political mercy of the barons of industry. (Fiske, 1987: 309)

An implication of Fiske's view is that, if fans are not dupes, then they must also bear some responsibility, at least in part, for what is socially negotiated as valuable in popular music. If the latter is no longer *singularly* determined by elite interests, then logically those interests cannot be *wholly* blameworthy. We return to this point – which is an aesthetic one about merit or value and a political one about power and culture – in Chapters 8 and 9, when considering Costello's disappointment in his sales and his public recognition, with his tendency to blame the record companies.

Whatever weight we give to this range of views about economic determinism, ideology and forms of resistance from below, and some of the time all of these writers are probably correct, what is clear is that we cannot discuss Costello or any other artist without some sensibility about the industrial context of their work. Despite the image of the auteur, their work exists and is rewarded or falls into disuse, in the setting of that context, which is full of contradictions.

---

[30] By 2005 there were only four major players (Vivendi/Universal, SonyBMG, AOL-Time Warner and EMI, which had absorbed Virgin Records). However, even as early as 1980 there were only six major global companies (MCA, CBS, Warner, RCA, Capitol/EMI and Polygram) (Bishop, 2005).

For example, artists can be oppressed *and* they can oppress others. They can champion social justice *and* can be the beneficiaries of current unjust socio-economic conditions. They can enjoy material excess *and* take social action about the needs of those in absolute poverty and starvation. Their products are commodities in the market place to create profits for capitalist organisations, but they can also be sources of critical emotional resonance in 'communities of affect' and political inspiration for ordinary people,[31] as well as sources of bland tranquillisation that can turn adults into children.

Costello and his contradictions in context

In the case of Costello in the 1980s, let us look at some examples of these contradictions, beginning with his protest about his treatment by the record companies. In 1977, at the start of his commercial success, he was signed to the independent label Stiff Records. Their scope of distribution was solely in the UK and his records could only be sent to the USA as imports. In frustration at the limitations this was placing upon his right to sing to the world (or at least the largest Anglophone market within it) he went to the convention of executives of CBS in London and busked outside to make his protest. He was arrested by the police. A few months later he was signed by Columbia Records (a wing of CBS).[32]

This highlights the first contradiction: the individual artist experiences their oppression by owners and managers of the means of production and distribution as idiosyncratic personal victimisation. This type of direct action is out of sync with our traditional understanding of collective opposition to employer power, in the collective struggles of the labour movement. Moreover, as Costello's CBS protest also makes clear, political opposition and self-promoting marketing opportunities can blend into one. Clayton-Lea describes this incident and Costello's arrest basically as a 'publicity stunt' to sell his album. As he puts it, 'the anti-rock star had arrived and everybody wanted to shake their hand' (Clayton-Lea, 1998: 27). This incident, 'stunt' or not, was hardly a principled opposition to political injustice but just an attempt to rectify a personal slight, with a commercial end in mind. It worked.

Costello played upon, and with, the image of being a victim of his trade and this was evident pictorially on the cover of *Spike*. Here, he is depicted as a trophy head to hang on the wall, with the label below bearing the ironic or

---

[31]   An example here in the West is the rallying point of the song 'Free Nelson Mandela' by Special AKA (The Specials) in 1984. Costello played on a remixed version as a backing musician in 1988. For Costello fans, 'Shipbuilding' and 'Tramp the Dirt Down' would be particular examples. As McClary and Walser (1990) note, an empirical challenge for new musicology is to understand what might 'trigger adulation in fans'.

[32]   Columbia became part of Sony. In 1987, Costello switched labels to Warner and thereafter his releases appeared on Rhino and Rykodisc.

sarcastic words 'The Beloved Entertainer'. The head has a grease-painted, glaring harlequin face with a sinister defiant laughing mouth. The 'I' of the word 'Spike' has become an image of a spike or nail hovering over the victim's scull, waiting to be driven home.[33]

His religious imagery (noted in Chapter 1) comes into play about his own victimhood at times. For example, in this 1982 interview with Neil Spencer in *NME* Costelllo emphasises both his role as an ordinary artisan and his special insights into his oppressive context:

> On the one hand, *I'm just a songwriter* who sings and puts my heart into it. On the other hand *I understand the business better* than a lot of people. I know where I stand in it. That side of me says 'hang on what is the point of bashing your head against a brick wall, to throw it away, because you're not going to put all this work in and people are not going to accept it *because of who you are? They've decided they don't like you,* so you might as well not bother to make records and be off like John the Baptist'... (Emphasis added)

Other indications of this defiant and angry attitude, in the face of victimisation, come through in the interviews we noted in earlier chapters in which he presents himself as being frustrated and misunderstood by those appraising his talents and creative outputs. He resents being called 'angry' or 'immature' or, later, 'mature'. It is as if the world, or at least those formally assessing his work, is out to wilfully misunderstand him and his existential plight.

This is pregnant with the possibility that really he does not *want* to be understood fully, because the melodrama between him and his unappreciative critics would then fizzle out.[34] This possible perversity actually inverts the plea of one of his covered songs, 'Don't Let Me Be Misunderstood' from *King of America*. If the tension were to melt away, then his identity as a romantic artist struggling to tell the truth within a culture of cynicism or disbelief would also be lost. Whilst this is a legitimate interpretation of Costello's marketing of the self in the 1980s, even if it is correct, then he may not have been wholly conscious of the tactic being deployed. When he

---

[33] In the song 'I Want to Vanish' from *All This Useless Beauty*, Costello uses the line 'To go where I cannot be captured. Laid on a decorated dish'. This continues a theme of a trophy being hunted down but this time just escaping the eventual fate of John the Baptist.

[34] 'Writing about music is like dancing about architecture – its a really stupid thing to want to do' (Costello in interview with Timothy Whit, in *Musician* magazine, October, 1983). A version of this sentiment has been attributed to others, such as Miles Davis, Thelonius Monk, Frank Zappa and Laurie Anderson. Whoever started the claim, it defends the power of the practising musician to go unchallenged by others. Similarly, in Chapter 1 we noted Costello evading Tracey MacLeod's reasonable invitation to articulate prosaically the meaning of 'Tramp the Dirt Down' and expressing a preference just to perform it. We can see a rhetorical pattern emerging here of protecting artistic mystique and authority. Performance becomes sovereign and performers become unaccountable.

adopts a 'who, me?' or 'poor me!' approach in his complaining public statements, it is impossible to know whether he really believes it at the time himself.

This sense of victimhood was used to good creative effect in his songs. He has been concerned to write about the pain and dark fate of others: miscarriages of justice for brutalised youth and consequent State executions; the victims of mindless post-colonial wars and diving for dear life rather than the pearls of peace; and the social and economic casualties of Thatcherism, who are broken and cannot be put back together again. In psychodynamic terms this is an example of 'projective identification' and its role in creativity. But, by the time that Costello becomes a successful artist with a dependent workforce, suddenly he is not the victim but the victimiser. In Chapter 2, we described the sacking of the engineer by Costello and the judgement of Griffiths about it. A second example is his (eventual) rejection of his bass player Bruce Thomas from The Attractions, which we turn to now.

Costello and his 'Subtractions'

Life on the road has its pros and cons for commercial touring musicians. As a successful young male group, Elvis Costello and The Attractions encountered a familiar pattern known to others. There was an imposed and prolonged intimacy. Band members spent hours together in hotels, backstage, onstage in rehearsal, sound-checks and performing, partying afterwards and, the greatest tedium of all, travelling from venue to venue. Much of the unrelenting feel of life on the road was broken by eating, listening to music, sleeping, practical joking, having casual sex, boozing and taking illicit drugs to varying degrees of excess.

The intimacy, homesickness, and disorientation engendered by perpetual venue-switching and substance use amplified the dynamics that would occur in any small group of human beings thrown together and unable to find much individual personal space. At points aggression broke out and individuals regressed in their psychological functioning, in their own particular ways. That picture is provided in *The Big Wheel* (2003), about life on the road with The Attractions, as seen from the very witty perspective of their bass player Bruce Thomas.

Thomas's book was written in 1990 and appeared again thirteen years later, with a new foreword. He is sarcastically perceptive and extremely funny. An even-handed appraisal of those around him is clearly not a priority in his writing, nor is there much serious self-analysis. Costello is not named because no one is; we have instead 'the Singer', 'the Drummer' and 'the Keyboard Player'. The author claims that the book was at the centre of Costello's personal rejection of him and states in the blurb that its contents put him 'in the unique position of being fired from the same job for the same reason – twice!'

However, the *exact* reasons for their alienation and separation are far from clear. Costello had become irritated with Thomas before the book appeared (and judging by what is said inside it, the feeling was mutual). Apart from the timing of the book's release, which casts doubt on the simple claim that it was the basis of Thomas's sacking, there are other aspects of Costello's decision-making to take into account. From 1984 he had intimated that The Attractions might no longer fit with his longer-term ambitions. Between 1984 and 1987 he rested them frequently in favour of using other musicians in the studio and on stage, but he did not sack them.

Costello's relationship with T-Bone Burnett and the ephemeral construction of 'The Coward Brothers', along with a range of new backing musicians playing on *King of America* could have given a signal that he may have been trying to 'constructively dismiss'[35] The Attractions or maybe let them down gently about a new career trajectory. There was procrastination from Costello but they did part company in 1987. However, starting almost immediately, for a good few years he continued to work with Pete Thomas and Steve Nieve. And further evidence of Costello's equivocation was that he even went on to give Bruce Thomas a second chance. Ambivalence and complexity seemed to dominate the relationship between Elvis Costello and The Attractions, from start to finish.

In 1993 (so after the release of *The Big Wheel*) the co-producer of *Brutal Youth*, Mitchell Froom, who had worked with Bruce Thomas on other records, involving Richard Thompson and Suzanne Vega, and with Costello on *King of America*, brokered a temporary professional reconciliation between the two men. Not surprisingly, there was great caution on both sides and personal trust never returned. By the end of the 1990s, their alienation was complete. It seems unlikely that the book or its prequel instalments were the prime cause of either their initial or eventual split. It is more likely that Thomas's caustic satire was symptomatic of that alienation. The book's highly disrespectful contents simply gave Costello further, quite understandable, grounds to reject his bass player.

In the pre-book instalments and then the book itself, not only is Thomas unappreciative of the good times to be remembered with Costello, he is actively contemptuous of him, when he emphasises at different points that 'the Singer' is an aggressive neurotic with an over-sized ego. To amplify this last point, 'the Singer' is only cast as one of a few players, not the main man in the story, creating an equalising effect about the targets of the author's amusement. However, there is one pointed passage, which is uncompromising in its attack on Costello (making, in the first part, observations of his presentation of self similar to our own in Chapter 1 about Costello's malleable accent and his performing personas[36]):

> The Singer ... had an accent that was given to wild variations, particularly during stage announcements. In Liverpool, it became a thick, nasal Scouse. It was top

---

[35]   This term is used to indicate when an employee resigns in frustration about the way in which they are being treated by their employer. It is a basis for legal action against the ex-employer.

[36]   Thomas used Costello's adaptive showmanship as a focus of scorn, whereas we simply note it as an undeniable aspect of his habitus and public impression management. Costello can ingratiate himself with audiences (but not always!) and this is just a standard trick of the trade, which he carries out in his own particular way.

o' the morning may the road rise to meet you, bejabbers brogue in Dublin. In London, it became a Cheltenham cockney that recalled the early Jagger. It was important only to remember what town you were actually in. The Singer might well have been called Curt Reply, but we simply called him 'The Pod' owing to the increasing tendency to resemble the shape of those creatures from Invasion of the Body Snatchers. (Thomas, 2003: 35)

Costello, as we have seen in earlier chapters, was thin-skinned. He could take offence very easily and, with his truculent and wary attitude to others, he could soon feel hurt and victimised, even if legitimate comment might come his way for cool consideration. At times, the sense was that he could start a fight in an empty house. Given the person involved, and him being well known to the author, the *Time Out* prequels to *The Big Wheel* were not going to be shrugged off with indifference. Costello was not likely to take joshing, from any quarter, with good humoured tolerance, especially when it came from a wayward and disloyal intimate.

One wonders quite what Thomas expected from Costello. Was it gratitude? Did Thomas underestimate the serious career-limiting powers Costello held over him? Had intimacy over the years meant that he had lost perspective on the reality of the power relationship involved between them? Maybe Thomas had simply had enough and no longer cared about any practical implications of his words. Whether it was from indifference, perversity or simple lack of insight, he did not concede that Costello was the very reason why he was there and enjoyed a commercial career.

An indication of the challenge for onlookers decoding what is happening in the politics of bands is the duplicity of Thomas. On the one hand he was writing material that was to become *The Big Wheel*, but on the other, in March 1987, he gave an interview with Dan Forte in *Guitar Player* in which he disclosed nothing of the tensions between him and Costello. Indeed, he depicts Costello as the rightful and legitimate leader of the band and someone who lets his colleagues, including Thomas, do their own thing as musicians. Any ambivalence is subtle and coded. For example, he concedes that, as he does not write or sing, he could not be the leader of a band but also admits that he does not like playing second fiddle. Thomas also mentions that occasionally Costello supplies the bass line but that he himself supplies ones missing from the writer in key bass-dominated songs like '(I Don't Want to Go To) Chelsea'. The disloyalty is there but it is barely visible, and the clues only make sense in the context of what ensued.

The elephant in the room, which Thomas ignored for his own reasons, was that The Attractions were constructed and hired by Costello and only played songs written by him, or covers of his choosing. Instead, Thomas created a counter-discourse of 'Elvis Costello and The Attractions', involving a whole system unit of musical creativity, success and warranted reputation. In the latter regard, Thomas was keen to foreground in the foreword to the second edition of *The Big Wheel* (hence it being cited here) a very brief meeting, not a reconciliation, on 10 March 2003, in which Elvis Costello and The Attractions – not just 'the Singer' – were inducted into the 'Rock and Roll Hall of Fame' in New York. This is an emphatic rhetorical message: the whole band, not just 'the Singer', made this ceremony possible. 'We were all in this together' can elide in meaning to 'we were all equally important' or even 'we were a band of equals', if that is how the story needs to be told or heard. But that story is self-deceiving and misleading.

As we noted in Chapter 1, music, when recorded and performed in a group, is indeed co-produced, no matter how its reputation is subsequently credited or its earnings distributed. However, as the leader in their midst, who jealously protected publication rights for his songs, Costello would take a hard line about any ambiguity. Moreover, the dominant and shared discourse of fans and critics about popular music is that the singer-songwriter at the centre of any musical outfit *is* that outfit really. The players are replaceable but 'the Singer' will survive as the central historical trace.

The Attractions may well be in the 'Rock and Roll Hall of Fame' but they are in the very large shadow of Elvis Costello's ego, particular writing talents, extraordinary voice, showmanship, musical preferences and political ownership. *He* continued to work successfully but by the mid-1990s The Attractions were finally defunct. They had been replaced with The Imposters – The Attractions but with a new bass player. With his irrepressible graveyard humour, Thomas called them 'The Subtractions'. By the time of their eventual split, Costello was complaining that Thomas was alternating between sloppy playing and going out of his way to upstage him during performances. It had been within Costello's gift to bring this mutual disaffection to a decisive end when the problem was first evident to him in 1984, but he vacillated.

A residual doubt is obvious, though, for both sides, which we return to in Chapter 9. Just as Costello could fairly recognise the important signature of Herbie Flowers' bass line in 'Take A Walk On The Wild Side' (see Chapter 2), try to imagine, say, 'Watching the Detectives' or '(I Don't Want to Go To) Chelsea' or 'Pump It Up' without Bruce Thomas's defining melodic contribution to each song. In terms of their lasting reputation, they were arguably as much his songs as Costello's. But the norm of popular music recording, and so not the unique demand of Costello as an individual, is that the singer-songwriter at the core of a band brings a lyric and tune into a studio and presents it for development through performance until a satisfactory version is captured.[37] This means that co-production process is not reflected in the publishing rights. It may not be fair, but that is how it works and The Attractions were not unique victims of this norm.

---

[37]   Many popular writer-performers do not read and write music (the case with Costello during our period of interest): they scribble down lyrics and remember a tune constructed on a guitar or piano and then capture it alone or with others during the recording process, when it then morphs. Most 'scores' of popular music are post-hoc indicators, not advance directives. Middleton (1990) calls this type of score 'a prognostic device or a beside-the-fact spin off'. As Tagg (2000) points out, popular music suffers less than classical music from 'notational centricity'.

At the end of it all, Costello sacked Thomas (twice) because he could. The music industry and reportage about its exotic lifestyle may create a recurring adolescent narrative of 'we are all in this together and having a devil-may-care time on the road'. However, the special authority of the single artist driving the project soon becomes evident, once they become displeased. That embodied authority means that they can do what they want. And they are in a position arbitrarily to withdraw the same freedom from others and end their career or stint of employment. Costello could get rid of a record engineer or a bass player and he did, even if one, for reasons of personal history and attachment, was harder to reject and in a position to wreak a little sneering public revenge.

Conclusion

This chapter has dealt with Costello and his position in the music industry during the 1980s. It highlights three major points about the tension between the subjective aspirations of a self-styled author of his own artistic destiny and the objective context of the industry in that period. First, he made a demonstrable and significant contribution to a minority critical social commentary within popular music. This was during a period when the norm of production in British popular music was of carefree individualistic froth, which was one response to the depressing socio-political impact of Thatcherism. However, he did not always make that progressive contribution in a spirit of solidarity with all musicians of the period. His appearances at left-of-centre concerts were the exceptions that proved this rule. At times he could deal with his competitors in the field in a disparaging and dismissive manner (see the third summary point below).

Second, there was a tension between the leftish and humanistic sentiments claimed by Costello, about the rights of others and our collective interdependence as a species (for example, when supporting progressive political causes in his concert work) and the micro politics of his own band. Bruce Thomas asked for trouble in writing his provocative book and its prequels, and was sacked because Costello could do that; the reverse scenario simply was not tenable politically. At that face-to-face or micro level of employment in the music industry, workers' rights are virtually non-existent. Thus, the brewing alienation and spats between Costello and Thomas exemplified a point about their career divergence, which recurred across the industry in large and small ways then and still occurs today.

Third, there is a tension between the real or apparent power of the auteur position and the immutable constraints of the economic environment. This becomes evident, and is effectively acknowledged, by the artist then protesting that their constraining environment turns *them* into an individual victim. Costello's exploitation by those in the industry was insignificant compared to that suffered by some others. For example, during the 1970s, under their original contract with a production company, the band Queen was hugely successful but remained stony broke for a good while, before obtaining a new manager to rectify the problem. All of their record and performance profits were sucked from them in the first 'deal'. (For an analysis of the corrupt dimension to the US record industry, see Dannen (2003).)

In the 1980s, the real and immediate power of the record companies cramped the style of all artists; the unbridled personal aspirations of any self-styled auteur were put into chains. This then confirms individual artists as being disconnected from the prospects of collective political action with those in their own trade. They become *both* victims of the industry *and* wary of sharing that position collectively with others. The latter are merely competitors in a market place to be disparaged, ignored, selectively co-opted for particular writing or recording purposes, or hired and fired. Costello adopted all of these positions at different times towards his colleagues in the industry (and he was not alone).

To summarise, we can position Costello in the social structure of 1980s Western capitalism, with its constraints and opportunities for ambitious commercial musicians. Above him, and his auteur resilience and industriousness, were international corporate interests, not all of which were legal and legitimate. In that super-ordinate position we find the record companies and the mass media, with their rapidly changing technologies of production and distribution. In a subordinate position, in socio-economic terms, were his consumer-fans and a small workforce he had the discretion to hire and fire. As with many in this position, he was sliding around somewhere in the ambiguous space between the ruling class, which expropriated the labour and commodified talents of musicians, and the mundane lives of most wage slaves, the unemployed and the unemployable, who were living in unremarkable anonymity.

In traditional Marxian terms, Costello could be described as a successful petit-bourgeois individualist. Although a fair description, this is also too general to capture the particular and nuanced character of *this* commercial musician, in the particular cultural field of the late 20th century. This basic Marxian-structural view of his position in society at the time is elaborated in the next chapter, with the emergence of newer postmodern considerations.

Chapter 8
Costello and Postmodernism

> We are what we pretend to be. So we must be careful about what we pretend to be.
> – Kurt Vonnegut Jr[1]

Introduction

The core chapters of this book have examined Costello's work during the 1980s, attending especially to the dimensions familiar to sociologists, of race, class and gender, as well as to the particularities of the music industry of the time. This view of the social context is within the traditions of sociology's founding fathers Marx (offering us an emphasis on class and political economy) and Weber (offering us the need to understand negotiated meaning by different groups in society and to take status and power seriously in social life). More recent concepts from Bourdieu of habitus and field have also guided our exploration from the outset. At times we have also drawn upon orientations and insights from psychoanalysis and existentialism.

All of these strands of reasoning, or social scientific resources, can be placed within a modernist current of thought. Words and things, ideologies and material forces, describable social groups and their covert and expressed interests, all have their place within this scheme of post-Enlightenment reasoning. However, Costello emerged as a commercially successful artist at the very time, whether he knew this or not then, of what came to be known as the 'postmodern turn'. Starting with Pop Art, postmodernism had established a strong position in the cultural field since the 1960s and some date its emergence in architecture specifically to 3.32pm on 15 July 1972.[2] But it was in the 1980s that postmodern ideas flourished in the academy and in serious cultural discussions.

The relevance for this book of the emerging intellectual vogue of postmodernism in the final quarter of the 20th century is twofold. First, Costello's musical products could be seen as *symptomatic* of postmodernism: they may exemplify its key characteristics. Second, he could be understood, quite differently, as part of a *modernist brake* on postmodern artistic expression, trying to hang on to older romantic impulses of early modernity. He might then be depicted as a conservative and nostalgic cultural exponent. Both of these readings of Costello will be explored below, but we can first note that the term 'postmodernism' is contested or 'polyvalent'; and so we outline three relevant connotations.

---

[1]   From *Mother Night* (1961).

[2]   This is when Le Corbusier's prize-winning tower block in St Louis (his 'machine for modern living') was dynamited because it had become uninhabitable (Jencks, 1984).

Three interweaving meanings of postmodernism

In its first connotation, 'postmodernism' is the state of the world under 'late' or 'high' capitalism and so it is simply a *societal description*. The world is now globalised yet differentiated, despite 'time-space compression' (Harvey, 1989). Though not totally homogenised, it is still under Western cultural domination, unevenly provoking older local traditions and political reactions. Concurrently it contains religious fundamentalism, secular indifference or hostility to faith as well as syncretism (for example in New Age spiritual movements). Global homogenisation, internationalism and secularism are offset by nationalisms and feudal religious traditions. Consumerism and service industries have now replaced the older emphasis on production ('post-Fordism'), a trend encouraged by electronic technological developments to produce a 'post-industrial society' (Bell, 1973; Castells, 1989).

Political ideologies have far less clear significance than in the past. Party politics in Western democracies have converged in their appeal to voters. Politics based on social class (following Marx) or professional moral communities (following Durkheim) are no longer as clearly visible and coherent as in the past. The Leninist experiments of the 20th century collapsed and the Eastern bloc learned to love capitalism. The opposition of capital and labour still shapes society. However, we also now encounter a multiplicity of 'new social movements' and 'identity politics' (for example, from women, gay and disabled people), whose demands in civil society are about human rights and preferred ways of living ('pre-figurative politics'). Political demands are no longer narrowly about access to material resources or the traditional political mechanisms governing the State. Laclau (1990) offers the concept of 'dislocation', when structures are displaced without replacement. This 'decentring' then leads to a multiplicity of forms of power in constant flux.

Moreover, if squaring the circle of individual liberty and social justice was the political challenge of the 20th century, by its end the emerging political priority was in stemming ecocide so that the human species avoided extinction (Seymour and Girardet, 1990). Those who provide this description of the state of society more or less endorse its human or political value, but they are all emphatic that we are now, in late capitalism, in a different sort of place to where we were in its early development (Jameson, 1991; Gorz, 1982; Baudrillard, 1983; Bell, 1973).

The second meaning is *philosophical* and is associated especially with French post-structuralism (with a nod towards American pragmatism), which challenged the idea of dominant or 'grand' narratives from Marx, Weber, Durkheim, Freud, Darwin and Lévi-Strauss. Instead, contingent context-dependent meanings are explored and multiple realities are describable and plural accounts given, even in the same situation. Unlike the above empirical description of the world, this connotation of postmodernism is about a philosophical movement, the start of which is attributed to Nietzsche and his critical analysis of the Enlightenment, though the idea of socially negotiated meanings began in earnest with Weberian sociology.

Those championing this approach to epistemology actively celebrate uncertainty as a political act against the amalgam of 'power/knowledge', with an emphasis on reading knowledge as a story in a variety of ways, rather than accepting it as a single source of authority (for example, Foucault, 1986; Lyotard, 1985; Derrida, 1981). Thus, this is not merely a description of how the world has changed but an active philosophical critique. It takes to task those in the academy who, after the Enlightenment, overconfidently sought to replace faith and religious superstition with the new – and, it is argued, unfounded – certainties of science (Bauman, 1988).

In this new philosophy, structural explanations and materialist assumptions about cause and effect are deemed to be suspect (hence 'post-structuralism'). All knowledge claims are contestable (the 'undecidability of propositions'). We cannot know the world, other than through the ways we represent it and so 'everything is socially constructed'. Reality, simply as reality, now becomes a joke and anyone still committed to its objective existence is now missing the postmodern point. The traditional faith in science is then critically undermined by that point and irony is enjoyed about how we understand ourselves and the world we inhabit.

We are left without the older modernist certainties of aggregating knowledge in the academy and simply now have unending 'discourses on discourses' (Lemert, 1985). Power is dispersed or 'de-centred' not locatable. Individual egos are not locatable either, but shifting identities can be explored in context. We now have 'history without a subject'. It is all about how we all see the world in different contexts. No one person's 'take'[3] on the world, or their morality, can be definitively deemed better or worse than another's. In sum, this reflects predominant philosophical assertions in the postmodern movement about idealism[4] and relativism.

The third connotation of postmodernism is *cultural* and refers to new artistic forms of expression which are characterised by pastiche and eclecticism, the old and the new mixed up selectively or randomly. In the 1980s, we saw this in architecture with glass and concrete being intermingled with steel and bricks, straight lines broken up with Norman arches.

The link between the postmodern architectural *style* of the 1980s and the societal *description* of the postmodern condition was that it was fitted for a landscape of consumerism: the shopping mall was privileged now, not the factory. Its pastiche could then blend unnoticed into any place in the world; hence

---

[3]   A noticeable shift in postmodern texts is the appearance of repeated (and not always consistent) use of speech marks, translating today into common showy or sarcastic performances, when the speaker uses one or two fingers on each hand to indicate imagined speech marks, so that their words denote irony or surface appearance. This leaves others with the question about the meaning of a word or statement if the speech marks were missing …

[4]   In philosophy 'idealism' refers to an emphasis on *ideas* in knowledge, rather than a focus on the facts linked to observable reality (empiricism). It is not a reference, as in the vernacular, to pure or romantic aspirations.

our perception now of the uniformity of the 'shopping experience'. Malls and a plurality of single storey retail outlets have become globalised in appearance. 'Retail parks', with their misleading connotations of health and recreation, are tedious in their *lack* of diversity, despite their superficial pluralism. These latter-day temples of Mammon could equally be in Newcastle, England, or Newcastle Australia – and all points in between.

By the late 1980s fashion-wise, potentially anything might be worn or worn together; incoherence and individuality were being celebrated. The visual arts emphasised 'bricolage': any object to hand could be picked up and added to something else and maybe installed for viewing using multi-media presentations. Moreover, art could be 'performed', shattering the boundaries between acting, dancing, music, film, painting and sculpting. Anything went and who was to say with certainty what was any good, beyond how it played in the market of arbitrary taste?

These three connotations of the word 'postmodern' provide us with relevant ways of dealing with Costello's work or construing his output in the 1980s. However, they are different ways and so postmodernism cannot be regarded as a single concept for consideration for our purposes. They are not totally separate in source and character though. For example, the cultural aspects of postmodernism (third connotation) have arisen because of the new conditions of possibility created by societal changes (first connotation).

And the second connotation simply claims that its approach to knowledge is now better aligned to understand the postmodern condition, and even advance its positive potential for humanity. However, its critics forcefully dispute this radical claim and argue that postmodernism is anti-rational and reactionary, not liberating and progressive (Callinicos, 1989), or it simply throws the baby out with the bathwater of the genuine, albeit limited, gains of the Enlightenment (Norris, 1993; Habermas, 1985). For Habermas, postmodernism leads to a 'neoconservative' form of politics because it has lost respect for the unfinished project of the Enlightenment, which sought to express three autonomous domains of reason (science, morality and art). He affirms the continued relevance of these three domains, proposed originally by Weber.

The three connotations of postmodernism noted above are held together firmly by the mixed glue of pluralism and relativism. This point was made evident publicly in Britain in the 1980s with the emergence of the popular magazine *Marxism Today* (reportedly read by Margaret Thatcher) which enthusiastically represented all three connotations. This post-Marxist shift in emphasis is important to note as part of the context of our time of interest. Many (though not all) of the champions of postmodernism in any of its connotations were those on the left, who had become disillusioned with the authoritarian intentions and outcomes of their forebears. Behind *Marxism Today* was the radically revised Communist Party of Great Britain, with its 'New Times' project responding to the late capitalism described in the first connotation of postmodernism.

Leninism in particular had been catastrophic, with its obsession with the superiority of the party vanguard and the power of the central committee. Stalin had invoked science to justify wild excesses of murder and persecution of real and imagined enemies. The USSR could send a man into space but the ordinary Soviet citizen could not buy a toothbrush. Pol Pot in Cambodia, using Mao as a role model and identifying with the pernicious paranoia of Stalin, murdered a large minority of his own population.[5]

The 'totalising' logic, then, of sources of legitimacy in the modern age, at its zenith in the middle of the 20th century, had led all too often to totalitarianism. Political authority promoting social equality and opposing exploitation frequently turned into the authoritarian state and just another depressing variant of barbarism. When gaining power, the revolutionary left simply offered its own version of what it sought to oppose in the fascisms of Italy, Spain, Japan and Germany. It was time for statues and walls to be pulled down, both literally and symbolically.[6]

Whether that ideological (or 'discursive') shift on the left was represented as liberal or libertarian (or even, according to Habermas, 'neoconservative') was open to debate but what was not in doubt was that all authority, whatever its source or justification, was now going to be exposed to rigorous challenge.

Assessing Costello's postmodern status

This, then, was the extant political and cultural milieu of the 1980s. Artist by artist, there may have been those who self-consciously took esoteric French post-structuralism as a cue for inspiration *and* those who were totally oblivious to this source of modish legitimacy in the 1980s. At the same time, the first connotation of 'postmodernism', relating to a description of a new sort of societal arrangement (not a philosophy but an observable outcome) meant that creative people, whatever their intellectual influences, were responding to that new context of possibility and constraint to some degree. For example, the bland, frothy individualism of the fellow musicians that Costello held in contempt (the 'pygmies' and 'dullards') were, in their own way, dancing to the tune of consumption not production, just as much as he was in his irritable and dour musical critique of Thatcherism.

One way and another we find the cultural avant-garde of the 1980s producing the eclectic multi-media mixture that came to be the third connotation of 'postmodern' and a rapidly adopted conformity in art and fashion. Our question here is whether

---

[5]   As part of the aftermath of the repeated bombing by the USA of Cambodia's innocent civilians, in the war against the Viet Cong, Pol Pot imposed agrarian socialism (mimicking Mao) and evinced a peculiar hybrid of communism and nationalism (mimicking Stalin). In the process around 2.5 million Cambodians were exterminated.

[6]   The Berlin Wall was pulled down by exasperated Germans in 1989. It had only been built in 1961. Democratic resistance can suddenly reverse the apparent permanency of authoritarian regimes.

Costello can or should be offered as a typical example of that trend. Was he a deliberate advocate of postmodern culture or was he an accidental postmodernist (because of the timing of his commercial success), with his real interests being more modernist and conservative in their intentions?

Given the three connotations of 'postmodern' noted above, we can examine how Costello and his work in the 1980s might be understood. Some of this exploration has to be tentative and interpretive because he is an elusive artist prone to laying false trails, perversity and jokiness. Also, our evidence comes from his products and secondary accounts (existing biographies and interview material he offered in a commercially sensitive context of self-promotion or self-defence). Nonetheless, there is enough to go on to make the exploration and offer our view.

Responding to the postmodern condition

Costello clearly dwelt upon adapting to the contingencies of his time. Whether his self-proclaimed shrewdness always led to successful outcomes in this regard is open to interpretation or judgment (from him or others). One reason for this was that, out of principle or perversity, he insisted on his way of doing things and would sometimes emphasise choices that seemingly were not in his own best commercial interests.[7] Notwithstanding this contradiction, by adapting to the contingencies of the period he was faced with two options: to outshine his fellow musicians by writing more cleverly in the orthodoxy of carefree individualism (discussed in Chapter 7); or to create an alternative, and even oppositional, form of song production.

Overwhelmingly he opted for the latter, though we noted in Chapter 7 that his self-pitying hit 'Good Year for the Roses' was against this trend in his work. However, he sang this song, he did not write it, which is pertinent here to our overall argument about his authored products in the 1980s.

An example of his attack upon the new mass consumerism is the song 'Worthless Thing' from *Goodbye Cruel World* (1984). This alludes to contestants in a popular television show of the time, milking greed and the cash nexus, and to its presenter's clichéd and manipulative script ('Come on down, the price is right, what's your name?'). It also alludes to the advertising industry and its conformist and pacifying messages for women: 'She's available and beautiful but with more time to devote. They're going to take this cable now and stick it down your throat.' This anticipated the growth of the shopping channel and the duped housewife. Another example of his sensibility about the impact of new technology is the song 'Satellite' from *Spike*. In it a young woman is distressed and a male viewer is sexually aroused. The scenario could be anything from soft pornography to the Eurovision Song Contest but what is not in doubt is Costello's sense of moral foreboding about the use of the new technology.

---

[7]   This was mainly in relation to the singles he opted to foreground and release, when fans and biographers could later spot the commercial possibilities of other tracks on his albums in the 1980s.

Thus Costello was more than capable of being observant of his contemporary social context. But this does not make him into a postmodern artist, only an artist who lived in postmodern times. In the latter, weaker, connotation of postmodernism, this sort of outcome applied to all of his peers in the music industry of the 1980s and so Costello was not unique. What made him different was his desire to critique the context he shared with other artists.

Evidence of Costello's philosophical orientation

We are not aware of Costello embracing post-structuralism as a philosophy. There is evidence though that he expressed himself in quite traditional modernist terms about his view of life. There are strong resonances of Catholicism (ingrained and evident in his habitus) and existentialism (learned as an intelligent questioning adult) in his musings and music. But more than this, he was a romantic egotist. In Chapter 7, we made a case for his position within longer traditions of Romanticism drawn from the 18th and 19th centuries and even the older one of the troubadours. We have used the unifying concept of the aspiring 'auteur' throughout the book to emphasise this identity.

What is difficult to appraise is the extent to which that auteur image and associated mixture of enthusiastic and unbounded artistic expression is *just* a public identity or whether it reflects an abiding or stable aspect of the *personality* of Declan MacManus. We are left to speculate how Declan would be, as a person, had his career not been successful and he had returned to a life of obscurity. Probably he would have still been egotistical and emotionally anguished in equal parts had he become an ordinary citizen. However, this is a guess about a path not taken.

But, once he took his path into show business, he gained confidence as a *general entertainer*[8] with a compulsive desire to express himself artistically. This translated into extra-ordinary productivity. Primarily a singer-songwriter, in his early career he also produced (Squeeze, The Pogues and The Specials) and even tried his hand at acting, with bit parts in the film *GBH* and the television series *Scully*. Apart from co-writing material with a long list of artists, he was often co-opted as a backing musician, mainly as a singer, but occasionally also with his guitar, as in the Roy Orbison television show in 1987.

What we have in the samples of interviews we have cited throughout the book is a man who puts himself firmly in the driving seat of his creative project and, despite him trying his hand (irrepressibly), at a number of roles within the entertainment industry, writing and singing music remained at the core. As he

---

[8]   Whether or not he was a *beloved* entertainer, his image on the front of *Spike* was a view that some, though not all, would have of him. But the notion of him being a *general* entertainer was not a variable subjective judgment; it had ample behavioural evidence. He was a modern version of a troubadour in action.

put it to David Hepworth in a 2003 interview in *The Word*: 'I am vocationally[9] an artist who happens to be a musician and I happen to make my livelihood at it.' Although his other roles were real enough, they reflected both personal ambition and a good deal of expressive versatility. These though do not make a case for him being a self-conscious exponent of artistic postmodernism. He could not exactly become 'Renaissance man' because of the objective limitations of his educational background but even this offered encouragement for versatility. As an autodidact he was unhampered by more limited and linear expectations of a focused middle-class career. His family script of musicianship was open-ended and he was not criticised for taking risks when trying his hand in show business, quite the reverse.

A good comparator here is the lead guitarist for Queen. The father of Brian May believed that his son had thrown his academic career away disastrously when joining a pop group. Many years of commercial success were required before this disapproval and disbelief were reversed. Costello had no such identity constrictions in his family of origin. For example, he appeared as a teenager with his father in a television advertisement for Whites Lemonade, catchy jingle and all; an impossible, not just an implausible, scenario for the young and bookish Brian May. In 2007, the latter returned to the academic fold to complete his PhD in astrophysics. Costello's *Honorary* Doctorate in Music, presented by the University of Liverpool around the same time, signals the difference in trajectory and outcome for the two musicians.

This personally liberating family context meant that he could experiment in the entertainment industry only *after* a core role of musician had been established commercially. As a producer of others, as a visual artist for his own record sleeves or as a bit part actor, he had to establish a core reputation *first* within a network of other opportunities. Thereafter, experimentation came naturally to him. It had never been knocked out of him, as can happen for many young people under risk-averse parental and schooling influences. It was not likely, though, that Costello could have gained immediate, or even eventual, success with those extended roles in the business, had he tried to put the cart before the horse.

Moreover, his personal experimentation ultimately remained within the field of entertainment. As he put it later in the Hepworth interview, with true or false modesty, in the company of serious academics he would not 'seem so smart'. Arguably, he *was* smart over quite a wide range of activities in the field of entertainment. Nonetheless, he wanted to emphasise his limitations: 'I have a one-trick talent to write songs. I've understood it instinctively since I was tiny.' That 'one-trick talent' was a springboard, though, for other avenues to be explored. His 'have a go' mentality meant that he went down them to see what he would find.[10]

---

[9]   The word 'vocationally' could be unpacked further. He did not use 'occupationally' or 'job-wise'. It is reasonable to see Costello's work as a sort of 'calling'. It is something he feels he simply must do. It has a driven feel to it, even though he is seemingly 'in the driving seat'.

[10]   In more recent times he has also tried his hand, with some success, as a television interviewer.

None of this demonstrable and demonstrative personal experimentation suggested a worked-out philosophical position-in-action of postmodernism. This point can even be upheld despite the challenging evidence about his name-switching. From the outset, Costello's stage name was part fantasy and part family history. Indeed, despite the apparent switches of identity over his career, unlike many commercial artists, he has never had a stage name simply plucked randomly from someone's imagination. The prefix 'Elvis' is an obvious and audacious allusion suggested by his manager. Elvis Presley dominated as a supreme pop identity in the 1960s and so to take his name risked accusations of disrespect or parody. This was a clever marketing provocation.

Moreover, Costello's family script hovers constantly in these name changes. 'Costello' was the surname of his great-grandmother. On his record credits we also had, 'D. MacManus'[11] and 'The Imposter aka E. Costello'. This is hardly a radical tactic to become someone else completely or nobody in particular at all. Outside of these very limited variations on his preferred writing credits on the record, he occasionally acquired other names on stage: for example, as part of the 'Coward Brothers' and as the 'MC Napoleon Dynamite'. But these were ephemeral and his audiences understood that it was Elvis Costello all along, in the same way that, as children, we knew that Santa Claus was some recognisable bloke dressed up for the occasion. The other identity adopted was for some of the artwork Costello produced himself for his record sleeves (as 'Eamonn Singer' for *Goodbye Cruel World* and *Blood & Chocolate*).

Compare that picture to artists with a self-declared postmodern intent, such as those who hide behind a strange identity or those whose identities seem to be rapidly distinct and complete reinventions. A good early example of this was David Bowie's identity switches in the 1970s. In a more recent example, we have Gorillaz, which is part live musicians and part cartoon characters, prompted by the vacuity of *MTV*. This project is a postmodern attack (cultural connotation) on an aspect of the commercial manifestation of postmodern times (societal connotation). The 'band' has, with postmodern irony, turned its critique into a commercial success.

Costello's identity switches were very modest compared to these examples and he has even commented on his strategy. For example, he notes this was not helped by his record company (see this theme in Chapter 7):

> it's obviously a blessing to have such a powerful image from your first few records but in another way it's limiting, *as people only see you in those terms*. And when your own record company defines you in those terms then it becomes difficult because they're not even helping to *promote the new image*. The country record [*Almost Blue*] was one attempt to escape. *Imperial Bedroom*

---

[11]   Even the name 'MacManus' had a movable history in his family. His paternal grandfather's surname was 'McManus' but his son Ross changed it to the alternative spelling. Thomson (2004) speculates that this switch to the more typically Scottish version was a way of escaping from anti-Irish prejudice.

was another and not just attempts either, I was actually doing it. It just goes to show how powerful the original image was. *Until you come up with a suitable contrasting one, you won't really get it over to people.* (Interview in *Record Collector*, October 1995, emphasis added)

This is not postmodern irony, or playfulness with situated identities, but good old-fashioned marketing of the self. It also reinforces our repeated thesis that Costello is positioning himself as a self-styled auteur in the long tradition of the romantic artist succeeding in an unsympathetic world, which fails to appreciate an extraordinary talent in its midst. He wants to portray himself as being in charge and that he can triumph over external constraints imposed on him. Costello, from his childhood, had learned about the industry and the importance of the impression created, when on public display and when selling his wares. As we noted in the previous chapter, this struggle for success and deserved recognition could even be elevated into a narrative of oppression (and see below).

Moreover, all artists are faced with the challenge of adapting to changing times if they wish to remain successful. There are only two options as the fashions of the industry shift. The first is to retain, defiantly, the original 'brand' and the second is to try something new. The second strategy risks alienating the existing fan base but it creates the new opportunity of winning them over *and* establishing a new audience and set of consumers. It is the clever thing to do but it does bring with it some commercial risk.[12] Costello is in this second category but that does not make him, or any other adaptive colleague taking the same risk, a postmodern artist.

Costello was struggling with what all ambitious artists, since the 1920s, had attempted: he was simply selling his image in the marketplace. He told David Fricke in *Rolling Stone* in April 1986 that he viewed his early image as a 'bit of a curse' and that his name was becoming a tedious brand name (like 'Durex'). And, as an another example of his exasperation with record companies blocking his attempts to move on from his narrow established reputation to create a new image, he complained in an interview in *Melody Maker* (13 May 1989) about the lack of promotion of *Blood & Chocolate*: 'They hated it and subsequently just fucking buried it.'

Similarly, his romantic modernism is clear in his pleas for his *individual* good faith and integrity. Here is an example of a contradictory narrative that the egotistical artist inevitably creates by first emphasising image creation above (inherently an exercise in dissimulation and marketing) and then, at other times, making a claim about his personal trustworthy authenticity:

... *everything* I've done on record – good or bad – I've done *with all my heart.* And I stand by every record I've done, even records I think these days don't

---

[12]   One of the best examples of this is when Bob Dylan 'went electric' in 1965 and was booed by his audiences and attacked as a traitor to the cause of folk music. With this storm weathered, he survived and thrived. Costello has persistently invited similar risky scenarios in his meandering interests and catholic musical tastes.

have any virtue. I've made bad records but I've never made a *dishonest* record, let's put it that way. (Costello in Kent, 2007: 217, emphasis added)

Whether we listen to Costello trying to market a new image or his stubborn declarations of sincere intentions, his sense of personal agency is at the centre at all times. Thus, notwithstanding the very limited switching of stage names, there is much that simply does not square with a postmodern picture of him as a musician. For example, he does not really endeavour to obscure his individual identity because of its irrelevance: this is not his confession of being part of 'history without a subject'.

The point of the identity-switching seemed to be consistent with a game of hide-and-seek – going back to his manager's marketing strategy, his father's caution about revealing too much and a temperamental suspiciousness, in which he simply did not want people to come too close. This mixture then translated into canny careerism, which permitted no self-doubt and created much intrigue for the music press.[13] Then and now, it also makes Costello very difficult to fathom as a person. Who is he, and what is he up to?[14]

Moreover, there is no evidence that he ever fundamentally queries his authorial position or authority (a requirement of a 'true' postmodern mind set). He takes himself very seriously and makes it clear to the world how his products are the direct outcome of his unique imagination, whether he goes by his given name of Declan MacManus or a stage name. There is little self-criticism, not much largesse about the role of others and little doubt about his creativity being anything but a function of his unusually talented musical mind.

Certainly the latter includes a regular honouring of the influence of other artists (for example in his liner notes). But even that honouring is a demonstration of his cleverness or 'encyclopaedic musical knowledge' (see below). In the 1980s he believed that he was riding the stallion of his imagination[15] and that he could easily win the race in competition with so many of his song writing inferiors, who were 'pygmies' and 'dullards'. Thus we should not confuse Costello's clever and deliberate game, of playing with his own recording personas and performance masks, with a knowing poststructuralist subversion of authorial intentionality.

---

[13] A good early example of this is when Costello was first becoming famous he held a press conference in which he insisted that no photographs were taken of his face. This was a very clever counter-intuitive gambit to stimulate press interest. It worked.

[14] Anyone approaching Costello and his work is then faced with this mystique. Griffiths (2007) notably begins his appraisal of whether or not the artist deserves the status of 'icon' with that dilemma, expressed for us all in an epigram, for his very first chapter, containing the question: 'Who (or what) exactly is Elvis Costello?' (taken from Bookmens 2004: 66).

[15] Freud used the metaphor of the horse and its rider, with the latter (the ego) believing erroneously that it was in charge of the former (the unconscious).

The style and content of Costello's work

Probably the most tempting empirical indication that Costello was a postmodern artist is the character of his work. Eclecticism was evident as time went on. He respected few boundaries in his sourcing of musical inspiration or his experimentation with his own songs. However, whilst all postmodernists are necessarily eclectic, not all eclectics are necessarily postmodernists. In this case, most of Costello's artistic exploration and allusions reflect his liberal catholic taste in music, simply derived from childhood exposure and his intelligent commercial adaptive strategy noted above. Thus, this pluralism is less about postmodern pastiche and more about affection and nostalgia, traceable to a smorgasbord of early musical influences in a hungry and impressionable young Declan MacManus (see Chapter 3), combined with a current shrewdness about the business.[16]

As far as the multi-media postmodern feature it is true that Costello generated some intriguing videos, but the use of the latter was a technological norm in postmodern society (connotation 1 noted above) not inherently an example of postmodern cultural experimentation (connotation 3 above). If we are to make a strong case for a postmodern label for any artist, it is that the third connotation should predominate because it refers to a cultural not just a societal description. This repeats the point for emphasis from above that Costello was an artist living in postmodern times, rather than a postmodern artist. But if we are correct in this interpretation, how do we account then for the fluidity of his musical interests?

The postmodern interpretation when answering this question would emphasise Costello's intertextuality. However, our argument is that a modernist explanation can be offered instead, which features allusion and derivation. Certainly the very wide spread of his musical content (in both lyrics and melody) show multiple and inter-penetrating influences. In postmodern times (first connotation from the introduction) the older strict rules of plagiarism had become lax. The enactment of so called 'sampling' reflected this shift. To our knowledge, Costello has not been sued for plagiarism, despite the uncanny resemblance of some of his song parts to past ones from other musicians. In the liner notes of the CD reissue of *Get Happy!!* Costello notes that he had a small early stab at 'sampling'. And within that ambiguity others resided. For example, the distinctive keyboard riff in 'Oliver's Army' is straight from Abba's 'Dancing Queen', which was slipped in, during recording, by Steve Nieve. Costello is quite open and even pernickety about declaring his allusions, as is evident in the liner notes to his reissued CDs.[17]

---

[16]   Costello's openness to experimentation has parallels with one of his successful collaborators, Paddy Moloney. Both artists will explore many hybrids of past traditions and seemingly unlikely partnerships, to try to discover a creative outcome and its commercial possibilities.

[17]   Griffiths (2007) notes that Costello's repeated and knowing allusions actually became more restricted in his later work. Griffiths gives examples of Costello being refused permissions for sampling when recording after 1990.

For example, when discussing *Armed Forces* he tells us that there are allusions to: Charlie Chaplin's speech in *The Great Dictator* (in 'Two Little Hitlers'); the 'great Don Covay' in the rhythmic quality of 'Goon Squad' and in one of its guitar parts being close to an early record by the New York group Television; Burt Bacharach's 'Anyone Who Had A Heart' and Randy Newman's 'I Don't Want to Hear It Anymore', when stylising 'Accidents Will Happen'; and David Bowie's music when shaping 'Moods for Moderns' and 'Senior Service'. This is not plagiarism or intertextuality[18] but simple and explicit indebtedness. It also demonstrates Costello's success as an autodidact, leaving us wondering whether he is constantly trying to make a showy point about his erudition, in reaction to his lack of formal higher education.

When we look at Costello's individual songs from the mid-1980s they are certainly saturated with ambiguity but this could reflect either the modish doubts of the time ('the undecidability of propositions') or, more plausibly for us, simply his love of wordplay. This came from a much older tradition. Edward Lear produced his *Book of Nonsense* in 1846 and Costello was emulating his tradition of scattergun word associations still in the late 20th century, with much success, just as John Lennon had done so twenty years previously in *In His Own Write* (1964) and *A Spaniard in the Works* (1965).[19] Like them, the sense from Costello was that it was an exercise with no particular end, other than to amuse the writer or their imagined audience; a point he conceded in later years. This capacity and compulsion was also an example of Costello's showy cleverness, noted above.

Also, surrealism had emerged in the first half of the 20th century, well before the 'post-modern turn'. Artists did not need postmodernism to tell them how to be funny, creative or weird; they had been doing it for ages. Thus, rather than Costello's work being a musical version of bricolage, more convincingly he was operating within the tradition of Edward Lear and James Joyce. These writers, like many others, existed on the intriguing borderline between madness and extraordinary creativity.[20]

Similarly, Costello's musical explorations about the absurdity of existence, or at least the absurd aspects of existence, therefore are not necessarily postmodern, even if

---

[18]   The problem with the concept of 'intertextuality', from the work of the poststructuralist philosopher Kristeva (1980), is that it adds very little, for our purposes, to old fashioned notions like 'allusion', 'derivation' 'influence', 'parody' or (more positively) 'indebtedness' (Irwin, 2004).

[19]   In the 1960s, The Beatles invented between themselves a strange Lear-type patois, which they employed in their Christmas records, produced just for the chummy amusement of their fan club members. John Lennon was the main proponent of funny nonsense, but Paul McCartney, George Harrison and Ringo Starr also made their contribution on the records.

[20]   There is a small psychiatric literature now demonstrating this point (for example, Post (1994) and Jamison (1993)). The novelist Jeanette Winterson, who has entered and returned from psychosis and tried to commit suicide, offers us this psychodynamic summary: 'Creativity is on the side of health – it isn't the thing that drives us mad; it is the capacity in us that tries to save us from madness' (Winterson, 2011: 171).

they could be read as such. They seem to be closer to existentialism, allegedly a spent and exhausted force of modernism, according to commentators about postmodernism in the academy like Jameson (1991). As an example of this uncertainty about where to place Costello, let us look at a song from *Blood & Chocolate*.

'Old School' aesthetic: the workings of 'Battered Old Bird'

This song describes the floors of a house, its inhabitants, neighbours and visitors, as well as sinister prospects and possibilities. Behind its closed doors there is a nightmare scenario of torture and terrifying abandonment. Child abuse and neglect (a boy being shut in the 'coal hole' and sent outside 'playing in the traffic') and substance misuse (pills and booze) weave in and out of the lyrics. The listener is being invited into a domestic version of Conrad's *Heart of Darkness* or its film sequel *Apocalypse Now*. A next-door neighbour, we are told, decapitated a 'visitor's child' and the song ends with the possibility of a boy's body parts being 'scattered in the attic'. There is 'a woman who teaches wrong from right'. She seems to be the child's mother (and the landlord the father). She, like the child, is a victim of abuse.

The prospect of honesty hovers as a dire threat, rather than an opportunity for its liberating authentic expression. Despite the idea of a mundane structure (the house), it seems to exist in world somewhere else that defies normal rules. The atmosphere of menace and absurd alienation is reinforced by the musical production and Costello's usual emotive voicing. Starting quietly, like a slowly burning fuse, the foreboding restraint culminates in a frenzied crime scene and a repeated cry of pain from the singer.

This song was emblematic of Costello in the middle of the 1980s and carried within it many of the themes we have described earlier in the book. First, there is a point about the powerful, even exciting, menace of sadism. Second, there is pessimism about intimacy. Third, there is anguish about the moral consequences of the abuse of power. Fourth, there is sensitivity and sensibility about the actual risks of innocence in childhood; but also this symbolises one aspect of human frailty unto death. Despite its many unnerving elements and its macabre depiction of brutality and abuse, the song is a sort of morality tale.

Consciously or not, Costello also points up the fragility of structures. This house, like others, has the apparently comforting solidity created by 'bricks and mortar' but, as was to soon be shown in Berlin, walls can break down and what they existed to protect is often not wholesome. In a limited way Costello may have shown some prophetic capability here; not so much that he could see into the future but that he provides us with an intuitive sense of things falling apart.[21] The grim lyrics and

---

[21]   In the mid-1980s it was the era of the 'New Times' of late capitalism, when much was 'dislocating' and structures crumbling. In tune with these prospects, in 1985 Paul Weller wrote 'Walls Come Tumbling Down' for his Style Council, when we were told that 'governments crack and systems fall'. Thus, in the 1980s there was some artistic sensibility and intuitive

emotive performance together draw our attention to a scandal about human suffering and exploitation in the midst of the mundane in an uncertain and fragmenting world.

This way of reasoning about the song might place Costello in the postmodern tradition of using ideas to challenge the authority of structures (the house and even the patriarchal power of the landlord who works for the central government – 'the Ministry'). An alternative reading is that he is playing with older modernist themes, exemplified by psychoanalysis about the dark side of the unconscious and its creation of neurosis (the 'two old maids' who wished that the other one was afraid). The other modernist resonance is with existentialism about bad faith: our denial or disowning of truths, which are at odds with our convenient view of our selves and the world, to ward off guilt and anxiety. Costello is violently puncturing pretence in the song.

Costello provides an account of the lyrical content of this song in the liner notes in the reissued CD of *Blood & Chocolate*. This account puts us all on the spot about authorial intentionality. Unlike some of his more typical, smart quick-fire reminders of the allusions to the work of others in his tracks over the years, this song is very personal. Allusion is there, but this time it is about his childhood and his own unconscious. This is what Costello says:

> It is a very long song based on the tenants of the house in which my family had the basement until I was five years old. Of course [*sic*] I changed some of the details. I was actually taught to swear in Welsh by our landlady but it doesn't rhyme. Some of the more nightmarish characters have been distorted by time but others, like the 'old maids', like the scriptwriter who drank burgundy for breakfast and the fellow who kept an old plastic christmas [*sic*] tree in cupboard [*sic*] by the stairs in case of emergencies were real enough. Because the song contained these alarming childhood memories, I found it hard to cut …

The note goes on a little more to explain the technicalities of two versions being spliced together to create some of the 'Strawberry Fields Forever'-type electronic distortion in the middle of the song. But the note is reproduced here because of its challenges and begged questions. Is this the nearest we are to get to an autobiographical account from Elvis Costello? Does it imply that he was abused as a child? Was there another child (maybe of the landlord and landlady)? How many of us could produce anything like a lived recollection of our place of residence before the age of five? How much of it was memory and, if so, how accurate were those recollections? How much has Costello added or subtracted when elaborating the associations through the filter of his imagination? (He calls them 'alarming childhood *memories*', not imaginings.) It is all very disturbing and perplexing for any reader, be they credulous or critical. Maybe Costello himself can't answer these questions and one wonders what his parents made of the song, when it appeared, if they heard it.

---

capability, when faced with the structural fragility of the period. Kurt Vonnegut compared artists to canaries in coal mines: they may keel over dead before those around notice there is a threat.

The anarchy in the lyric is carried over into the lo-fi, 'garage band' production of the track with off-kilter mixing and overdubs of dubious efficacy. The bulk of *Blood & Chocolate* was recorded 'live' in the studio, an unusual choice within the context of mid-1980s rock; by this point, most artists were recording multi-tracked songs, consisting of individually recorded instrumental and vocal tracks layered over a foundation of bass and drums, frequently accompanying a metronome (click track) heard in headphones that would not be audible in the final mix.

The benefits of multi-tracking are vast and predominantly in the realm of production – the producer retains full sonic control of every instrument independently, the auditory 'space' a song occupies can be finely manipulated throughout the production process. The direction or concept of the track can be altered, perhaps radically, right up until the stage of mastering. This brings all the individual tracks together into a (usually) stereo mix and finalising the audible relationships between each individual track of the song.

The alternative to multi-track recording is to record every musician performing his or her part live, simultaneously, 'in the room'. This 'live' performance – essentially referring to the continuous single-take quality of the recording, although some bands invite an audience into the studio to improve the ambience – can then be recorded from a point within the space. (This happened in early recordings, when ensembles would have to gather around a recording horn, each musician positioned spatially according to the relative volume of their instrument). Alternatively, each instrument is individually mic'd, as in the multi-tracking process, with the acceptance that there will be a substantial amount of audible 'bleed' of louder instruments into the mic channel of quieter ones. This 'bleeding' can be attenuated, with variable success, by mic and instrument placement and dense screens that are used as acoustic baffles.

The benefits of 'in the room' recording lie mainly with the performers: instrumentalists and vocalists can respond to each others' performances, taking advantage of their own talent and using the split-second reactions of the subconscious to create a performance in real time. A prime example of multi-track recording is a Pop album (the realisation of a concept designed for mass appeal), of 'in the room' recording an acoustic Jazz album (the faithful documentation of inter-musician relationships).

Every individual song analysed within this book was recorded in multiple layers, using overdubs.[22] According to Costello's liner notes:

> We set up in the studio as we would in rehearsals, using monitor speakers rather than headphones. We also played a lot closer to 'stage' volume so that there was little or no separation ... This made for a booming, murky sound that made

---

[22]   Admittedly, 'Alison' only uses one overdub – Costello's backing vocal – but this just shows how ubiquitous the technique is, and how useful. Even when artists make commitments to record live, as on *Blood and Chocolate*, the temptation to improve the end product using overdubs is ever present.

subtly [*sic*] impossible. If we tried anything fancy it sounded like we were playing wearing boxing gloves ... Because of the volatile nature of both the method and the musicians many of the tracks were either first takes or took no more than three or four attempts ...

With this knowledge under our belts, what is immediately noticeable about the recording of 'Battered Old Bird' is the peculiarly unbalanced mix: this track has the kind of balance one would expect to hear on a demo. In particular, the drums sound thin, as if they were missed out in the mixing process. Compare the sound of the piano or vocal, rich and present, with the drums. The recording of the individual elements of the kit is clear and detailed, but everything is very small. Cymbal crashes and thudding rock tom hits are almost laughably miniscule. Returning to the liner notes, Costello comments: 'If there was too much bass "spill" on the drum mikes we simply turned down the direct bass channel.'

This is an oversimplification from Costello. If there is too much bass in your drum mic, you will indeed need less bass from other sources, but you will also have less control over the drums. Drums frequently have more mics on them than any other instrument – one for each drum (at least four), one for hi-hat and overheads to pick up the cymbals (and everything else in the room, if no effort is made to get any separation). Costello's description implies that *any* source is appropriate – that the bass sound in the drum mics will do as well as the *actual* recorded bass sound, mic'd from the bass amp or DI'd.[23] If only this was the case – sound engineers could set up a couple of mics and record any ensemble with equal ease! What we hear on 'Battered Old Bird' betrays the actual (and opposite) course of events – the close-mic'd vocals, keys, bass and guitar channels have been mixed and balanced together, whilst the drum channels with a little bass, a little guitar, a little piano and vocals, have been mixed out, resulting in a thin and distant drum sound. As far as the arrangement goes, Costello has more to say on the topic (*Blood & Chocolate* reissue liner notes again):

We seemed unable to agree about anything to do with Battered Old Bird. We tried it in faster tempi, different keys and vocal deliveries but nothing could be sustained for the entire song ... One night, during mixing Nick hit on the solution. By a combination of vari-speeding and bold editing, two separate versions were spliced into one (a lesson learned from "Strawberry Fields Forever"). A growling harmonium was dubbed onto the cracks and while the hybrid isn't perfect, I'm glad we didn't simply scrap the song entirely.

Rarely are edits so blatantly flagged up – the first harmonium 'growl' occurs at 00:26 and lasts about seven seconds, presumably covering a splice between two

---

[23] A DI (direct input) box takes the electrical signal from the instrument to the mixer before it becomes amplified and reaches the speaker, resulting in a sound that is effectively 'raw', despite being processed to balance and boost the signal.

lines of the second verse. Certainly the first two minutes of the track sound like the same track, or close takes; the really noticeable splice happens at 02:21, where a brief swell (that sounds more like a guitar reverse effect than a harmonium) leads us into the second half of a far more energised take of the song, with a crunchier, livelier guitar tone and a more open vocal tone. This lasts until about 04:45 when yet another take gradually fades in, again featuring what sounds like reverse-effect on either harmonium or guitar, during which Costello can be heard echoing his final lines from the previous edit, literally catching up with himself.

It is a sign of how much Costello valued this lyric that this edit (by far the clumsiest on an album of far more raw material than Costello had presented for some years) was retained. Its precarious fate mirrored that of the band. By now they did not seem prepared to work together constructively on the arrangement necessary to record the tune again, using this Frankenstein's edit as a template.

Conclusion

We have ended this chapter deliberately with a song that allows us to reinforce two clear features that we emphasised in our preface. First, we have approached Costello, his work, and their time and place from a fairly traditional position of humanistic social science. We have taken seriously what he said about the biographical resonances of 'Battered Old Bird' and his turmoil in making it work in the studio, in the context of much personal disaffection in the band. There is more than a strong possibility that the distressed and distressing content of the song had *current* resonances in Costello's life. If this is the case, then we may be observing in the song and its fractious and inefficient recording an example of 'regression in service of the ego', with an intriguing, if somewhat unnerving, creative outcome.

Second, and following from the first point, not only have we resisted any attempt to read his work as a discourse, we have sought to retain his 'messy' humanity as a named person. This has been done with due consideration to the risks of overly respecting authorial intentionality (which we consider to be an overstated caution from structuralism within literary criticism) and the claims of postmodernists that context is all important but that the *objectivity* of that context is beyond proof or comprehension.

From our perspective, real social forces not only exist objectively but their role and relevance can in part (but never totally) be demonstrated empirically. As far as our topic is concerned, these empirical claims can gain a reasonable consensus. British colonialism, with its faded grandeur and ongoing violence, shaped the position taken by both Thatcher and Costello in the 1980s. The protection of elite interests by an industrial military complex was as relevant in late capitalism as it was in its earlier days. The class-based interests of the Conservative Party ensured that Thatcher's style of leadership was going to be tolerated until those interests were de-stabilised by policies like the Poll Tax. Costello's aspirations as an auteur ultimately were going to be constrained by the changing character of the field of the music industry. His products were also going to be assessed within an emerging cultural critique derived from identity politics, especially from second-wave feminism (points we explored in Chapters 6 and 7).

We are coming to the end of the book, then, by making a double claim about and from modernism. First, our own analytical approach has eschewed a commitment to post-structuralism. Second, we are claiming that Costello was a modernist not a postmodernist artist (except in the weak or limited sense of him living, like everybody else, in the post-modem world of globalised advanced capitalism in the 1980s).

The song just examined represents a turning inwards to the recesses of the artist's memory and imagination. If Costello would make a poor psychoanalytical patient (because of his irritable defensiveness) that does not mean at all that he was incapable of exploring his inner life, via his writing and performances. A song like 'Battered Old Bird', with its acute emotional rawness in form and content, resonated with his life in two periods (his eccentric childhood in the 1950s and his emotional fragility in the 1980s). With this type of personal capability in mind, running alongside a career in which his authenticity has been claimed and disputed by onlookers (including, to an extent, us now), we are left with many contradictions about the artist. We begin our next and final chapter with that sense of uncertainty.

Chapter 9
Macbeth at the Foam Party

Nearly all our originality comes from the stamp that time impresses upon our sensibility.

– Charles Baudelaire[1]

This book has moved to and fro between the sides of the triangle we noted in our preface: the musician, his music, and his time and place. We hope that this has provided some illumination for the reader about the triangle as a whole. As we have put the book together we have tried to keep to that declared aim and it has generated a fair bit of ambiguity.

This outsiders-looking-in conclusion probably reflects, in large part, the ambivalence of Elvis Costello. He is not sure who he is, at least for public consumption. Is he from London, Liverpool, Ireland or (latterly) the USA? He is uncertain about his creative path and so has been restless. He loves women but gets fairly irritated with them as well. He espouses progressive political or humanistic values but can be ruthless in his treatment of others; but not always. He is a proven anti-racist tainted by a single incident suggesting the opposite, which has left him in a state of impotent guilt. The USA is there to be loved and loathed, though we suspect mainly the former. He can adore fellow musicians but also treat them with utter contempt. He is blatantly nostalgic but flatly denies this position.

When we come to appreciate the content of Costello's songs, traces of his personal life and the social context of their production in the 1980s are equally important. Between them, they created extensive conditions of possibility then, as well as interpretive options with hindsight now. Moreover, the contemporary juxtaposition of that particular young man with those particular times contained important historical traces.

Without a faded colonial past, Thatcher could not have indulged in a spasm of opportunistic military reaction in the South Atlantic, left Bobby Sands to die as a common criminal or made a fetish of casino capitalism to save the City of London. Without the same past, Costello could not have been fired up and inspired by the turbulence of a post-colonial Anglo-Irish identity or inhabited his particular family script to creative effect. In the present of the 1980s, Thatcher both furnished Costello with creative indignation and provided him with the content of some of his songs. What they had in common was a shared history, albeit with contrasting views on what to do with its legacy.

---

[1]   From 'The Painter of Modern Life', in *Selected Writings on Art and Artists*, ed. Charvet (1972).

The romantic troubadour in postmodern times

Groping back further for our understanding, Costello's work can be aligned with the Romantic tradition. From further back we can hear echoes of the idiosyncratic professed wisdom of the troubadours. Indeed, to this day, the peculiar form of organic scholarship (not just artistic expression and desire to entertain) of the troubadours has a resonance in Costello's autodidactic identity and his occasional preachy ways. As we argued in Chapter 8, this presentation of self from Costello has little to do with being fashionably postmodern and everything to do with a set of complex conditions and cultural traditions that well preceded his birth.

Post-modernism may well now dutifully challenge the claims of scientific progress and sensible rationality offered by the Enlightenment, but the first powerful reaction to the latter came from Romanticism in the arts, from the mid-18th century onwards. And it is in that tradition that we can reasonably locate Elvis Costello. Together, these older cultural traces gave a web of apparent substance and confidence to his auteur image. This prospect of a unique and extraordinary artistic talent occurred in a field which, according to Costello, was occupied mainly by 'dullards' and 'pygmies'. Some of this sedimented artistic legacy from past decades, and even centuries, seemed to be within his awareness but much was undoubtedly unconscious. The role of unconscious sources and impulses in some part explains both the mystery of his creativity (a mystique he sometimes uses to his own commercial advantage) and his recurring confusion and ambivalence about who he is and how he should relate to others.

Given all of this uncertainty, as a person Elvis Costello inevitably remains puzzling. His songs are easier to decode than the man himself and, as we have demonstrated, they are by no means *easy* to interpret. We were given fair warning about this challenge before we started, from previous Costello-watchers like Bookmens (2004) and Griffiths (2007).

Moreover, we are faced with a wider interpretive dilemma, when discussing *any* recognised and commercially successful musician. Our struggle to understand Elvis Costello throws into relief a general analytical challenge, about understanding those in the field of popular music who 'make it'. We only ever really know any of them via their performances, their lyrics, the odd publicised scandal and the interviews they supply to the world, with the occasional contribution from hagiography or those with axes to grind.

Commercial artists are still just human beings, and saints are rare and few of us are all bad. We will never know any successful artists as would an honest supportive friend, a loving relative or empathic but frank psychotherapist. Moreover, in this case, Costello has yet to offer the world a warts-and-all autobiography to analyse carefully. Given his history of defensive self-promotion, we doubt that he will ever provide the world with such an account, in the tradition of Rousseau's *Confessions*.

Sense-making about artistic integrity

By necessity, then, it is the public displays and words that we are left decoding in the field of popular music: we can only study personas and the particular artist's preferred style of impression-management in a 'commercially sensitive' context. For some in the music industry, the notion of a 'commercial artist' is inherently pejorative. By contrast, we have used the phrase as a neutral description, simply to mean musicians who seek to establish and sustain a good income in a competitive context. This disparity between our use and its negative connotation, within the artistic culture of music itself, deserves a little attention here. It is relevant when appraising Costello's individual work but it also raises recurring general questions about the industry for all involved.

How do those who wish to 'make it' commercially also manage to be 'authentic', 'honest' or retain their 'integrity'? Does this mean doing what is comfortable or is consistent with their conscience? Is 'integrity' what they consider themselves to have but others they disapprove of do not? Is it about insisting on doing things on their own terms and not those determined by others? If this is the case, then what is the difference between honesty and egotism? How can artists in a commercial context remain 'honest' when they *have* to market themselves and their wares?

Thus the notion of 'artistic integrity' is an attractive one for those wishing to make strong claims about good faith, but all of these questions remain open. The devoted fan *wants* to have integrity affirmed in the music they prefer, because their own experience resonates with the topics, desires and sentiments of its content. For some contingent existential reason or other they find that it 'speaks to them' (it could even change their life). In that context of meeting between the product and the consumer, there is a strong need for the listener to believe in the honesty of the speaker for their own experience to be fulfilling and meaningful. When and if fans find themselves sharing that experience, they then become a 'community of affect' (Hebdige, 1979).[2]

Moore (2002) makes the point that authenticity has a useful remaining conceptual role to play in the analysis of popular music. However, it is a situated *ascription*, requiring case-by-case examination. It is not something that is indwelling in a musical product (an *inscription*). Instead, it is about the sincere intentions of artists, as writers and performers, *and* the recognition of that effort by listeners, especially when the latter believe the artist is articulating a shared sense of being-in-the-world. We made this point in relation to Costello in Chapter 6. 'Telling it like it is' or singing 'from the heart' are ascribed aspects of authenticity using personal criteria of fans and critics.

---

[2] It is from this conclusion that we can understand why some sociologists are now singularly concerned with the contingent experience of listeners. However, Moore's point is that authenticity is best framed as a *relational* concept – it emerges as an interaction of the product of a writer, the performer and the interpretive apprehension of particular listeners. Therefore all of these elements are relevant to understand. We noted at the outset that this book was not an empirical investigation of the last of these.

Following Moore's point, while Costello may have considered that he had made 'bad' records but they were never 'dishonest', he is claiming an inscribed form of authenticity, which strictly we can, and should, query. Ultimately the ascribed authenticity of his music also arises from the judgment of others. It is not *only* the business of Costello, the auteur, no matter how strongly he might insist on his personal ownership of musical meaning. The fact that he does consider it to be his role alone to judge (as with his pronouncement that 'Tramp the Dirt Down' was not 'subversive', when we say now that it was) emphasises why Moore's framing of authenticity is critically important to consider.

Integrity might also be judged by technical aspects, especially the strict adherence to a 'pure' musical tradition, such as soul or folk. Bob Dylan's 'betrayal' of the acoustic folk tradition is the best example of this, but Punk's self-satisfied amateurism is another. The matter of amateurism raises another aspect of integrity: maybe those, like Costello, who are seeking earnings from producing music are *ipso facto* straying from the path of authenticity.[3]

Thus 'authenticity' is a polyvalent concept in musicology, and we have to unpick our assumptions about the word from one analytical situation to another. Its relevance for us here is that Costello makes strong rhetorical claims in this regard. For him, and many for other artists who strain for sincerity within record company constraints, the tension created is about how to remain honest *despite* those constraints. This, then, accounts for Costello being able to develop a narrative of oppression about his own plight in relation to record company managers and corporate profit-seeking.

Musicians, like anyone else, want to make a living but it is not always easy to do that in a context in which many forces draw them away from their creative intent and direct expressiveness. Regrettable compromise, unseemly competitiveness, opportunism and subterfuge can soon become part of a career trajectory. Elements of all these could be found in Costello's work in the 1980s; but this was the case, to some extent, for any commercial artist from the period.

Nowadays the performing elites of the industry have been disturbed by the internet and the loss of power of the record industry, as we noted in Chapter 7. These elites may have resented the constraints of the record companies but their success and privileged 'lifestyle' were also products of those constraints. As a

---

[3]   A parallel for fans of rugby and cricket, who know their history, was the traditional distinction between purity in the game offered by gentleman amateurs, and wage slavery then sullying that authenticity, with the emergence of professionalism. But the latter was about those who had to earn a living. Analogously, in popular music, we have the artist who simply cannot afford to indulge in a pure hobby. Ultimately it is a matter of social class but with the chance of a 'rags to riches' trajectory. Popular music is dominated by successful artists who came from ordinary or even very humble backgrounds. That underlying ordinariness increases the likelihood that, should they become famous, their fans will like them and at the same time the rising artists know how best to appeal to their former peer group (see note 4 below on Bruce Springsteen). Their shared origins lay the ground for a 'community of affect'.

result of the disturbance in the economy of music arising from technological shifts, any appraisal of new artists means now that we must re-orientate our assumptions in a changed field of competition, fame and fortune.

This point about the 'nature' of being-a-commercial-artist-in-the-world during the 1980s and how much of it was about bad, or good, faith has come up repeatedly in our chapters, when we have explored Costello as an aspiring auteur. With these questions in mind, any extrapolation we try to make from Elvis Costello to Declan MacManus has to be done with some caution or even shrugged shoulders. But even in this case, when we limit ourselves to his career persona from interviews and his stage performances in the flesh, much ambiguity still remains.

For example, we thought that the story had been told about his hiring and firing of The Attractions but we are now not really sure what it was all about. The more it is viewed, the more it becomes cloudy. And this links, in part, to another ambiguity. Costello developed a reputation for ruthless aggression. He was a young man, to use the recollection from Charlie Dore, 'who did not suffer fools gladly' (see Chapter 7). And yet, despite Bruce Thomas doing his level best to provoke his boss, Costello tolerated him for several years without taking decisive action. He then let him back into his professional life after the break in 1987 and even after the appearance of the highly disrespectful *The Big Wheel*.

Was this about one musician or the whole of The Attractions? If it was the latter, why did Costello go on to re-employ Steve Nieve and Pete Thomas, with apparent equanimity, well into the 1990s? If, between 1984 and 1987, his pointed solo tours and experimentation with alternative backing musicians and collaborators was a way of driving The Attractions out of his life, then Costello did not carry his intention through very efficiently. If all of the displacements of the role of The Attractions, which stretched over years not just months, were only focused on expelling the bass player, then this seemed like a sledgehammer to crack a walnut. Why did he not just fire him in 1984 as he had done the engineer clowning around in the studio (see Chapter 2), and why did he agree to Thomas coming back in the 1990s? Was Mitchell Froom really that silver-tongued as a peace-broker?

We struggle then, to pass a clear judgement on Costello's artistic integrity. In part this is because the criteria used in this procedure are highly variable amongst musicologists; our point made above about authenticity being a polyvalent concept. If we use first-person ascriptions, then by his own account Costello has made bad records but 'never a dishonest one': he is saying to the world 'please trust me, my aim is true'.

If we use the judgment of adoring music critics, such as Schruers noted in Chapter 6, then his expressiveness which 'approaches rage' is evidence of his integrity. At the point of musical production there is little or no space between his direct emotional expression and what the listener then hears: he is telling it like it is and speaking the truth in the troubadour tradition and his appreciative listeners believe him. But emotions can be performed-they are not *inherently* sincere. Insincere sincerity is what makes a good actor, but maybe we expect more of musicians than of actors in this regard.

Costello's habitus highlights this ambiguity for us when interpreting his intentions. He explores, at times with some dangerous candour, the implications of heterosexual intimacy but, like Norman Mailer and his novels, the characters in his songs are not literally Elvis Costello. However, the 'tell-it-and-be-damned' stance he takes could also be an ingenious way of making his mark, compared to his anodyne competitors in the singer-songwriter trade. He learned the tricks of that trade early on in his life: he certainly had Bourdieu's 'feel for the game'.

As for another traditional definition of musical authenticity (loyalty to a tradition, style or genre) then this is tricky as well. Costello clearly honours a range of musical traditions but has championed no one of these in particular for a prolonged period. His catholic tastes and his experimentation with hybrids were noted in Chapter 8. And when, for example, he immersed himself, probably sincerely, in say the tradition of Country and Western music (see Chapter 3), doing his best to be true to the instrumentation required in his pilgrimage to a Nashville studio, arguably he lacked an authentic mandate.

This inadequacy came from a geographical fact of his life: he was temporarily adopting a cultural tradition that was never his own. He is not from Tennessee and only knew of its musical products, albeit 'with curiosity and affection', as a foreigner. This is a probable reason why the producer of *Almost Blue* could play with him so cruelly.[4] It is also why we noted in our analysis of 'Good Year For The Roses' the struggle Costello had in trying to write himself into the authentic script of the Country and Western tradition.

Gender and race

Continuing with the theme of interpretive ambiguity, there is the matter of his attitude towards women. The journalistic consensus that Costello was misogynistic did not fully hold water, as we pointed out in Chapter 6. Or if he had hostile feelings about women he also loved them. We are back to ambivalence. Certainly women have fallen in love with him. Three wives and an intense love affair suggest that something happens in his intimacy with women that hooks them rather than hurts them, at least in a period of romantic development.

---

[4]   Compare this with the work of Bruce Springsteen who, despite being a multi-millionaire, continues to persuade his fans that his direct experience authentically reflects that of the working (or even unemployed) man in impoverished urban America *now* (Seymour, 2012). For example, 'That was my story. I've written about it for 30 years, because I lived that story as a child, and I saw its effects. I saw the crisis it creates' (from interview in *Rolling Stone*, March 2012). Springsteen's claim to authenticity here is about his own US culture. Costello could only contingently appropriate an American musical style, with a passport of 'curiosity and affection'. And as for social class, Costello's bohemian musical family of origin does not provide us with a simple cultural norm equivalent to that claimed as a creative mandate by Springsteen.

The remaining ambiguity, which we were keen to highlight but could not resolve, was how far it is legitimate to conflate his lyrics, and their occasional creepy perverted meanderings, with Costello's actual dealings with women in his personal life. We simply do not know the answer to this because it is connected to a wider question about all human beings. How much do we let our unconscious thoughts and feelings, revealed in our dreams and imagination, become our private or public conduct?

For Costello, we cannot assume that what he says in his lyrics necessarily reflects the way that he then conducts himself. However, as we noted in Chapter 6, if there were any hint of a scandal about the way he treated women in his life, the mass media would have surely seized upon it. It is very unlikely that Costello's highly cautious attitude towards public exposure of his personal life would have been sufficient to suppress serious scandal. His sulky contempt, and that of Nick Kent, for the 'girl', who intruded on their pub conversation in 1991, hardly indicated a respectful approach to women. However, the reason for their collusive machismo might have been traceable to her employers (their bête noire of the record industry). Costello might have been just as obnoxious to a male 'suit', so gender could be a red herring here in our *post hoc* judgement of a single reported event.

And even when his lyrics expressed anger, despair and confusion about women, all that this demonstrates is that there is more to the mind than the conscience and more to free communication than cautious social rectitude or the pieties of political probity. If Costello, or any other artist in any field of expression, is not permitted to explore diverse erotic experiences or our chaotic intimacy, from his or her unique experience and unbridled imagination, then where else in life should unflinching candour appear, if ever? Apart from risking dire authoritarian consequences, knee-jerk ideological rejections of artistic exploration, which are normative in intent by suppressing unwelcomed news, will generate heat but not much light. Costello faced accusations of misogyny from his critics and so this point is relevant to our appraisal of his work in the 1980s.

As for the post-feminist music industry, Costello has left its flourishing to others, who have been intent on turning pop videos into soft pornography. In the light of the way the industry unfolded in the wake of *MTV*, who has done a greater disservice to women's rights in popular music, Elvis Costello or the oxymoronic 'girl power' from the likes of the Spice Girls, the Pussycat Dolls, Madonna, Beyoncé, Britney Spears, Shakira and Christina Aguilera, with their faux-feminist lyrics, scanty dress and formulaic pelvic gyrations and thrusts? In what sense do these artists champion feminism, if at all? These (rhetorical) questions suggest that Costello's reputation as a misogynist needs to be placed into a wider industrial context.

Accusations of racism against Costello, we think, are the easiest to deal with: his anti-racism was confirmed by his political commitments and by his collegial work with black musicians. What is remarkable, which we came across when writing Chapter 4, was the inconsistency with which he was judged in comparison to those like David Bowie (subsequently contrite) and Eric Clapton (subsequently not contrite) about their odious right-wing outpourings. Why are we still preoccupied by a single inebriated, and then spitefully-leaked, private incident, involving what Ray Charles maturely dismissed as 'stupid bar talk', when other artists carrying far more grounds for guilt and remorse have been left unchallenged and even venerated as 'gods'? Our partial answer to this question was Costello's progressive aspirations and claimed ideology, which made him a bigger target to hit.

If there is any residual matter about racism it is maybe Costello's contempt for the English, given that 'England was the whore of the world' (and thus, given his place of upbringing, possibly contempt for himself). This opens up a deeper question, which is not unusual in a post-colonial context and which only he knows the answer to. With his Anglo-Irish roots, he has been at some points 'Irish' and at other points not. He is certainly eligible for an Irish passport but that is an only an objective administrative quirk of history still permitted by the Dublin government to honour the Irish diaspora. We do not know how he sees his national identity subjectively, if indeed he even thinks in these terms any longer.

'Inarticulate speech of the heart'

Turning to his music and his reputation as a wordsmith, the songs we have scrutinised in the book demonstrate that Costello was not condemned to the word salads and tangential associations he revelled in during his early writing. Generally, as time progressed, his lyrics denoted more than they connoted but they remained multi-layered in their allusions. His 'way with words' was not consistent in a different sense though, because he did not always speak with a high degree of fluency. In contrast with his sophisticated lyrics, his conversational style often could tend towards the inarticulate.

His tendency to lapse into clumsy swearing for emphasis (for example, his allusion to satellite television and 'fuckin' Madonna' in the 1991 interview with Nick Kent, noted in Chapter 7) hardly marked him out, on that evidence alone, as being always comfortable with *conversational dialogues*. He was becoming drunk at the time, but this is not likely to be the whole explanation. When asked, reasonably, simply to provide a cool critique of Thatcherism during the interview with Tracey MacLeod discussed in Chapter 1, he ended up in an ashen-faced, tongue-tied, swearing fit of pique. Thousands of viewers with considered criticisms of Margaret Thatcher would have probably made a better fist of an articulate analytical statement. He was at his best when planning his lyrics (and his liner notes then, or posted statements now on the internet about politics): he then shone brightly. This suggests that the mono-logical character of writing suited him better than the dialogical nature of live conversations.

He was clearly inspired by some topics more than others. Intimacy was the obvious one, with its recurring dramas of 'birth and copulation and death'.[5] Also

---

[5]   This term was made famous by T.S. Eliot when summarising the basics of life (from 'Sweeney Agonistes').

memories in his life or musings about past generations hooked his imagination. As for politics, when we looked at songs like 'Tramp The Dirt Down', 'Shipbuilding' and 'Peace in Our Time', these were outstanding musical contributions to a wider cultural critique of Thatcherism. From our perspective, he was not alone in two senses in his subversive project, as part of that critique. First, some of his best recordings were written with others (exemplified by 'Shipbuilding'). Second, the performers he worked with shaped the overall aesthetic merit of particular tracks (exemplified by 'Tramp the Dirt Down'). But, even without conceding the pure auteur role he at times wanted to claim for himself, Costello's very powerful presence still invites our respect and recognition.

Within his preferred songwriting themes, there was much about Thatcherism that did not engage his curiosity or fire his imagination and we listed these in Chapter 1. We do not know why some items on the list were ignored by Costello. But what he did provide were some important rallying points of cultural resistance against Thatcherism, suggesting that, as far as Costello's fans were concerned, Fiske (1987) was right to warn us against stereotyping *all* consumers of popular music as 'cultural dopes' (even if many of them could be legitimately described in that way – see below).

Moreover, and this links to the remaining ambiguity about judging him in a post-feminist context, the emotional range of his inner life did not translate fully into his favoured forms of lyrical production. We noted in Chapter 6 that, despite the shallow rhetoric of the oft-quoted 'revenge and guilt' interview in 1977, he had very tender emotions. However, he opted most of the time to sing songs in the latter vein, when they were written by *other* people. It is as if there was a block from within to do this alone; possibly some sort of 'taboo on tenderness', embodying his own personal version of the modern crisis of masculinity.

He could do indignant self-pity and masochistic obeisance in his own lyrics and furious accusations also came readily. But true tenderness *for others*, when and if it was there, was usually drowned out by other, more stormy, feelings nearby. This might account for why he was stereotyped as 'Mr. Angry', when he thought of himself, maybe quite sincerely, as 'Mr. Love'. It might also account for why he could not bring himself to state the obvious, that he was a nostalgic writer (see Chapter 3); a denial maybe reinforced by his fear of public exposure about the vagaries of his private life. That is our conclusion, unless we have missed something in his writing in the 1980s, and it is completely at odds with his stated view.

The context of Thatcherism

When we turn from Costello and his music to the social context of his work, then Thatcherism provided him with rich material for his political songs. He wanted to remain angry and critical in the 1980s and refused to join the throng of zany abandon. By the end of the decade he had declared his wish for the death of an elected Prime Minister, condemned a whole nation for being a prostitute and was echoing the despair of Alan Bleasdale's 'Yosser Hughes', who symbolised Thatcher's destruction of male working-class potency.

New technology and changes in the music business inspired some of his contemptuous lyrics. The record companies and their domination in the field provided him with a narrative about his *own* victimhood. At the same time, the new identity politics, especially about race and gender, formed a pointed context of judgement for his work, sometimes with negative outcomes for him. Thus, Costello was both moralistic and was being subjected to the moralisations of others, with the former rather encouraging the latter.

Taking these points together, with hindsight his limited audiences and disappointing sales were predictable. If his fans, more than others in the new land of atomised consumerism, indeed were not simply dupes of the record industry, maybe they were self-selecting in their attraction to a particular type of artist and music. Given Costello's clever wordplay, obscure allusions, and earnest and dour political view of life, we can see how only a limited market niche might have developed within the frothy confection of 1980s music. Costello was staging *Macbeth* in the midst of a foam party. Some people could see it but most could not. Most of the young record-buying public would not be educated enough to understand and appreciate his allusions, and the few that were would not necessarily share his political value system.

This point about a recurring division in the field of popular music, between frothy confection and genuine intellectualism worthy of careful consideration and reflection, is pertinent to consider when estimating the reputation of Costello and his limited commercial success. Inglis (2000) commends some writers (such as Lennon and McCartney) as unrecognised but legitimate critical intellectuals. He is hostile to those in social science who refuse to recognise such a presence in popular culture. However, arguably Costello drove intellectualism within popular music just a little too far for his own good. As one music critic from *The Guardian* noted sarcastically, confirming the point from Inglis about British anti-intellectualism, Costello was one of those songwriters 'who reads too many books'.

Whether or not that is accurate and pertinent (what is wrong with reading books?), Costello ended up blaming the record companies, when in truth this is a complex matter and must also have implicated the buying public. It also implicated the demands his elaborate products at times placed upon their appreciation of what he was trying to achieve. If consumers of popular music are not all, or merely, cultural dupes then they must also, to some extent, be blameworthy for the choices they make (see our discussion of this in Chapter 7). If they are agents, not just victims, then they, *not just* record companies and participating artists, are culpable in co-constructing the nature of that culture. We consider that this point is fair, even though we accept the caveat that consumers have less power than those seeking to tranquillise and manipulate them (Barber, 2007). When Costello warned, in his song 'You Worthless Thing', 'they're going to take this cable now and stick it down your throat', he was making a legitimate point. The buying public could heed this sort of warning (or not).

Given this scenario about Costello, the complexity of his offerings and the limited tastes of mass consumers for him to turn his attention resentfully and pointedly onto the constraints of his record company would only tell part of a complicated story. The venom with which he attacked artists like Madonna also reveals, by implication, something bigger that was going on about the core business of *MTV* land: it was becoming slicker, and more eroticised and manipulative, as we noted earlier. In that context, artists like Costello were unlikely to be 'mainstreamed' or sell their wares in vast amounts. Other artists would put themselves forwards to perform the antics that Costello despised. 'Sex positive' feminism could be commodified and it was – and still is. This trend was complemented by cheesy 'boy bands' fulfilling their role in the common process of consumers opting for form over content. They supplied the musical equivalent of Mills and Boon novels for women of any age.

Costello's limited public recognition in the 1990s, not just the 1980s, went on to confirm these norms of a new type of commercialised music. The extent of his success was never aligned with his own view of his talents, or probably that of those who loved and respected his work. We would concur with Bookmens and Griffiths that Costello may have missed out on 'icon' status but we have also argued that the grain of his voice was unique. Moreover, as Griffiths noted, Costello 'hung out' with a lot of people who were icons. Those high-status friends and collaborators were clearly very respectful of his talents. Within the field of music in the 1980s (and afterwards) he may well be remembered as a 'musician's musician', which, if the case, is no mean feat.[6]

Conclusion

In formal socio-political terms, Costello could be fairly described as a successful petit-bourgeois individualist. He was also a self-defined auteur and proud autodidact; a product of mid-20th-century modernity but inherited by the particular 'New Times' of the 1980s. He was not a capitalist but he certainly was not one of the workers. He competed with fellow musicians, but sometimes collaborated with them for commercial or political reasons. He respected and even venerated some, but poured scorn on others. He hired and he fired, but not always terribly convincingly or efficiently. He expertly produced the work of others, especially in the cause of anti-racism, and dabbled in acting and drawing, with mixed results.

Here was Costello during postmodern times and so he might be judged as an avant-garde exponent of musical bricolage, given his wide-ranging willingness to experiment with the unexpected. As we noted in the previous chapter, we are

---

[6]   However, this prospect can be put in the context of some writings on popular music to date, which do not even acknowledge Costello's presence, let alone his reputation. His name is missing from some key texts, for example, Clayton *et al* (2003), Bennett et al., (1993) and Bennett (2000).

not convinced by this way of understanding him and his work. Our judgement is that he was an old-fashioned kind of a guy in more ways than one. Maybe he was largely 'his father's son', only much more successful, as time proved.[7] He was a hard working modernist, who was trying to pay his due respects to the traditions of music he had learned to love in his childhood and formative years as a performing musician.

Given the dismissals from some of his critics during the 1980s and since, we find no reason at all to query Costello's political or aesthetic worth because of suspected or attributed racism or misogyny. He made some undeniably racist comments in a foul-mouthed drunken private spat. He was eternally ashamed after the event and his public role in the anti-racist cause is now well proven. Ray Charles was right to judge Costello by his actions, not his 'stupid bar talk'.

Moreover, the world is not simply divided into those harbouring pure racial hatred and those with none at all (white anti-racist activists are conscious of this about their inner worlds). And if all of our private follies were put on public parade, we would all be found guilty of something. We are all, to some degree, liars, cheats and hypocrites. The worst that Costello could be reasonably accused of was low-grade depressive misanthropy (he was a grumpy young man), as well as evident arrogance, grandiosity and occasional political hypocrisy in his dealings with others. These are within the range of pride and prejudice familiar to us all, to some degree. Read all about it: Declan MacManus was human!

He was an indefatigable and prolific entertainer, 'beloved' by some but not others, who was good at his job and he knew it. He had a big head but it had much talent to contain. He wanted to be the author of his own creative destiny but, like all of us, ultimately had to accept external constraints. The adolescent vanity of the self-defined auteur soon hits the buffers of real forces beyond his or her control, though those forces also might feed their imagination. All of Costello's favoured personal expression was occurring in an intensifying period of finance capitalism, which was soon to beget casino capitalism. This created norms of infantilising consumerism, shameless greed, the pornification of popular culture, atomised individualism and, most depressingly, unremitting military violence in the world. In a variety of ways, today we are paying the price of this recent legacy.

When many others in the music industry were fiddling while Rome burned, or mollifying us with bread and circuses, Costello delivered his view of events in his own particular way. As we note throughout the book, he was not alone. However, he was part of a memorable minority of artists, whose legacy is likely to endure when the cultural resistance to Thatcherism is appraised in the future.

---

[7]   An irony here is that his father was technically a much better singer. But if there was an Oedipal drama then the son won out, if we adhere to external criteria of commercial success.

References

Abbotts, J., Williams, R. and Ford, G. (2001) Morbidity and Irish Catholic descent in Britain: relating health disadvantage to socio-economic position. *Social Science & Medicine* 52(7): 999–1005.

Adams, T. (2010) Interview with Elvis Costello. *Observer*, 17 October.

Adorno, T. (1990) On popular music. In S. Frith and A. Goodwin (eds) *On Record: Rock, Pop and the Written Word*. London: Routledge.

Adorno, T.W., Frenkel-Brunswik, E., Levinson, D.J. and Sanford, R.N. (1950) *The Authoritarian Personality*. New York: Harper & Brothers.

Attwood, F. (2009) *Mainstreaming Sex: The Sexualization of Western Culture*. London: I.B. Tauris.

Barber, B.R. (2007) *Consumed: How Markets Corrupt Children, Infantalize Adults and Swallow Citizens Whole*. New York: Norton.

Barthes, R. (1967) *The Death of the Author*, trans. R. Howard. *Aspen*, 5–6.

Barthes, R. (1977) *Image, Music, Text*. New York: Hill and Wang.

Baudelaire, C. (1972) *Selected Writings on Art and Artists*, trans. P.E. Charvet. New York: Penguin.

Baudrillard, J. (1983) *Simulations*. New York: Semiotext(e).

Bauman, Z. (1988) *Legislators and Interpreters*. Cambridge: Polity Press.

Bell, D. (1973) *The Coming of Post-Industrial Society*. New York: Basic Books.

Bennett, A. (2000) *Popular Music in Youth Culture: Music Identity and Place*. Basingstoke: Palgrave.

Bennett, T., Frith, S., Grossberg, L., Shepherd, J. and Turner, G. (eds) (1993) *Rock and Popular Music*. London: Routledge.

Berne, E. (1964) *Games People Play*. New York: Grove Press.

Bhaskar, R. (1991) *Philosophy and the Idea of Freedom*. Oxford: Blackwell.

Bion, W. R. (1961) *Experiences in Groups*. London: Tavistock.

Bishop, J. (2005) Building international empires of sound: concentrations of power and property in the 'global' music market. *Popular Music and Society* 28: 443–71.

Bookmens, R. (2004) Uncanny identities: high and low and global and local in the music of Elvis Costello. *European Journal of Cultural Studies* 7(1): 59–74.

Bourdieu, P. (1977) *Outline of a Theory of Practice*, trans. R. Nice. Cambridge: Cambridge University Press.

Bourdieu P. (1993) *The Field of Cultural Production*. Columbia: Columbia University Press.

Callenicos, A. (1989) *Against Post-modernism: A Marxist Critique*. Cambridge: Polity Press.

Campbell, B. (1987) *The Iron Ladies: Why Do Women Vote Tory?* London: Virago.

Camus, A. (1961) *The Outsider.* Harmondsworth: Penguin.

Castells, M. (1989) *The Informational City.* Oxford: Basil Blackwell.

Church of England (1985) *Faith in the City: A Call for Action by Church and Nation. The Report of the Archbishop of Canterbury's Commission on Urban Priority Areas.* London: Church House.

Clark, T.J. (2012) For a Left with no future. *New Left Review* 74: 53–76.

Clayton, M., Herbert, T. and Middleton, R. (eds) (2003) *The Cultural Study of Music: A Critical Introduction.* London: Routledge.

Clayton-Lea, T. (1998) *Elvis Costello: A Biography.* London: Andre Deutsch.

Cohen, M. (1978) Review of *My Aim Is True. Creem*, February.

Cohen, S. and Taylor, L. (1976) *Escape Attempts: The Theory and Practice of Resistance in Everyday Life.* London: Routledge.

Cole, J. (1987) *The Thatcher Years: A Decade of Revolution in British Politics.* London: BBC.

Covach, J. (2003) Pangs of history in late 1970s New Wave rock. In A.F. Moore (ed.) *Analysing Popular Music.* Cambridge: Cambridge University Press.

Curra, J. (2011) *The Relativity of Deviance.* London: Sage.

Dannen, F. (2003) *Hit Men: Powerbrokers and Fast Money Inside the Music Business.* London: Helter Skelter Publications.

Dempsey, J.M. (2004) McCartney at 60: a body of work celebrating home and hearth. *Popular Music and Society* 27(1): 27–40.

Derrida, J. (1974) *On Grammatology.* New York: The Johns Hopkins University Press.

Derrida, J. (1981) *Writing and Difference.* London: Routledge.

Elias, N. (1969) *The Court Society.* Oxford: Blackwell.

English, R. (2005) *Armed Struggle: The History of the IRA.* Oxford: Oxford University Press.

Feld, S. (1974) Linguistic models in ethnomusicology. *Ethnomusicology* 18(2): 197–217.

Fiske, J. (1987) *Television Culture.* London: Methuen.

Forte, D. (1987) Bruce Thomas Pumps It Up With Elvis Costello. *Guitar Player*, March.

Foucault, M. (1973) *The Order of Things: The Archaeology of Knowledge*, trans. A.M. Sheridan. London: Tavistock.

Foucault, M. (1986) The subject and power. In J. Dreyfus and P. Rabinow. *Michel Foucault: Beyond Structuralism and Hermeneutics.* Brighton: Harvester.

Freud, S. (1989) *The Standard Edition of the Complete Works of Sigmund Freud.* New York: Vintage.

Fricke, D. (1983) Review of Van Morrison's 'Inarticulate Speech of the Heart'. *Rolling Stone*, 28 April.

Friedman, M. (1970) The social responsibility of business is to increase its profits. *The New York Times Magazine*, 13 September.

Frith, S. (1983) *Sound Effects: Youth Leisure and the Politics of Rock*. London: Constable.

Frith, S. (1988) *Music for Pleasure: Essays in the Sociology of Pop*. Cambridge: Polity.

Frith, S. (1996) *Performing Rites: On the Value of Popular Music*. Oxford: Oxford University Press.

Frith, S. and Goodwin, A. (eds) (1990) *On Record: Rock, Pop and the Written Word*. London: Routledge.

Fromm, E. (1976) *The Anatomy of Human Destructiveness*. Harmondsworth: Penguin.

Garfield, S. (1986) *Expensive Habits: The Dark Side of the Music Industry*. London: Faber.

Gerson, G. (2009) Culture and ideology in Ian Suttie's theory of mind. *History of Psychology* 12(1): 19–40.

Goffman, E. (1959) *The Presentation of Self in Everyday Life*. New York: Anchor Books.

Gorz, A. (1982) *Farewell to the Working Class: An Essay on Post-Industrial Socialism*. London: Pluto Press.

Gouldstone, D. (1989) *Elvis Costello: A Man Out of Time*. London: Sidgwick and Jackson.

Graña, C. (1964) *Bohemian versus Bourgeois: French Society and the French Man of Letters in the Nineteenth Century*. New York: Basic Books.

Greenacre, P. (1960) Woman as artist. *Psychoanalytical Quarterly* 29: 208–27.

Griffiths, D. (2002) Cover versions and the sound of identity in motion. In D. Hesmondhalgh and K. Negus (eds) *Popular Music Studies*. Oxford: Oxford University Press.

Griffiths, D. (2007) *Elvis Costello*. London: Equinox.

Grossberg, L. (1983) The politics of youth culture: some observation on rock and roll in American culture. *Social Text* 8: 104–26.

Habermas, J. (1985) Modernity: an incomplete project. In H. Foster (ed.) *Postmodern Culture*. London: Pluto Press.

Hall, S. (1980) Thatcherism: A New Stage? *Marxism Today*, February: 22–28.

Hall, S. and Jefferson, T. (eds) (1976) *Resistance Through Rituals: Youth Subcultures in Post-War Britain*. London: Hutchinson.

Hanisch, C. (1970) The personal is political. In S. Firestone and A. Koedt (eds) *Notes from the Second Year: Women's Liberation, Major Writings of the Radical Feminists*. New York: Radical Feminism.

Harvey, D. (1989) *The Condition of Postmodernity*. Oxford: Blackwell.

Hebdige, D. (1979) *Subculture: The Meaning of Style*. London: Routledge.

Hepworth, D. (2003) Nobody talks like Elvis. *Word*, April.

Hepworth, D. (2007) Interview with Elvis Costello. *Word*, February.

Hesmondhalgh, D. and Negus, K. (2002) Introduction: popular music studies: meaning, power and value. In D. Hesmondhalgh, and K. Negus (eds) *Popular Music Studies*. London: Hodder Education.

Hoskyns, B. (1991) El Have No Fury. *The Wire*, June.

Hutcheon, L. (1985) *A Theory of Parody: The Teachings of Twentieth-Century Art Forms*. New York: Methuen.

Inglehart R., Foa, R., Peterson, C. and Welzel, C. (2008) Development, freedom, and rising happiness: a global perspective (1981–2007). *Perspectives on Psychological Science* 3(4): 264–85.

Inglis, I. (2000) Men of ideas? Popular music, anti-intellectualism and The Beatles. In I. Inglis (ed.) *The Beatles, Popular Music and Society*. Basingstoke: Macmillan.

Irwin, W. (2004) Against intertextuality. *Philosophy and Literature* 28(2): 227–42.

Jakobovits, I. (1986) *From Doom to Hope: A Jewish View of Faith in the City*. London: Office of the Chief Rabbi.

James, O. (2008) *Affluenza*. London: Vermillion.

Jameson, F. (1991) *Post-modernism or the Cultural Logic of Late Capitalism*. London: Verson.

Jamison, K.R. (1993) *Touched with Fire*. New York: Free Press.

Jencks, C. (1984) *The Language of Postmodern Architecture*. London: Academy

Jessop, B., Bonnett, K. and Bromley, S. (1990) Farewell to Thatcherism? Neo-Liberalism vs New Times. *New Left Review* 179: 81–102.

Jessop, B., Bonnett, K., Bromley, S. and Ling, T. (1988) *Thatcherism: A Tale of Two Nations*. Cambridge: Polity.

Kelly, K. and McDonell, E. (eds) (1999) *Stars Don't Stand Still in the Sky: Music and Myth*. London: Routledge.

Kent, N. (1977) The man who would be king. *NME*, 27 August.

Kent, N. (1978) Welcome to the working of Elvis Costello's mind. *Creem*, February.

Kent, N. (1978) Elvis Costello interviewed by Nick Kent. *NME*, 25 March.

Kent, N. (2007) *The Dark Stuff: Selected Writings on Rock Music*. London: Faber and Faber.

Kris, E. (1952) *Psychoanalytic Explorations in Art*. New York: International University Press.

Kristeva, J. (1980) *Desire in Language: A Semiotic Approach to Literature and Art*. New York: Columbia University Press.

Laclau, E. (1990) *New Reflections on the Revolution of Our Time*. London: Verso.

Langer, S. (1942) *Philosophy in a New Key: A Study in the Symbolism of Reason, Rite, and Art*. Cambridge Mass.: Harvard University Press.

Lawson, N. (1980) *The New Conservatism*. London: The Centre for Policy Studies.

Layard, R. (2005) *Happiness*. London: Allen Lane.

Leavey, G., Rozmovits, L. and Ryan, L. and King, M. (2007) Explanations of depression among Irish migrants in Britain. *Social Science & Medicine* 65(2): 231–44.

Leppert, R.D. and McClary, S. (1987) *Music and Society*. Cambridge: Cambridge University Press.

Levy, A. (2005) *Female Chauvinist Pigs*. London: Barnes and Noble.

Longhurst, B. (2007) *Popular Music and Society*, 2nd edition. Cambridge: Polity.

Lopez, J. and Potter, G. (2001) *After Postmodernism: An Introduction to Critical Realism*. London: The Athlone Press.

Lukes, S. (1967) Alienation and anomie. In P. Laslett and W.G. Runciman (eds) *Philosophy, Politics and Society*. Oxford: Blackwell.

Lyotard, J.-F. (1985) *The Postmodern Condition: A Report on Knowledge*. Manchester: Manchester University Press.

Machin, D. (2010) *Analysing Popular Music: Image, Sound and Text*. London: Sage.

Marcus, G. (1993) *In the Fascist Bedroom: Writings on Punk (1977–1992)*. London: Viking.

Marcuse, H. (1964) *One Dimensional Man*. Boston: Beacon Press.

Marr, A. (2007) *A History of Modern Britain*. London: Macmillan.

Marshall, L. (2011) The sociology of popular music, interdisciplinarity and aesthetic autonomy. *British Journal of Sociology* 62(1): 154–74.

Martin, P.J. (1995) *Sounds and Society: Themes in the Sociology of Music*. Manchester: Manchester University Press.

Martin, P.J. (2006) *Music and the Sociological Gaze: Art Worlds and Cultural Production*. Manchester: Manchester University Press.

McClary, S. and Walser, R. (1990) Start making sense! Musicology wrestles with rock. In S. Frith and A. Goodwin (eds) *On Record*. London: Routledge.

Merton, R. (1996) *On Social Structure and Society*, ed. P. Sztompka. Chicago: Chicago University Press.

Meyer, L. (1958) *Emotion and Meaning in Music*. Chicago: Chicago University Press.

Middleton, R. (1990) *Studying Popular Music*. Milton Keynes: Open University Press.

Milgram, S. (1963) Behavioral study of obedience. *Journal of Abnormal and Social Psychology* 67(4): 371–8.

Moore. A. (1993) *Rock: The Primary Text*. Milton Keynes: Open University Press. 2nd revised edition (2001), Aldershot: Ashgate.

Moore, A. (2002) Authenticity as authentication. *Popular Music* 21(2): 209–23.

Mortimer, J. (1985) *Paradise Postponed*. London: Penguin.

Murdoch, I. (1978) *The Red and the Green*. London: Panther.

Nattiez, J. (1975) *Fondements d'une sémiologie de la musique*. Paris: Union Générale d'Editions.

Nazroo, J. and Iley, K. (2010) Ethnicity, race and mental disorder in the UK. In D. Pilgrim, A. Rogers and B. Pescosolido (eds) *The SAGE Handbook of Mental Health and Illness*. London: Sage.

Norris, R. (1993) *The Truth About Postmodernism*. London: Macmillan.

Nunn, H. (2002) *Thatcher, Politics and Fantasy*. London: Lawrence & Wishart.

Nuttall, J. (1968) *Bomb Culture*. London: MacGibbon & Kee.

Oates, J.C. (1971) 'Out of the Machine': review of Norman Mailer's 'Prisoner of Sex'. *The Atlantic*, July: 43.

Offe, C. (1984) Reflections on the welfare state and the future of socialism. (Interviewed by David Held and John Keane) In J. Keane (ed.) (1984) *Contradictions of the Welfare State*. London: Hutchinson.

Offe, C. (2005) *Reflections on America: Tocqueville, Weber and Adorno in the United States*. Cambridge: Polity.

Paasonen, S., Nikunen, K. and Saarenma, L. (eds) (2007) *Pornification: Sex and Sexuality in Media Culture*. Oxford: Berg.

Pardini, S.F.S. (2012) Bruce Zirilli: The Italian sides of Bruce Springsteen. In K. Womack, J. Zolten and M. Bernhard (eds) (2012) *Bruce Springsteen, Cultural Studies and the Runaway American Dream*. Farnham: Ashgate.

Perone, J.E. (1998) *Elvis Costello: A Bio-Bibliography*. Westport, Conn.: Greenwood Press.

Post, F. (1994) Creativity and psychopathology: a study of 291 world famous men. *British Journal of Psychiatry* 165: 22–34.

Proust, M. (1995) *In Search of Lost Time*, trans. C. Prendergast. London: Penguin.

Reese, K. (1981) *Elvis Costello*. New York: Proteus Books.

Reisner, R.G. (1977) *Bird: The Legend of Charlie Parker*. New York: De Capo Press.

Riddell, P. (1983) *The Thatcher Government*. Oxford: Martin Robertson.

Roberts, K. (1993) Career trajectories and the mirage of increased social mobility. In I. Bates, and J. Riseborough (eds), *Youth and Inequality*. Buckingham: Open University Press.

Rogers, A. and Pilgrim, D. (2003) *Mental Health and Inequality*. Basingstoke: Palgrave.

Roth, P. (1997) *American Pastoral*. London: Jonathan Cape.

Rogers, A. and Pilgrim, D. (2010) Mental disorder and danger. In D. Pilgrim, A. Rogers and B. Pescosolido (eds) *SAGE Handbook of Mental Health and Illness*. London: Sage.

St. Michael, M. (1986) *Elvis Costello: An Illustrated Biography*. London: Omnibus.

Saks, M. (1983), Removing the blinkers? A critique of recent contributions to the sociology of professions *The Sociological Review* 31: 3–21.

Sartre, J.-P. (1958) *Search for a Method*, trans. H. Barnes. New York: Norton.

Schruers, F. (1978) Elvis Costello is angry and convincing: *This Year's Model* fulfils every New Wave expectation. *Circus*, 22 June.

Sedikides, C., Wildschut, T. and Baden, D. (2004) Nostalgia: conceptual issues and existential functions. In J. Greenberg, S.L. Coole and T. Pyszczynski, (eds) *Handbook of Experimental Existential Psychology*. New York: Guilford.

Seymour, E.M. (2012) Where dreams are lost and found. In K. Womack, J. Zolten and M. Bernhard (eds) *Bruce Springsteen, Cultural Studies and the Runaway American Dream*. Farnham: Ashgate.

Seymour, J. and Girardet, H. (1990) *Far from Paradise: the Story of Human Impact on Environment*. London: Green Print.

Shepherd, J. (1991) *Music as Social Text*. Cambridge: Polity.

Simons, H. (ed.) (1989) *Rhetoric in the Human Sciences*. London: Sage.

Smith, L.D. (2004) *Elvis Costello, Joni Mitchell and the Torch Song Tradition*. London: Praeger.

Spinoza, B. *Ethics*, trans. E. Curtley. London: Penguin Books.

Stratton, J. (1983) The contemporary music industry: organisations and ideology. *Popular Music* 3: 143–56.

Street, J. (1986) *Rebel Rock: The Politics of Popular Music*. Oxford: Basil Blackwell.

Suttie, I.D. (1935) *The Origins of Love and Hate*. London: Kegan Paul, Trench Trubner and Co.

Tagg, P. (2000) Analysing popular music: theory, method and practice. In R. Middleton (ed.) *Reading Pop: Approaches to Textual Analysis in Popular Music*. Oxford: Oxford University Press.

Thatcher, M. (1996) *The Path to Power*. London: Harper Collins.

Thomas, B. (2003) *The Big Wheel*, 2nd edition. London: Helter Skelter Publications.

Thomson, G. (2004) *Complicated Shadows: The Life and Music of Elvis Costello*. Edinburgh: Canongate.

Thurlow, R. (1987) *Fascism in Britain: A History 1918–1985*. London: Tauris.

Thurschwell, P. (1999) Elvis Costello as cultural icon and cultural critic. In K.J.H. Dettmar and W. Richey (eds) *Reading Rock and Roll: Authenticity, Appropriation, Aesthetics*. New York: Columbia University Press.

Vonnegut, K., Jr (1961) *Mother Night*. New York: Gold Medal Books.

White, T. (1983) A Man Out of Time Beats the Clock. *Musician* 60, October.

Wikstrom, P. (2009) *The Music Industry*. Cambridge: Polity.

Wild, D. (1989) Interview with Elvis Costello. *Rolling Stone*, 1 June.

Wilden, A. (1980) *System and Structure: Essays in Communication and Exchange*. London: Tavistock.

Wilkinson, R.G. (2005) *The Impact of Inequality: How to Make Sick Societies Healthier*. London: Routledge.

Wimsatt, W.K. and Beardsley, M.C. (1946) The intentional fallacy. *Sewanee Review* 44 468–88.

Winterson, J. (2011) *Why Be Happy When You Could Be Normal?* London: Jonathan Cape.

Wollstonecraft, M. (1972) *A Vindication of the the Rights of Woman: With Strictures on Political and Moral Subjects*. London: Joseph Johnson.

Womack, K., Zolten, J. and Bernhard, M. (eds) (2012) *Bruce Springsteen, Cultural Studies and the Runaway American Dream*. Farnham: Ashgate.

Young, H. (1995) *One Of Us*. London: Macmillan.

Young, H. and Sloman, A. (1986) *With Respect, Ambassador*. London: BBC.

Zaborowski, R. (2012) Is the control of emotions possible? *History & Philosophy of Psychology* 14(1): 34–52.

Zimbardo, P.G. (1972). *The Stanford Prison Experiment: A Simulation Study of the Psychology of Imprisonment*. Stanford: Philip G. Zimbardo, Inc.

Index

Elvis Costello is referred to as EC throughout the index, except for his own main entry where he is entered as Costello, Elvis.

References to music examples are in **bold**.